TM

References for the Rest of Us!®

P9-CEG-149

BESTSELLING BOOK SERIES

Do you find that traditional reference books are overloaded with technical details and advice you'll never use? Do you postpone important life decisions because you just don't want to deal with them? Then our *For Dummies*® business and general reference book series is for you.

For Dummies business and general reference books are written for those frustrated and hard-working souls who know they aren't dumb, but find that the myriad of personal and business issues and the accompanying horror stories make them feel helpless. *For Dummies* books use a lighthearted approach, a down-to-earth style, and even cartoons and humorous icons to dispel fears and build confidence. Lighthearted but not lightweight, these books are perfect survival guides to solve your everyday personal and business problems.

> *"More than a publishing phenomenon, 'Dummies' is a sign of the times."*
>
> — The New York Times

> *"A world of detailed and authoritative information is packed into them..."*
>
> — U.S. News and World Report

> *"...you won't go wrong buying them."*
>
> — Walter Mossberg, Wall Street Journal, on For Dummies books

Already, millions of satisfied readers agree. They have made For Dummies the #1 introductory level computer book series and a best-selling business book series. They have written asking for more. So, if you're looking for the best and easiest way to learn about business and other general reference topics, look to For Dummies to give you a helping hand.

Wiley Publishing, Inc.

5/09

English Grammar For Dummies®

Cheat Sheet

Parts of Speech

- **Noun:** names a person, place, thing, idea (*Lulu, jail, cantaloupe, loyalty*, and so on)
- **Pronoun:** takes the place of a noun (*he, who, I, what*, and so on)
- **Verb:** expresses action or being (*scrambled, was, should win*, and so on)
- **Adjective:** describes a noun or pronoun (*messy, strange, alien*, and so on)
- **Adverb:** describes a verb, adjective, or other adverb (*willingly, woefully, very*, and so on)
- **Preposition:** relates a noun or a pronoun to another word in the sentence (*by, for, from*, and so on)
- **Conjunction:** ties two words or groups of words together (*and, after, although*, and so on)
- **Interjection:** expresses strong emotion (*yikes! wow! ouch!* and so on)

Parts of a Sentence

- **Verb (also called the predicate):** expresses the action or state of being
- **Subject:** the person or thing being talked about
- **Complement:** a word or group of words that completes the meaning of the subject-verb pair
- **Types of complements:** direct and indirect objects, subject complement, objective complement

Pronouns Tips

- Pronouns that may be used only as subjects or subject complements: I, he, she, we, they, who, whoever.
- Pronouns that may be used only as objects or objective complements: me, him, her, us, them, whom, whomever.
- Common pronouns that may be used as either subjects or objects: you, it, everyone, anyone, no one, someone, mine, ours, yours, theirs, either, neither, each, everybody, anybody, nobody, somebody, everything, anything, nothing, something, any, none, some, which, what, that.
- Pronouns that show possession: my, mine, your, yours, his, her, hers, its, our, ours, their, theirs, whose.

For Dummies: Bestselling Book Series for Beginners

English Grammar For Dummies®

Cheat Sheet

Subject-Verb Agreement Tips

- Match singular subjects with singular verbs, plural subjects with plural verbs.
- Amounts of time and money are usually singular (ten dollars *is*).
- *Either/or* and *neither/nor:* Match the verb to the closest subject (neither the boys nor the girl *is*).
- *Either* and *neither*, without their partners *or* and *nor,* always take a singular verb (*either* of the apples *is*).
- All subjects preceded by *each* and *every* take a singular verb.
- Both, few, several, many are always plural.

Punctuation Tips

- **Endmarks:** All sentences need an endmark: a period, question mark, exclamation point, or ellipsis. Never put two endmarks at the end of the same sentence.
- **Apostrophes:** For singular ownership generally add *'s;* for plural ownership generally add *s'.*
- **Commas:** In direct address use commas to separate the name from the rest of the sentence. In lists place commas between items in a list, but not before the first item. Before conjunctions, when combining two complete sentences with a conjunction, place a comma before the conjunction. If you have one subject and two verbs, don't put a comma before the conjunction.

Verb Tense Tips

- **Simple present tense:** tells what is happening now
- **Simple past tense:** tells what happened before now
- **Simple future:** talks about what has not happened yet
- **Present perfect tense:** expresses an action or state of being in the present that has some connection with the past
- **Past perfect tense:** places an event before another event in the past
- **Future perfect tense:** talks about something that has not happened yet in relation to another event in the future

For Dummies: Bestselling Book Series for Beginners

English Grammar
FOR
DUMMIES®

by Geraldine Woods

WILEY

Wiley Publishing, Inc.

English Grammar For Dummies®

Published by
Wiley Publishing, Inc.
111 River St.
Hoboken, NJ 07030
www.wiley.com

Library of Congress Control Number: 2001089309

ISBN: 0-7645-5322-4

Manufactured in the United States of America

15 14 13 12

1B/RT/QT/QT/IN

About the Author

Geraldine Woods' career as a grammarian began in her elementary school, which in those days was called "grammar school" for very good reason. With the guidance of a series of nuns carrying long rulers (good for pointing at the board and slapping unruly students), she learned how to diagram every conceivable type of sentence. She has been an English teacher for 25 years and has written 40 books, give or take a few. She loves minor-league baseball, Chinese food, and the novels of Jane Austen. The mother of a grown son (Tom, a lawyer), she lives in New York City with Harry (her husband of 30 years) and parakeets Alice and Archie.

Dedication

For my husband and son, the hearts of my life.

Author's Acknowledgments

I offer thanks to my students, whose intelligence and curiosity never fail to inspire me. I also thank technical editor Tom LaFarge, whose good sense of humor and knowledge of grammar vastly improved this book. I am grateful to my project editor Linda Brandon, whose thoughtful comments challenged me to clarify my explanations and whose encouragement changed many a bad day into a good one. I appreciate the hard work of copy editors Billie Williams and Ellen Considine, who constantly reminded me to focus on you, the reader. I am also grateful to acquisitions editors Joyce Pepple, Roxane Cerda, and Susan Decker, who encouraged me at every opportunity. I owe a debt of gratitude to my agent, Carolyn Krupp, who calmed my nerves and answered my e-mails with unfailing courtesy and valuable assistance. Lastly, I thank my colleagues in the English Department, whose passion for teaching and love of our subject make my time at work a pleasure.

Publisher's Acknowledgments

We're proud of this book; please send us your comments through our online registration form located at www.dummies.com/register.

Some of the people who helped bring this book to market include the following:

Acquisitions, Editorial, and Media Development

Project Editor: Linda Brandon

Acquisitions Editor: Susan Decker

Copy Editors: Ellen Considine, Billie A. Williams

Technical Editor: Thomas LaFarge

Editorial Manager: Christine Beck

Editorial Assistant: Jennifer Young

Cover Photos: ©1996 Rob Gage/FPG

Composition

Project Coordinator: Regina Snyder

Layout and Graphics: Amy Adrian, Karl Brandt, Joyce Haughey, Jill Piscitelli, Betty Schulte, Brian Torwelle, Julie Trippetti, Jeremey Unger

Proofreaders: Angel Perez, TECHBOOKS Production Services

Indexer: TECHBOOKS Production Services

Special Help
Jennifer Ehrlich

Publishing and Editorial for Consumer Dummies

Diane Graves Steele, Vice President and Publisher, Consumer Dummies

Joyce Pepple, Acquisitions Director, Consumer Dummies

Kristin A. Cocks, Product Development Director, Consumer Dummies

Michael Spring, Vice President and Publisher, Travel

Brice Gosnell, Associate Publisher, Travel

Suzanne Jannetta, Editorial Director, Travel

Publishing for Technology Dummies

Andy Cummings, Vice President and Publisher, Dummies Technology/General User

Composition Services

Gerry Fahey, Vice President of Production Services

Debbie Stailey, Director of Composition Services

Contents at a Glance

Cartoons at a Glance

By Rich Tennant

page 337

page 283

page 7

page 219

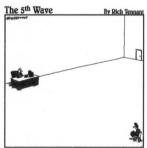

page 81

page 147

Cartoon Information:
Fax: 978-546-7747
E-Mail: richtennant@the5thwave.com
World Wide Web: www.the5thwave.com

Table of Contents

• •

Introduction

• •

A few years ago, a magazine sponsored a contest for the comment most likely to end a conversation. The winning entry? *I teach English grammar.* Just throw *that* line out at a party. Everyone around you will clam up or start saying *whom.*

Why does grammar make everyone nervous? As an English teacher, I have to take part of the blame. Some of us make a big deal out of grammar in our classrooms, drilling the parts of speech, clauses, and verbals until our students beg for mercy. Centuries ago when I was in elementary school — which, by the way, was called grammar school in those days for very good reasons — I had to diagram sentences. It's a wonder I ever learned to communicate at all by the time those lessons were over.

Happily, you don't have to learn all those technical terms of English grammar — and you certainly don't have to diagram sentences — in order to speak and write correct English. In this book I tell you the tricks of the trade, the strategies that help you make the right decision when you're facing such grammatical dilemmas as the choice between *I* and *me, had gone* and *went,* and so forth. I explain *what* you're supposed to do, but I also tell you *why* a particular word is correct or incorrect. You won't have to memorize a list of meaningless rules (well, maybe a couple from the punctuation chapter!) because when you understand the reason for a particular choice, you'll pick the correct word automatically.

About This Book

In this book, I concentrate on what English teachers call the common errors. I tell you what's what in the sentence, but I do it in logical, everyday (pardon the term) English, not in obscure terminology. You don't have to read this book in order, though you can, and you don't have to read the whole thing. Just browse through the table of contents and look for things that you often get wrong. For example, if you know that verbs are your downfall, check out Chapters 2 and 3 for the basics. Chapters 11 and 18 show you how to pick the correct verb in a variety of situations, and Chapter 22 gives you the equivalent of a doctorate in verbology. You decide how picky you want to be.

How to Use This Book

Each chapter in this book introduces some basic ideas and then shows you how to choose the correct sentence when faced with two or three alternatives. If I define a term — linking verbs, for example — I show you a practical situation in which identifying a linking verb helps you pick the right pronoun. I center the examples in the text so that you can find them easily. One good way to determine whether or not you need to read a particular section is to check the pop quizzes that are sprinkled around every chapter. If you get the right answer, you probably don't need to read that section. If you're puzzled, however, backtrack and read the chapter. Also, watch for Demon icons. They identify the little things — the difference between two similar words, commonly misused words, and so on — that may sabotage your writing.

What You Are Not to Read

Here and there throughout this book, you see some items marked with the Black Belt icon. No human being in the history of the world has ever needed to know those terms for any purpose connected with speaking and writing correct English. In fact, I recommend that you skip them and go skateboarding instead. For those of you who actually enjoy obscure terminology for the purpose of, say, clearing a room within ten seconds, the Black Belt icons define such exciting grammatical terms as *subjective complement* and *participial phrase*. Everyone else, fear not: These terms are clearly labeled and completely skippable. Look for the Black Belt icons and avoid those paragraphs like the plague.

Foolish Assumptions

I wrote *English Grammar For Dummies* with a specific person in mind. I assume that you, the reader, already speak English to some extent and that you want to speak it better. I also assume that you're a busy person with better things to do than worry about *who* and *whom*. You want to speak and write well, but you don't want to get a doctorate in English Grammar. (Smart move. Doctorates in English probably move you up on the salary scale less than any other advanced degree, except maybe Doctorates in Philosophy.)

This book is for you if

- You want better grades.
- You aspire to a higher-paying or higher-status job.

✔ You want your speech and writing to present you as an educated, intelligent person.

✔ You want a good score on the SATIIW, formerly known as the English Achievement Test.

✔ You want your writing and your speech to be clear and to say exactly what you mean.

✔ You want to polish your skills in English as a second language.

✔ You simply want to use better grammar.

How This Book Is Organized

The first two parts of this book cover the basics, the minimum for reasonably correct English. Part III addresses what English teachers call *mechanics* — not the people in overalls who aim grease guns at your car, but the nuts and bolts of writing: punctuation and capital letters. Parts IV and V hit the finer (okay, pickier) points of grammar, the ones that separate regular people from Official Grammarians. If you understand the information in this section, you'll have a fine time finding mistakes in the daily paper.

Here's a more specific guide to navigating *English Grammar For Dummies*.

Part I: The Parts of Speech and Parts of the Sentence

This part explains how to distinguish between the three Englishes — the breezy slang of friend-to-friend chat, the slightly more proper conversational language, and the I'm-on-my-best-behavior English. I explain the building blocks of a sentence, subjects and verbs, and show you how to put them together properly. In this part, I also provide a guide to the complete sentence, telling you what's grammatically legal and what's not. I also define objects and linking verb complements and show you how to use each effectively.

Part II: Avoiding Common Errors

In this part, I describe the remaining members of Team Grammar — the other parts of speech that can make or break your writing. I show you how to join short, choppy sentences into longer, more fluent ones without incurring a visit from the grammar police. I also explain the two types of descriptive words and show you how the location of a description may alter the meaning of the sentence. Prepositions — the bane of many speakers of English as a second language — are in this part, too, as well as some tips for correct usage. Finally, in this part I tell you how to avoid mismatches between singular and plural words, by far the most common mistake in ordinary speech and writing. Part II also contains an explanation of pronoun gender. In addition, reading this section may also help you avoid sexist pronoun usage.

Part III: No Garage, But Plenty of Mechanics

If you've ever asked yourself whether you need a comma or if you've ever gotten lost in quotation marks and semicolons, Part III is for you. I explain all the rules that govern the use of the worst invention in the history of human communication: the apostrophe. I also show you how to quote speech or written material and where to place the most common (and the most commonly misused) punctuation mark, the comma. Lastly, I outline the ins and outs of capital letters: when you need them, when you don't, and when they're optional.

Part IV: Polishing Without Wax — The Finer Points of Grammar

Part IV inches up on the pickiness scale — not all the way to Grammar Heaven, but at least as far as the gate. In this part, I tell you the difference between subject and object pronouns and pronouns of possession. (You need an exorcist.) I also go into detail on verb tenses, explaining which words to use for all sorts of situations. I show you how to distinguish between active and passive verbs and how to use each type properly. I illustrate some common errors of sentence structure and tackle comparisons — both how to form them and how to insure that your comparisons are logical and complete. Finally, I explain parallelism, an English teacher's term for balance and order in the sentence.

Part V: Rules Even Your Great-Aunt's Grammar Teacher Didn't Know

Anyone who masters the material in Part V has the right to wear a bun and tsk-tsk a lot. This part covers the moods of verbs (ranging from grouchy to just plain irritable) and explains how to avoid double negative errors. Part V also gives you the last word on pronouns, those little parts of speech that make everyone's life miserable. The dreaded *who/whom* section is in this part, as well as the explanation for all sorts of errors of pronoun reference. I explain subordinate clauses and verbals, which aren't exactly a hot stock tip, but a way to bring more variety and interest to your writing. I also give you the lowdown on the most obscure punctuation rules.

Part VI: The Part of Tens

Part VI is the Part of Tens, which offers some quick tips for better grammar. Here I show you ten ways to fine-tune your proofreading skills. I also give you a quick summary of the top ten (some would call them the bottom ten) most common errors along with their corrections. Finally, I suggest ways (apart from *English Grammar For Dummies*) to improve your ear for proper English.

Icons Used in This Book

Wherever you see this icon, you'll find helpful strategies for understanding the structure of the sentence or for choosing the correct word form.

Not every grammar trick has a built-in trap, but some do. This icon tells you how to avoid common mistakes as you unravel a sentence.

Think you know how to find the subject in a sentence or identify a pronoun? Take the pop quizzes located throughout this book to find out what you know and what you may want to learn.

Keep your eye out for these little devils; they point out the difference between easily confused words and show you how to make your sentence say what you want it to say.

Here's where I get a little technical. If you master this information, you're guaranteed to impress your oldest neighbor and bore all of your friends.

Where to Go from Here

Now that you know what's what and where it is, it's time to get started. Before you do, however, one last word. Actually, two last words: *Trust yourself.* You already know a lot. If you're a native speaker, you've communicated in English all of your life, including the years before you set foot in school and saw your first textbook. If English is an acquired language for you, you've probably already learned a fair amount of vocabulary and grammar, even if you don't know the technical terms. For example, you already understand the difference between

The dog bit Agnes.

and

Agnes bit the dog.

You don't need me to tell you which sentence puts the dog in the doghouse and which sentence puts Agnes in a padded room. So take heart. Browse the table of contents, take a few pop quizzes, and dip a toe into the Sea of Grammar. The water is fine.

Part I

The Parts of Speech and Parts of the Sentence

The 5th Wave   By Rich Tennant

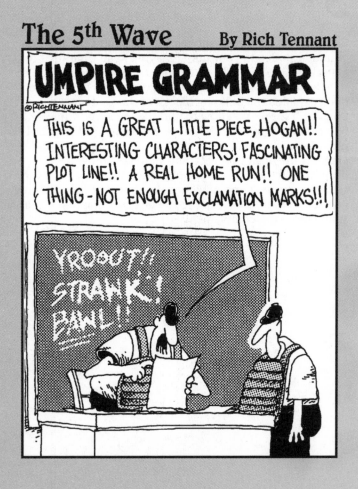

In this part . . .

So it's like, communication, y'know?

Can you make a statement like that without bringing the grammar police to your door? Maybe. Read Chapter 1 for a discussion of formal and informal language and a guide to when each is appropriate. The rest of this part of the book explains the building blocks of the sentence. Chapter 2 shows you how to find the verb, and Chapter 3 tells you what to do with it once you've got it. Chapter 4 provides a road map to the subject of the sentence and explains the basics of matching subjects and verbs properly. Chapter 5 is all about completeness — why the sentence needs it and how to make sure that the sentence gets it. In Chapter 6, I explore the last building block of a sentence — the complement.

Chapter 1

I Already Know How to Talk. Why Should I Study Grammar?

*Y*ou may be reading this book for any of a number of reasons. Perhaps you're in the cafeteria, hoping to impress a nearby English teacher — the one who recently told you that handing in the fifteen essays you're missing will raise your grade all the way to F–. Or maybe you're reading this book on a bus, hoping that such a scholarly pursuit will convince the love of your life, who is sitting across from you, that you're a serious person and completely date-worthy. (Hey, it can happen.) Or you may be reading this book in the office lounge, assuming that your boss will glance over and decide that you want to improve yourself and therefore deserve a promotion.

The most likely reason that you're reading this book, however, is that you want to learn better grammar. In this chapter I show you how the definition of *better grammar* changes according to your situation, purpose, and audience. I also tell you what your computer can and can't do to help you write proper English.

Living Better with Better Grammar

The curtain goes up, and you step on stage. One deep breath, and you're ready. *Ladies and gentlemen, it's an honor to be speaking . . . to speak . . . to have spoken . . . to you this evening.* You clear your throat and go on. *I offer my best efforts to whomever . . . whoever the committee decides . . . will decide should receive the nomination.* You begin to sweat, but you go on. *Now if everyone will rise to his . . . to their . . . to your feet, we'll sing the national anthem.* Out of breath from sheer panic, you run off the stage and search frantically for a grammar book.

Does this sound like you? Do your words turn into pretzels, twisting around themselves until you don't know why you ever thought to open your mouth (or your computer word processing program)? If so, you have lots of company. Nearly everyone in your class or office (or squadron or terrorist cell or whatever) has the same worries.

Stuck in English class, you probably thought that grammar was invented just to give teachers something to test. But in fact grammar — or to be more precise, formal grammar lessons — exists to help you express yourself clearly. Without a thorough knowledge of grammar, a little thread of doubt will weave its way across your speech and writing. Part of your mind will string words together, and another part will ask, *Is that correct?* Inevitably, the doubts will show.

You should also learn grammar because, rightly or wrongly, your audience or readers will judge you by the words you use and the way you put them together. Ten minutes at the movies will show you the truth of this statement. Listen to the speech of the people on the screen. An uneducated character sounds different from someone with five diplomas on the wall. The dialogue reflects reality: Educated people follow certain rules when they speak and write. If you want to present yourself as an educated person, you have to follow those rules also.

Deciding Which Grammar to Learn

I can hear the groan already. *Which* grammar? You mean there's more than one? Yes, there are actually several different types of grammar, including *historical* (how language has changed through the centuries) and *comparative* (comparing languages). Don't despair; in *English Grammar For Dummies,* I deal with only two — the two you have to know in order to improve your speech and writing.

Descriptive grammar gives names to things — the parts of speech and parts of a sentence. When you learn descriptive grammar, you understand what every word *is* (its part of speech) and what every word *does* (its function in the sentence). If you're not careful, descriptive grammar can go overboard fast, and you end up saying things like *"balloon" is the object of the gerund, in a gerund phrase that is acting as the predicate nominative of the linking verb "appear."* Never fear: I wouldn't dream of inflicting that level of terminology on you. However, there is one important reason to learn some grammar terms — to understand *why* a particular word or phrase is correct or incorrect.

Functional grammar makes up the bulk of *English Grammar For Dummies.* Functional grammar tells you how words behave when they are doing their jobs properly. Functional grammar guides you to the right expression — the one that fits what you're trying to say — by insuring that the sentence is put together correctly. When you're agonizing over whether to say *I* or *me,* you're actually solving a problem of functional grammar.

So here's the formula for success: A little descriptive grammar plus a lot of functional grammar equals better grammar overall.

Distinguishing between the Three Englishes

Better grammar sounds like a great idea, but *better* is tough to pin down. Why? Because the language of choice depends on your situation. Here's what I mean. Imagine that you're hungry. What do you say?

Wanna get something to eat?

Do you feel like getting a sandwich?

Will you accompany me to the dining room?

These three statements illustrate the three Englishes of everyday life. I call them friendspeak, conversational English, and formal English.

Before you choose, you need to know where you are and what's going on. Most important, you need to know your audience.

What is grammar anyway?

In the Middle Ages, *grammar* meant the study of Latin, because Latin was the language of choice for educated people. In fact, grammar was so closely associated with Latin that the word was also used to refer to any kind of learning. (You may have heard people from earlier generations — your grandparents, perhaps — talk about their *grammar school,* not their elementary school. The term *grammar school* is a leftover from the old days. The very old days.)

However, these days grammar is the study of language, specifically, how words are put together to create meaning. Because of all of those obsessive English teachers and their rules, grammar also means a set of standards that you have to follow in order to speak and write correctly. This set of standards is also called *usage,* as in *standard* and *non-standard* usage. Standard usage is the one that earns an A grade. It is the commonly accepted, correct patterns of speech and writing that mark an educated person in our society. You'll find standard usage in government documents, in newspapers and magazines, and in textbooks. Non-standard usage draws red ink from a teacher's pen faster than a bullet cuts through butter. It includes slang, dialect, and just plain bad grammar.

Wanna get something to eat? Friendspeak

Friendspeak is informal and filled with slang. Its sentence structure breaks all the rules that English teachers love. It's the language of *I know you and you know me and we can relax together*. In friendspeak the speakers are on the same level. They have nothing to prove to each other, and they're comfortable with each other's mistakes. In fact, they make some mistakes on purpose, just to distinguish their personal conversation from what they say on other occasions. Here's a conversation in friendspeak:

> Me and him are going to the gym. Wanna come?
>
> He's like, I did 60 pushups, and I go like, no way.
>
> I mean, what's he think? We're stupid or something? Sixty? More like one.
>
> Yeah, I know. In his dreams he did 60.

I doubt that the preceding conversation makes perfect sense to many people, but the participants understand it quite well. Because they both know the whole situation (the guy they're talking about gets muscle cramps after .4 seconds of exercise), they can talk in shorthand.

I don't deal with friendspeak in this book. You already know it. In fact, you've probably created a version of it with your best buds.

Do you feel like getting a sandwich? Conversational English

A step up from friendspeak is *conversational English*. Although not quite friendspeak, conversational English includes some friendliness. Conversational English doesn't stray too far from your English class rules, but it does break some. For example, it says that you can relax, but not completely, and it's the tone of most everyday speech, especially between equals. Conversational English is — no shock here — usually for conversations, not for writing. Specifically, conversational English is appropriate in these situations:

- Chats with family members, neighbors, acquaintances
- Informal conversations with teachers and co-workers
- Friendly conversations (if there are any) with supervisors
- Notes and e-mails to friends
- Comments in Internet chat rooms, bulletin boards, and so on
- Friendly letters to relatives

Phat grammar

Psst! Want to be in the in-crowd? Easy. Just create an out-crowd and you're all set. How do you create an out-crowd? Manufacture a special language (slang) with your friends that no one else understands, at least until the media picks it up. You and your pals are on the inside, talking about a *bad* song that everyone likes (*bad* means good). Everyone else is on the outside, wondering how to get the *411* (information). Should you use slang in your writing? Probably not, unless you're sending an e-mail or a personal note to a good friend. The goal of writing and speaking is communication. Also, because slang changes so quickly, even a short time after you've written something, the meaning may be obscure. Instead of cutting-edge, you sound dated.

When you talk or write in slang, you also risk sounding uneducated. In fact, sometimes breaking the usual rules is the point of slang. In general, you should make sure that your readers know that you understand the rules before you start breaking them (the rules, not the readers) safely.

Conversational English has a breezy sound. Letters are dropped in contractions (don't, I'll, would've, and so forth). You also drop words (*Got a match? See you later. Be there soon.* and so on). In written form, conversational English relaxes the punctuation rules too. Sentences run together, dashes connect all sorts of things, and half sentences pop up regularly. I'm using conversational English to write this book because I'm pretending that I'm chatting with you, the reader, not teaching grammar in a classroom situation.

Will you accompany me to the dining room? Formal English

You're now at the pickiest end of the language spectrum: formal, grammatically correct speech and writing. Formal English displays the fact that you have an advanced vocabulary and a knowledge of etiquette. You may use formal English when you have less power, importance, and/or status than the other person in the conversation. Formal English shows that you've trotted out your best behavior in his or her honor. You may also speak or write in formal English when you have *more* power, importance, and/or status than the other person. The goal of using formal English is to impress, to create a tone of dignity, or to provide a suitable role model for someone who is still learning. Situations that call for formal English include:

- Business letters (from or between businesses as well as from individuals to businesses)
- Letters to government officials
- Office memos

✔ Reports

✔ Homework

✔ Notes or letters to teachers

✔ Speeches, presentations, oral reports

✔ Important conversations (for example, job interviews, college interviews, parole hearings, congressional inquiries, inquisitions, sessions with the principal in which you explain that unfortunate incident with the stapler, and so on)

Think of formal English as a business suit. If you're in a situation where you want to look your best, you're also in a situation where your words matter. In business, homework, or any situation in which you're being judged, use formal English.

Using the Right English at the Right Time

Which type of English do you speak? Friendspeak, conversational English, or formal English? Probably all of them. (See preceding section for more information.) If you're like most people, you switch from one to another without thinking, dozens of times each day. Chances are, the third type of English — formal English — is the one that gives you the most trouble. In fact, it's probably why you bought this book. (Okay, there is one more possibility that I haven't mentioned yet. Maybe your nerdy uncle, the one with ink stains on his nose, gave *English Grammar For Dummies* to you for Arbor Day and you're stuck with it. But you're not playing a heavy-metal CD at high volume and surfing the Internet, so you must be reading the book. Therefore, you've at least acknowledged that you have something to think about, and I'm betting that it's formal English.) All the grammar lessons in this book deal with formal English, because that's where the problems are fiercest and the rewards for knowledge are greatest.

Which is correct?

A. Hi, Ms. Sharkface! What's up? Here's the 411. I didn't do no homework last night — too much going on. See ya! Love, Legghorn

B. Dear Ms. Sharkface,

Just a note to let you know that I've got no homework today. Had a lot to do last night! I'll explain later!

Your friend,

Legghorn

C. Dear Ms. Sharkface:

I was not able to do my homework last night because of other pressing duties. I will speak with you about this matter later.

Sincerely,

Legghorn

Answer: The correct answer depends upon a few factors. How willing are you to be stuck in the corner of the classroom for the rest of the year? If your answer is very willing, send note A, which is written in friendspeak. (By the way, *the 411* is slang for "information.") Does your teacher come to school in jeans and sneakers? Does he or she have the self-image of a 1960s hippie? If so, note B is acceptable. Note B is written in conversational English. Is your teacher prim and proper, expecting you to follow the Rules? If so, note C, which is written in formal English, is your best bet.

Relying on Computer Grammar Checkers Is Not Enough

Your best friend — the one who's greasing the steps to the cafeteria while you're reading *English Grammar For Dummies* — may tell you that learning proper grammar in the third millennium is irrelevant because computer grammar checkers make human knowledge obsolete. Your friend is wrong about the grammar programs, and the grease is a very bad idea also.

It is comforting to think that a little green or red line will tell you when you've made an error and that a quick mouse-click will show you the path to perfection. Comforting, but unreal. English has a half million words, and you can arrange those words a couple of gazillion ways. No program can catch all of your mistakes, and most programs identify errors that aren't actually wrong.

Spelling is also a problem. Every time I type *verbal,* the computer squawks. But *verbal* — a grammar term meaning a word that comes from a verb but does not function as a verb — is in the dictionary. Nor can the computer tell the difference between *homonyms* — words that sound alike but have different meanings and spelling. For example, if I type

Aren't you glad you don't have to do this?

Imagine that you're in fifth grade in a dusty classroom, counting the number of nano-seconds until recess. Ms. Sharkface assigns yet another page of unbelievably boring work. Before you pass out (of the room or of reality, depending upon the length of your lesson), you take out a ruler. Yes, a ruler, and no, it's not math class. Ms. Sharkface is one of a long line of English teachers who teach sentence structure with diagramming.

Diagramming is still in use, but its heyday has long since passed. The theory of diagramming is that a picture helps students understand the function of each word and how the word relates to others in the sentence. The theory is correct; diagramming actually does help you *see* the sentence. Unfortunately, it also forces you to spend a great deal of time drawing little lines and deciding non-language-related issues, such as whether a particular section should be straight or tilted. Just to show you how lucky you are that you don't have to diagram, here's a sentence and its diagram.

Sentence: When Lochness is pooped and yearns for vacation, he goes to spycamp.com, if he can pay for it.

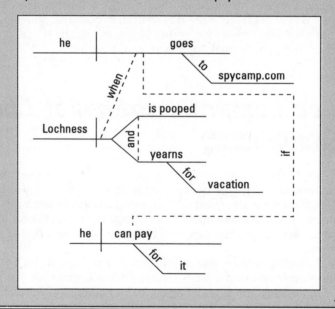

Eye through the bawl at hymn, but it went threw the window pain instead.

the computer underlines nothing. However, I was actually trying to say

I threw the ball at him, but it went through the window pane instead.

In short, the computer knows some grammar and spelling, but you have to know the rest.

Chapter 2

Verbs: The Heart of the Sentence

Think about a sentence this way: A sentence is a flatbed truck. You pile all of your ideas on the truck, and the truck takes the meaning to your audience (your reader or your listener). The verb of the sentence is a set of tires for the truck. Without the verb, you may get your point across, but you're going to have a bumpy ride.

In other words, every sentence needs a verb. The verb is what the sentence rests on and what gives the sentence movement. Verbs are the heart of the sentence because you start with the verb when you want to do anything to your sentence — including correct it. And as the old song goes, "you gotta have heart."

Verbs come in all shapes and sizes: linking and action; helping verb and main verb, regular and irregular; singular and plural; and present, past, and future. In this chapter, I unravel the first two categories — linking and action, helping verb and main verb — and show you how to choose the right verb for each sentence.

Linking Verbs: The Giant Equal Sign

Linking verbs are also called *being verbs* because they express states of being — what is, will be, or was. Here's where algebra intersects with English. You can think of linking verbs as giant equal signs plopped into the middle of your sentence. For example, you can think of the sentence

Legghorn's uncle *is* a cannibal with a taste for finger food.

as

Legghorn's uncle = a cannibal with a taste for finger food.

Or, in shortened form,

Legghorn's uncle = a cannibal

Just as in an algebra equation, the word *is* links two ideas and says that they are the same. Thus, *is* is a linking verb. Here are more linking verbs:

Lulu *will be* angry when she hears about the missing bronze tooth.

Lulu = angry (*will be* is a linking verb)

Lochness *was* the last surfer to leave the water when the tidal wave approached.

Lochness = last surfer (*was* is a linking verb)

Even in the dark, Lucrezia's red hair and orange eyes *were* completely visible.

hair and eyes = visible (*were* is a linking verb)

Ludwig *has been* depressed ever since the fall of the House of Usher.

Ludwig = depressed (*has been* is a linking verb)

Earwigs *are* a constant problem for that pink elephant.

Earwigs = problem (*are* is a linking verb)

You may wonder (okay, only if you're having a no-news day) whether *become* is a linking verb. Grammarians argue this point often (maybe because they tend to have no-news lives). The problem is that *become* is part *being*, part *action*. For example:

Zud's single eyebrow *becomes* obvious only when he steps into the light.

On the one hand, you may say that

eyebrow = obvious

but you may also say that the sentence shows action. Zud's single eyebrow is hidden and then exposed.

So what is *become* — an action or being? A little of each. In the real world, the answer doesn't matter unless you're completing the sentence with a pronoun. (See "Placing the Proper Pronoun in the Proper Place," later in this chapter.) Frankly, I can't think of any sentence with *become* as a verb that ends with a pronoun. Well, except one:

> "Moonlight becomes you," declared Legghorn as he strummed a guitar under Lola's window.

However, in this sentence the verb means *to look attractive on, to suit.* Therefore, *becomes* in this sample sentence is definitely an action verb.

Being or linking — what's in a name?

In the preceding section, you may have noticed that all the linking verbs in the sample sentences are forms of the verb *to be,* which is (surprise, surprise) how they got the name *being verbs.* When I was a kid (sometime before they invented the steam engine), these verbs were called *copulative,* from a root word meaning "join." However, copulative is out of style with English teachers these days (perhaps because you can also use the root for words referring to sex). I prefer the term *linking* because some equal-sign verbs are not forms of the verb *to be.* Check out these examples:

> With his foot-long fingernails and sly smile, Lochinvar *seemed* threatening.
>
> Lochinvar = threatening (*seemed* is a linking verb)
>
> A jail sentence for the unauthorized use of a comma *appears* harsh.
>
> jail sentence = harsh (*appears* is a linking verb in this sentence)
>
> The penalty for making a grammar error *remains* severe.
>
> penalty = severe (*remains* is a linking verb in this sentence)
>
> Lochness *stays* silent whenever monsters are mentioned.
>
> Lochness = silent (*stays* is a linking verb in this sentence)

Seemed, appears, remains, and *stays* are similar to forms of the verb *to be* in that they express states of being. They simply add shades of meaning to the basic concept. You may, for example, say that

> With his foot-long fingernails and sly smile, Lochinvar *was* threatening.

But now the statement is more definite. *Seemed* leaves room for doubt. Similarly, *remains* (in the third sample sentence) adds a time dimension to the basic expression of being. The sentence implies that the penalty was and still is severe.

No matter how you name it, any verb that places an equal sign in the sentence is a *being, linking,* or *copulative verb.*

Savoring sensory verbs

Sensory verbs — verbs that express information you receive through the senses of sight, hearing, smell, taste, and so forth — may also be linking verbs:

> Two minutes after shaving, all of Legghorn's three chins *feel* scratchy.
>
> all of Legghorn's three chins = scratchy (*feel* is a linking verb)

> Lola's piano solo *sounds* horrible, like barking inside a paint can.
>
> piano = horrible (*sounds* is a linking verb)

> The ten-year-old lasagna in your refrigerator *smells* disgusting.
>
> lasagna = disgusting (*smells* is a linking verb)

> The ten-year-old lasagna in your refrigerator also *looks* disgusting.
>
> lasagna = disgusting (*looks* is a linking verb)

> Needless to say, the ten-year-old lasagna in your refrigerator *tastes* great!
>
> lasagna = great (*tastes* is a linking verb)

Some verbs, especially those that refer to the five senses, may be linking verbs, but only if they act as an equal sign in the sentence. If they aren't equating two ideas, they aren't linking verbs. In the preceding example sentence about Legghorn's chins, *feel* is a linking verb. Here's a different sentence with the same verb:

> With their delicate fingers, Lulu and Lochness *feel* Legghorn's chins.

In this sentence, *feel* is not a linking verb because you're not saying that

> Lulu and Lochness = chins.

Instead, you're saying that Lulu and Lochness don't believe that Legghorn shaved, so they went stubble hunting.

Which sentence has a linking verb?

A. That annoying new clock sounds the hour with a recorded cannon shot.

B. That annoying new clock sounds extremely loud at four o'clock in the morning.

Answer: Sentence B has the linking verb. In sentence B, clock = extremely loud. In sentence A, the clock is doing something — sounding the hour — not being. (It's also waking up the whole neighborhood, but that idea isn't in the sentence.)

Try another. Which sentence has a linking verb?

    A. Ludwig stays single only for very short periods of time.

    B. Stay in the yard, Fido, or I'll cut your dog-biscuit ration in half!

Answer: Sentence A has the linking verb. In sentence A, Ludwig = single (at least for the moment — he's asking Ludmilla to marry him as you read this sentence). In sentence B, Fido is being told to do something — to stay in the backyard — clearly an action.

Linking verbs connect the subject and the subject complement. For more on complements, see Chapter 6. For the truly terminology-obsessed only: two other names for subject complements are *predicate nominative* and *predicate adjective*.

Here is a list of the most common linking verbs:

- ✔ Forms of *to be:* am, are, is, was, were, will be, shall be, has been, have been, had been, could be, should be, would be, might have been, could have been, should have been, shall have been, will have been, must have been, must be.

- ✔ Sensory verbs: look, sound, taste, smell, feel.

- ✔ Words that express shades of meaning in reference to a state of being: appear, seem, grow, remain, stay.

Completing Linking Verb Sentences Correctly

A linking verb begins a thought, but it needs another word to complete the thought. Unless all your friends have ESP (extrasensory perception), you can't walk around saying things like

    President Murgatroyd is

or

    The best day for the party will be

and expect people to know what you mean.

Due to a grammar error

The picnic has been cancelled *due to? because of?* the arrival of killer sparrows from their Southern nesting grounds.

Okay, which one is correct — *due to* or *because of?* The answer is *because of.* According to a rule that people ignore more and more every day:

✔ *Due to* describes nouns or pronouns. It may follow a linking verb if it gives information about the subject. (See "Linking Verbs: The Giant Equal Sign," earlier in the chapter, for more information.)

✔ *Because of* is a description of an action. (See "Lights! Camera! Action Verb!" later in this chapter for information on action verbs.)

The semi-logical reasoning that underlies this rule draws you deep into grammatical trivia, so keep reading only if you're daring (or bored). *Due to,* by definition, means "owing to." *Owing* is an adjective, and an adjective is a description of nouns and pronouns. In a linking verb sentence, the subject (always a noun or pronoun) may be linked to a description following the verb. An example:

Lola's mania for fashion is *due to* her deprived upbringing in an all-polyester household.

Due to her deprived upbringing in an all-polyester household describes *mania.*

Because of and *on account of* describe an action, usually answering the question why. An example:

The bubble-gum gun that Ratrug likes to carry is no longer being manufactured *because of* protests from the dental association.

Why is the gun no longer being manufactured? Because of protests from the dental association.

In real life (that is to say, in everyday conversational English), *due to* and *because of* are interchangeable. When you need your most formal, most correct language, be careful with this pair! One easy solution (easier than remembering which phrase is which) is to avoid them entirely and simply add *because* with a subject–verb pair.

You have three possible completions for a linking verb. One is a description:

After running 15 miles in high heels, Ludmilla's thigh muscles are *tired.*

thigh muscles = *tired* (tired is a description, an adjective in grammatical terms)

Ludmilla's high heels are *stunning,* especially when they land on your foot.

high heels = *stunning* (stunning is a description, also called an adjective)

Oscar's foot, wounded by Ludmilla's heels, seems particularly *painful.*

foot = *painful* (painful is a description, an adjective)

Lola's solution, to staple Oscar's toes together, is not very *helpful.*

solution = *helpful (helpful* is a description, an adjective. The other descriptive words, *not* and *very,* describe *helpful,* not *solution.)*

You may also complete a linking verb equation with a person, place, or thing — a noun, in grammatical terms. Here are some examples:

The most important part of a balanced diet is *popcorn.*

part of a balanced diet = *popcorn (popcorn* is a thing, and therefore a noun)

Lulu will be *president* of the Popcorn Club someday.

Lulu = *president (president* is a noun)

Legghorn's nutritional consultant has always been a complete *fraud.*

Legghorn's nutritional consultant = *fraud (fraud* is a noun)

Similarly, sometimes you complete a linking verb sentence with a *pronoun,* a word that substitutes for the name of a person, place, or thing. For example:

The winner of the all-state spitball contest is *you!*

winner = *you (you* is a substitute for the name of the winner, and therefore a pronoun)

Whoever put glue in the teapot is *someone* with a very bad sense of humor.

Whoever put glue in the teapot = *someone (someone* is a substitute for the name of the unknown prankster and therefore a pronoun)

You can't do much wrong when you complete linking verb sentences with descriptions or with nouns. However, you can do a lot wrong when you complete a linking verb sentence with a pronoun. In the next section, I show you how to avoid common linking verb–pronoun errors.

Placing the Proper Pronoun in the Proper Place

How do you choose the correct pronoun for a sentence with a linking verb? Think of a linking verb sentence as reversible. That is, the pronoun you put after a linking verb should be the same kind of pronoun that you put before a linking verb. First, however, I give you an example with a noun, where you can't make a mistake. Read these sentence pairs:

Ruggles is a *resident* of Red Gap.

A *resident* of Red Gap is *Ruggles*.

Lulu was a resident of Beige Gap.

A resident of Beige Gap was Lulu.

Both sentences in each pair mean the same thing, and both are correct. Now look at pronouns:

The winner of the election is *him!*

Him is the winner of the election!

Uh oh. Something's wrong. You don't say *him is,* unless you're in an old Tarzan movie. You say *he is.* Because you have a linking verb (*is*), you must put the same word after the linking verb that you would put before the linking verb. Try it again:

The winner of the election is *he!*

He is the winner of the election!

Now you've got the correct ending for your sentence.

If you pay attention to linking verbs, you'll choose the right pronouns for your sentence. Subject pronouns are *I, you, he, she, it, we, they, who,* and *whoever.* Pronouns that are not allowed to be subjects include *me, him, her, us, them, whom,* and *whomever.*

Remember that in the previous examples, I discuss formal English, not conversational English. In conversational English, this exchange is okay:

Who's there?

It is me.

or

Who's there?

It's me.

In formal English, the exchange goes like this:

Who is there?

It is I.

Because of the linking verb *is,* you want the same kind of pronoun before and after the linking verb. You can't start a sentence with *me* (unless, as I said earlier, you're in a Tarzan movie). But you can start a sentence with *I.*

Now you've probably, with your sharp eyes, found a flaw here. You can't reverse the last reply and say

I is it.

I takes a different verb — *am.* Both *is* and *am* are forms of the verb *to be* — one of the most peculiar creations in the entire language. So yes, you sometimes have to adjust the verb when you reverse a sentence with a form of *to be* in it. But the idea is the same; *I* can be a subject. *Me* can't.

Pronouns are divided into groups called *cases.* One group, the nominative or subject case, includes all the pronouns that may be subjects. The pronoun that follows the linking verb should also be in nominative, or subject, case. Another group of pronouns, those in objective case, acts as objects. Avoid object pronouns after linking verbs. These are a few examples of terminology designed by grammarians with nothing better to do. (For more information on pronoun case, see Chapter 17.)

Lights! Camera! Action Verb!

Linking verbs are important, but unless you're in some sort of hippie commune left over from the Sixties, you just can't sit around being all the time. You have to do something. It is here that action verbs come into the picture. Everything that is not *being* is *action,* at least in the verb world. Unlike the giant equal sign associated with linking verbs (see "Linking Verbs: The Giant Equal Sign," earlier in the chapter), something *happens* with an action verb:

Drusilla *slapped* the offending pig right on the snout. (*Slapped* is an action verb.)

Wynfred *will steal* third base as soon as his sneezing fit *ends.* (*Will steal* and *ends* are action verbs.)

According to the teacher, Ruggles *has shot* at least 16 spitballs in the last ten minutes. (*Has shot* is an action verb.)

You can define action verbs as all the verbs that don't express being. Don't let the name *action* fool you. Some action verbs aren't particularly energetic: *think, sit, stay, have, sleep, dream,* and so forth. Besides describing my ideal vacation, these words are also action verbs! Think of the definition this way: if the verb is *not* a giant equal sign (a linking verb), it's an action verb.

Getting by with a Little Help from My Verbs

You've probably noticed that some of the verbs I've identified throughout this chapter are single words and others are made up of several words. The extra words are called *helping verbs*. They don't carry out the trash or dust the living room, but they do help the main verb express meaning, usually changing the time, or *tense,* of the action. (For more on tense, see Chapter 3.)

Here are some sentences with helping verbs:

Allergia *will have sung* five arias from that opera by the time her recorder *runs* out of tape and her listeners *run* out of patience.

(In *will have sung, sung* is the main verb; *will* and *have* are helping verbs; *runs* and *run* are both main verbs without helping verbs.)

Legghorn *should have refused* to play the part of the villain, but his ego simply *would* not *be denied.*

(In *should have refused, refused* is the main verb; *should* and *have* are helping verbs; in *would be denied, denied* is the main verb; *would* and *be* are helping verbs.)

Distinguishing between helping verbs and main verbs isn't particularly important, as long as you get the whole thing when you're identifying the verb in a sentence. If you find only part of the verb, you may confuse action verbs with linking verbs. You want to keep these two types of verbs straight when you choose an ending for your sentence, as I explain in "Placing the Proper Pronoun in the Proper Place," earlier in the chapter.

To decide whether you have an action verb or a linking verb, look at the main verb, not at the helping verbs. If the main verb expresses action, the whole verb is action, even if one of the helpers is a form of *to be.* For example:

is going

will be sung

has been painted

should be strangled

are all action verbs, not linking verbs, because *going, sung, painted,* and *strangled* express action.

Pop the Question: Locating the Verb

A scientific study by a blue-ribbon panel of experts found that 90 percent of all the errors in a sentence occurred because the verb was misidentified. Okay, there was no study. I made it up! But it is true that when you try to crack a sentence, you should always start by identifying the verb. To find the verb, read the sentence and ask two questions:

- ✔ What's happening?
- ✔ What is? (or, What word is a "giant equal sign"?)

If you get an answer to the first question, you have an action verb. If you get an answer to the second question, you have a linking verb.

For example, in the sentence

Archie flew around the room and then swooped into his cage for a bird-seed snack.

you ask "What's happening?" and your answer is *flew* and *swooped. Flew* and *swooped* are action verbs.

If you ask, "What is?" you get no answer, because there's no linking verb in the sentence.

Try another:

Ludmilla's new tattoo will be larger than her previous fifteen tattoos.

What's happening? Nothing. You have no action verb. What is? *Will be. Will be* is a linking verb.

Pop the question and find the verbs in the following sentences. For extra credit, identify the verbs as action or linking.

A. Ludmilla scratched the cat almost as hard as the cat had scratched her.

B. After months of up and down motion, Lester is taking the elevator sideways, just for a change of pace.

C. The twisted frown on Legghorn's face seems strange because of the joyful background music.

Answers: A. *scratched* is an action verb, *had scratched* is an action verb. B. *is taking* is an action verb. C. *seems* is a linking verb.

Strictly speaking, the term *verb* is the name of the part of speech. In the sentence, the action or being is expressed by the *predicate*. (The *subject* is who or what you're talking about and the *predicate* is what you're saying about the subject.) The *complete predicate* is everything that you say about the subject. The *simple predicate* is the plain old verb. I've never been able to figure out why anyone would want to identify the complete predicate. The simple predicate, yes, but the simple predicate is the same as the verb, so you may as well call it the verb and be done with it.

Forget To Be or Not To Be: Infinitives Are Not Verbs

Here and there in this chapter I say "all forms of the verb *to be*." But *to be* is not actually a verb. In fact, it's an infinitive. An *infinitive* is *to + a verb* (yet another mixing of math and English). Here are some examples:

to laugh

to sing

to burp

to write

to be

Infinitives are the great-grandparents of verb families. Everything in the verb family descends from the infinitive, but like the retired, elderly relative who sits on the porch all day, infinitives don't perform any verb jobs in a sentence. In fact, if they do show up in the sentence, they take on a different job. (Sort of like a retired postmaster who refuses to carry a letter anywhere but plays racquetball all afternoon.) Infinitives may act as subjects or objects. They may also describe other words in the sentence. I discuss infinitives in more detail in Chapter 24.

The way it's suppose to be?

Do these sentences look familiar?

Lola *was suppose* to take out the garbage, but she refused to do so, saying that garbage removal was not part of her creative development.

Legghorn *use* to take out the trash, but after that unfortunate encounter with a raccoon and an empty potato chip bag, he is reluctant to venture near the cans.

Lochness *is suppose* to do all kinds of things, but of course he never does anything he *is suppose* to do.

If these sentences look familiar, look again. Each one is wrong. Check out the italicized verbs: *was suppose, use,* and *is suppose.* All represent what people hear but not what the

speaker is actually trying to say. The correct words to use in these instances are *supposed* and *used* — past tense forms. Here are the correct sentences:

Lola *was supposed* to take out the garbage, but she refused to do so, saying that garbage removal was not part of her creative development.

Legghorn *used* to take out the trash, but after that unfortunate encounter with a raccoon and an empty potato chip bag, he is reluctant to venture near the cans.

Lochness *is supposed* to do all kinds of things, but of course he never does anything he *is supposed* to do.

The most important thing to know about infinitives is this: When you pop the question to find the verb, don't choose an infinitive as your answer. If you do, you'll miss the real verb or verbs in the sentence. Other than that, forget about infinitives!

Okay, you can't forget about infinitives completely. Here's something else you should know about infinitives in formal English: Don't split them in half. For example, you commonly see sentences like the following:

Mudbud vowed to really study if he ever got the chance to take the flight instructor exam again.

This example is common, but incorrect. Grammatically, *to study* is a unit — one infinitive. You're not supposed to separate its two halves. Now that you know this rule, read the paper. Everybody splits infinitives, even the grayest, dullest papers with no comics whatsoever. So you have two choices. You can split infinitives all you want, or you can follow the rule and feel totally superior to the professional journalists. The choice is yours.

DEMONS

Two not for the price of one

Here's a spelling tip: the following words are often written as one — incorrectly! Always write them as two separate words: a lot, all right, each other.

Example: Ludmilla has *a lot* of trouble distinguishing between the sounds of "l" and "r," so she tries to avoid the expression *"all right"* whenever possible. Ludmilla and Ludwig (who also has pronunciation trouble), help *each other* prepare state-of-the-union speeches every January.

Here's another tip. You can write the following words as one or two words, but with two different meanings:

Altogether means "extremely, entirely."

All together means "as one."

Example: Lochivar was *altogether* disgusted with the way the entire flock of dodo birds sang *all together*.

Another pair of tricky words:

Sometime means "at a certain point in time."

Some time means "a period of time."

Example: Lochness said that he would visit Lulu *sometime,* but not now because he has to spend *some time* in jail for murdering the English language.

Still more:

Someplace means "an unspecified place" and describes an action.

Some place means "a place" and refers to a physical space.

Example: Lochness screamed, "I have to go *someplace* now!" Lulu thinks he headed for *some place* near the railroad station where the pizza is hot and no one asks any questions.

And another pair:

Everyday means "ordinary, common."

Every day means "occurring daily."

Ludwig loves *everyday* activities such as cooking, cleaning, and sewing. He has the palace staff perform all of those duties *every day*.

Last set, I promise:

Anyway means "in any event."

Any way means "a way, some sort of way."

Example: *"Anyway,"* added Ratrug, "I don't think there is *any way* to avoid jail for tax evasion."

Chapter 3

Relax! Understanding Verb Tense

*Y*ou can tell time lots of ways: look at a clock, dial a number and listen to that annoying mechanical voice ("At the tone the time will be. . . ."), or check the verb. The verb shows the action or state of being in the sentence. In English, the verb also shows the time the action or "being" took place. (For more information on finding the verb in a sentence, see Chapter 2.)

In some lucky languages — Thai, for example — the verb has basically one form. Whether the sentence is about the past, the present, or the future doesn't matter; the verb is the same. Extra words — yesterday, tomorrow, now, and so forth — indicate the time. Not so in English (sigh). In English, six different tenses of verbs express time. In other words, each tense places the action or the state of being of the sentence at a point in time.

Before you start complaining about learning six tenses, spend a moment being grateful that you don't speak Latin. In case you're wondering why it's a dead language that no one speaks anymore, each verb in Latin has 120 different forms!

Three of the six English tenses are called *simple*. In this chapter, I explain the simple tenses in some detail, such as the difference between *I go* and *I am going*. The other three tenses are called *perfect*. (Trust me, the perfect tenses are far from it.) I touch upon the basics of the perfect tenses: present perfect, past perfect, and future perfect in this chapter. Then I dig a little more deeply into present perfect tense. The other two perfect tenses — past and future — are real headaches and far less common than present perfect, so I save them for later. For an in-depth explanation of the past perfect and future perfect tenses, see Chapter 18.

Simplifying Matters: The Simple Tenses

The three simple tenses are present, past, and future. Each of the simple tenses (just to make things even *more* fun) has two forms. One is the unadorned, no-frills, plain tense. This form doesn't have a separate name; it is just called *present, past,* or *future.* It shows actions or states of being at a point in time, but it doesn't always pin down a specific moment. The other form is called *progressive.* The progressive form is not politically active; it doesn't make speeches about minimum wage reform or campaign finance. Instead, the *progress*ive form shows actions or a state of being *in progress.*

Present tense

Present tense tells you what is going on right now. This simple tense has two forms. One is called *present,* and the other is *progressive.* The present form shows action or state of being that is occurring now, that is generally true, or that is always happening. The present *progressive* form is similar, but it often implies a process. (The difference between the two is subtle. I go into more details about using these forms below.) For now, take a look at a couple of sentences in the no-frills present tense:

> Rugelach *rolls* his tongue around the pastry. (*rolls* is in present tense)
>
> Legghorn *plans* nothing for New Year's Eve because he never *has* a date. (*plans, has* are in present tense)

Now here are two sentences in the present progressive form:

> Alexei *is axing* the proposal to cut down the national forest. (*is axing* is in present progressive form)
>
> Murgatroyd and Lulu *are skiing* far too fast down that cliff. (*are skiing* is in present progressive form)

Past tense

Past tense tells you what happened before the present time. This simple tense also has two forms — plain and chocolate-sprinkled. Sorry, I mean plain, which is called *past,* and *past progressive.* Consider these two past-tense sentences:

> When the elastic in Ms. Belli's girdle *snapped,* we all *woke* up. (*snapped* and *woke* are in past tense)

Despite the strong plastic ribbon, the package *became* unglued and *spilled* onto the conveyor belt. (*became* and *spilled* are in past tense)

Here are two more examples, this time in the past progressive form:

While Buzzy *was sleeping,* his cat Catnip *was* completely *destroying* the sofa. (*was sleeping* and *was destroying* are in the progressive form of the past tense)

Lola's friends *were passing* tissues to Lulu at a rate of five per minute. (*were passing* is in the progressive form of the past tense)

You can't go wrong with the past tense, except for the irregular verbs — I get to them later in this chapter. But one very common mistake is to mix past and present tenses in the same story. Here's an example:

So I go to the restaurant looking for Cindy because I want to tell her about Grady's date with Eleanor. I walk in and I see Brad Pitt! So I went up to him and said, "How's Jennifer?"

The speaker started in present tense — no problem. Even though an event is clearly over, present tense is okay if you want to make a story more dramatic. (See the sidebar "The historical present," later in this chapter.) But the last sentence switches gears — suddenly we're in past tense. Problem! Don't change tenses in the middle of a story. And don't bother celebrities either.

Future tense

Future tense talks about what has not happened yet. This simple tense is the only one that always needs helping verbs to express meaning, even for the plain, no-frills version.

Helping verbs such as *will, shall, have, has, should,* and so forth change the meaning of the main verb. (See Chapter 2 for more information.)

Future tenses — this will shock you — come in two forms. I'm not talking about alternate universes here; this book is about grammar, not sci-fi adventures! One form of the future tense is called *future,* and the other is *future progressive.* The unadorned form of the future tense goes like this:

Nutrella *will position* the wig in the exact center of the dragon's head. (*will position* is in future tense)

Ludmilla and I *will* never *part*! (*will part* is in future tense)

A couple of examples of the future progressive:

During the post-election period, Gumpus *will be pondering* his options. (*will be pondering* is in the progressive form of the future tense)

Lola *will be sprinkling* the flowers with fertilizer in a vain attempt to keep them fresh. (*will be sprinkling* is in the progressive form of the future tense)

Find the verbs and sort them into present, past, and future tenses.

A. When the tornado whirls overhead, we run for the camera and the phone number of the television station.

B. Shall I compare you to a winter's day?

C. When you were three, you blew out all the candles on your birthday cake.

Answers: In sentence A, the present tense verbs are *whirls* and *run*. In sentence B, the future tense verb is *shall compare*. In sentence C, the past tense verbs are *were* and *blew*.

Now find the verbs and sort them into present progressive, past progressive, and future progressive forms.

A. Exactly 5,000 years ago, a dinosaur was living in that mud puddle.

B. Agamemnon and Apollo are enrolling in a union of mythological characters.

C. The pilot will be joining us as soon as the aircraft clears the Himalayas.

Answers: In sentence A, the past progressive verb is *was living*. In sentence B, the present progressive verb is *are enrolling*. In sentence C, the future progressive verb is *will be joining*.

Using the Tenses Correctly

What's the difference between each pair of simple tense forms? Not a whole lot. People often interchange these forms without creating any problems. But shades of difference in meaning do exist.

Present and present progressive

The single-word form of the present tense may be used for things that are generally true at the present time but not necessarily happening right now. For example:

Ollie *attends* wrestling matches every Sunday.

If you call Ollie on Sunday, you'll get this annoying message he recorded on his answering machine because he's at the arena (*attends* is in present tense). You may also get this message on a Thursday (or on another day) and it is still correct, even though on Thursdays Ollie stays home to play chess. Now read this sentence:

Ollie *is playing* hide-and-seek with his dog Spot.

This sentence means that right now (*is playing* is in the progressive form of the present tense), as you write or say this sentence, Ollie is running around the living room looking for Spot, who is easy to find because he never stops barking.

Past and past progressive

The difference between the plain past tense and the past progressive tense is pretty much the same as in the present tense. The single-word form often shows what happened in the past more generally. The progressive form may pinpoint action or state of being at a specific time or occurring in the past on a regular basis.

Gulliver *went* to the store and *bought* clothes for all his little friends.

This sentence means that at some point in the past Gulliver whipped out his charge card and finished off his Christmas list (*went* and *bought* are in past tense).

While Gulliver *was shopping,* his friends *were planning* their revenge.

This sentence means that Gulliver shouldn't have bothered because at the exact moment he was spending his allowance, his friends were deciding what time to pour ink into his lunchbox (*was shopping* and *were planning* are in the progressive form of the past tense).

Gulliver *was shopping* until he *was dropping,* despite his mother's strict credit limit.

This sentence refers to one of Gulliver's bad habits, his tendency to go shopping every spare moment (*was shopping* and *was dropping* are in the progressive form of the past tense). The shopping was repeated on a daily basis, over and over again. (Hence, Gulliver's mom imposed the strict credit limit.)

Future and future progressive

You won't find much difference between these two. The progressive gives you slightly more of a sense of being in the middle of things. For example:

Hammy *will be playing* Hamlet with a great deal of shouting.

Hammy's actions in the sentence above may be a little more immediate than

Hammy *will play* Hamlet with a great deal of shouting.

In the first example, *will be playing* is in the progressive form of the future tense. In the second example, *will play* is in future tense.

Understanding the difference between the two forms of the simple tenses entitles you to wear an Official Grammarian hat. But if you don't catch on to the distinction, don't lose sleep over the issue. If you can't discern the subtle differences in casual conversation, your listeners probably won't either. In choosing between the two forms, you're dealing with shades of meaning, not Grand-Canyon-sized discrepancies.

Perfecting Grammar: The Perfect Tenses

Now for the hard stuff. These three tenses — present perfect, past perfect, and future perfect — may give you gray hair, even if you are only twelve. And they have progressive forms too! As with the simple tenses, each tense has a no-frills version called by the name of the tense: present perfect, past perfect, and future perfect. The progressive form adds an "ing" to the mix. The progressive is a little more immediate than the other form, expressing an action or state of being in progress.

In this section, I state the basics and provide examples. For a complete explanation of present perfect and present perfect progressive tense, see "Using Present Perfect Tense Correctly," later in this chapter. For a full discussion of the correct sequence with past and future perfect tenses, see Chapter 18.

Present perfect and present perfect progressive

The two present perfect forms show actions or states of being that began in the past but are still going on in the present. These forms are used whenever any action or state of being spans two time zones — past and present.

The historical present

Not surprisingly, you use present tense for actions that are currently happening. But (Surprise!) you may also use present tense for some actions that happened a long time ago and for some actions that never happened at all. The historical present is a way to write about history or literature:

> On December 7, 1941, President Franklin Delano Roosevelt *tells* the nation about the attack on Pearl Harbor. The nation immediately *declares* war.

> Harry Potter *faces* three tests when he *represents* Hogwarts in the tournament.

In the first sentence, *tells* and *declares* are in present tense, even though the sentence concerns events that occurred decades ago. Here the historical present makes the history more dramatic. In the second sentence, *faces* and *represents* are in present tense. The idea is that for each reader who opens the book, the story begins anew. With the logic that we have come to know and love in English grammar, the events are always happening, even though Harry Potter is a fictional character and the events never happened.

First, check out examples with present perfect tense:

> Rumpus and his friends *have spent* almost every penny of the inheritance. (*have spent* is in present perfect tense)

> Lulu's mortal enemy, Rumpus, *has pleaded* with her to become a professional tattooist. (*has pleaded* is in present perfect tense)

Now peruse these progressive examples:

> Rumpus *has been studying* marble shooting for fifteen years without learning any worthwhile techniques. (*has been studying* is in the progressive form of the present perfect tense)

> Lulu and her mentor Lola *have been counting sheep* all night. (*have been counting* is in the progressive form of the present perfect tense)

Past perfect and past perfect progressive

Briefly, each of these forms places an action in the past in relation to another action in the past. In other words, a timeline is set. The timeline begins some time ago and ends at NOW. At least two events are on the timeline. For more information about how to use the past perfect, see Chapter 18. Here are a couple of examples of the past perfect tense:

> After she *had sewn* up the wound, the doctor realized that her watch was missing! (*had sewn* is in past perfect tense)

The watch *had ticked* for ten minutes before the nurse discovered its whereabouts. (*had ticked* is in past perfect tense)

Compare the preceding sentences with examples of the past perfect progressive (try saying *that* three times fast without spraying your listener!):

The patient *had been considering* a lawsuit but changed his mind. (*had been considering* is in the progressive form of the past perfect tense)

The doctor *had been worrying* about a pending lawsuit, but her patient dropped his case. (*had been worrying* is in the progressive form of the past perfect tense)

Future perfect and future perfect progressive

These two forms talk about events or states of being that have not happened yet in relation to another event even further in the future. In other words, another timeline, with at least two events or states of being on it. For more information on how to use the future perfect tense, see Chapter 18.

First, I give you the plain version of the future perfect:

Appleby *will have eaten* the entire apple by the time the bell rings at the end of recess. (*will have eaten* is in future perfect tense)

When Appleby finally arrives at grammar class, Appleby's teacher *will have* already *outlined* at least 504 grammar rules. (*will have outlined* is in future perfect tense)

Now take a look at the progressive form of the future perfect tense:

When the clocks strikes four, Appleby *will have been chewing* for 29 straight minutes without swallowing even a bite of that apple. (*will have been chewing* is in the progressive form of the future perfect tense)

By the time he swallows, Appleby's teacher *will have been explaining* the virtues of digestion to her class for a very long time. (*will have been explaining* is in the progressive form of the future perfect tense)

Using Present Perfect Tense Correctly

This mixture of present (*has, have*) and past is a clue to its use: present perfect tense ties the past to the present. This tense probably won't give you many problems. Just be sure you include an element of the past and an element of the present in the idea you are expressing.

I *have gone* to the cafeteria every day for six years, and I *have* not yet *found* one edible item.

This sentence means that at present I am still in school, still trying to find something to eat and for the past six years I was in school also, trudging to the cafeteria each day, searching for a sandwich without mystery meat in it.

Bertha *has* frequently *buzzed* Bubba, but Bubba *has* not *buzzed* Bertha back.

This sentence means that in the present Bertha hasn't given up yet; she's still trying to buzz Bubba from time to time. In the past Bertha also buzzed Bubba. In the present and in the past, Bubba's been daydreaming, ignoring the buzzer, and not bothering to let Bertha in.

As with the simple present tense, the present perfect tense takes two forms. One is called *present perfect*, and the other *present perfect progressive*. Shades of difference in meaning exist between the two — the progressive is a little more immediate — but nothing you need to worry about.

Which one is correct?

A. Bertha moved into Bubba's building in 1973 and lived there ever since.

B. Bertha has moved into Bubba's building in 1973 and lived there ever since.

C. Bertha moved into Bubba's building in 1973 and has lived there ever since.

Some tense pairs

Helping verbs, as well as main verbs, have tenses. Some of the most common pairs are *can/could* and *may/might.* The first verb in each pair is in present tense; the second is in past tense. If you *can* imagine, you are speaking about the present. If you *could* imagine, you are speaking about the past. More and more people interchange these helping verbs at random, but technically, the verbs do express time. So remember:

Now you *may* talk about how much you hate writing school reports.

Yesterday you *might* have gone to the store if the sky hadn't dumped a foot of snow on your head.

After six years of lessons, you *can* finally dance a mean tango.

No one ever danced as well as Fred Astaire *could* in those old movie musicals.

Answer: Sentence C is correct. You cannot use the simple past, as in sentence A, because a connection to the present exists (the fact that Bertha still lives in Bubba's building). Sentence B is wrong because the moving isn't connected to the present; it's over and done with. So you can't use present perfect for the move. Sentence C has the right combination — the move, now over, should be expressed in simple past. The event that began in the past and is still going on (Bertha's living in the building) needs present perfect tense.

Forming Present and Past Participles of Regular Verbs

I used to tell my classes that my gray hair came from my struggles with *participles,* but I was just trying to scare them into doing their grammar homework. Participles are not very mysterious; as you may guess from the spelling, a *part*iciple is simply a *part* of the verb. Each verb has two participles — a present participle and a past participle. You may have noticed the *present participle* in the present progressive tenses. The present participle is the *ing* form of the verb. The past participle helps form the present perfect tense since this tense spans both the past and present. Regular past participles are formed by adding *ed* to the verb. Table 3-1 shows a selection of regular participles.

Table 3-1	Examples of Regular Participles	
Verb	*Present Participle*	*Past Participle*
ask	asking	asked
beg	begging	begged
call	calling	called
dally	dallying	dallied
empty	emptying	emptied
fill	filling	filled
grease	greasing	greased

Just to Make Things More Difficult: Irregular Verbs

When you're out bargain hunting, irregulars look good. Just a tiny difference between an irregular shirt and a regular one, and the irregular one costs less. Unfortunately, an irregular is not a bargain in the grammar market. It's just a pain. In this section, I break down the irregulars into two parts. The first part is the mother of all irregular verbs, *to be*. Second is a list of irregular past tense forms and past participles.

"To be or not to be" is a complete pain

Possibly the weirdest verb in the English language, the verb *to be,* changes more frequently than any other. Here it is, tense by tense.

Present Tense	Singular	Plural
I am	you are	you are, we are
you are	he, she, it is	they are

Note that the singular forms are in the first column and plural forms are in the second column. Singulars are for one person or thing and plurals for more than one. "You" is listed twice because it may refer to one person or to a group. (Just one more bit of illogic in the language.)

Past Tense	Singular	Plural
I was	you were	you were, we were
you were	he, she, it was	they were

Future Tense	Singular	Plural
I will be	you will be	you will be, we will be
you will be	he, she, it will be	they will be

Present Perfect	Singular	Plural
I have been	you have been	you have been, we have been
you have been	he, she, it has been	they have been

Past Perfect	*Singular*	*Plural*
I had been	you had been	you had been, we had been
you had been	he, she, it had been	they had been

Future Perfect	*Singular*	*Plural*
I will have been	you will have been	you will have been, we will have been
you will have been	he, she, it will have been	they will have been

Irregular past and past participles

Are you having fun yet? Now the true joy begins. Dozens and dozens of English verbs have irregular past tense forms, as well as irregular past participles. (The present participles, except for the occasional change from the letter *y* to the letter *i*, are fairly straightforward. Just add *ing*.) I won't list all the irregular verbs here, just a few you may find useful in everyday writing. If you have questions about a particular verb, check your dictionary. In Table 3-2, the first column is the infinitive form of the verb. (The infinitive is the "to + verb" form — to laugh, to cry, to learn grammar, and so on.) The second column is the simple past tense. The third column is the past participle, which is combined with *has* (singular) or *have* (plural) to form the present perfect tense. The past participle is also used with *had* to form the past perfect tense.

Table 3-2	Examples of Irregular Participles	
Verb	*Past*	*Past Participle*
begin	began	begun
bite	bit	bitten
break	broke	broken
bring	brought	brought
catch	caught	caught
choose	chose	chosen
come	came	come
do	did	done
drive	drove	driven
eat	ate	eaten
fall	fell	fallen

Verb	Past	Past Participle
fly	flew	flown
get	got	got or gotten
go	went	gone
know	knew	known
lead	led	led
lend	lent	lent
lie	lay	lain
lose	lost	lost
ride	rode	ridden
ring	rang	rung
rise	rose	risen
run	ran	run
say	said	said
see	saw	seen
shake	shook	shaken
sing	sang	sung
sink	sank or sunk	sunk
sit	sat	sat
speak	spoke	spoken
steal	stole	stolen
take	took	taken
write	wrote	written

Who made these rules anyway? Old guys in England?

The next time you try to decide whether you *had run* or *had ran* home, thank the Angles and the Saxons. Those old guys were members of Germanic tribes who invaded England about 1500 years ago. Their languages blended into Anglo-Saxon, which came to be called Englisc. Nowadays it's called "Old English."

Old English lasted about 400 years; this English would look and sound like a foreign language to English-speakers today. Although it's gone, Old English isn't forgotten. Remnants remain in modern speech. You can thank (or blame) the Anglo-Saxons for most of the irregular verbs, including the fact that you say *ran* instead of *runned*.

In the Middle English period (1100 to about 1450) England was speckled with local dialects, each with its own vocabulary and sentence structure. Nobody studied grammar in school, and nobody worried about what was correct or incorrect. (There were a few more important items on the agenda, including starvation and the bubonic plague.)

In the fifteenth century the printing press was invented and the era of Modern English began. At this time, folks were more interested in learning to read and also more interested in writing for publication. But writers faced a new problem. Sending one's words to a different part of the country might mean sending them off to someone whose vocabulary or sentence structure was different. Not to mention the fact that spelling was all over the place! Suddenly, rules seemed like a good idea. London was the center of government and economic life — and also the center of printing. So what the London printers decided was right soon *became* right. However, not until the eighteenth century did the rules really become set. Printers, in charge of turning handwriting into type, were guided by "printers' bibles," also known as the rules.

Schoolmasters tried to whip the English language into shape by writing the rules down. But they grafted Latin concepts onto English, and it wasn't always a good fit. In fact, some of the loonier rules of English grammar come from this mismatch. In Latin, for example, you can't split an infinitive because an infinitive is a single word. In English, infinitives are formed with two words *(to* plus a *verb,* as in *to dance, to dream).* Nevertheless, the rule was handed down: no split infinitives.

Chapter 4

Who's Doing What? How to Find the Subject

In Chapter 2 I describe the sentence as a flatbed truck carrying your meaning to the reader or listener. Verbs are the wheels of the truck, and subjects are the drivers. Why do you need a subject? Can you imagine a truck speeding down the road without a driver? Not possible, or, if possible, not a pleasant thought!

Who's Driving the Truck or Why the Subject Is Important

All sentences contain verbs — words that express action or state of being. (For more information on verbs, see Chapter 2.) But you can't have an action in a vacuum. You can't have a naked, solitary state of being either. Someone or something must also be present in the sentence — the *who* or *what* you're talking about in relation to the action or state of being expressed by the verb. The "someone" or "something" doing the action or being talked about is the subject.

A "someone" must be a person and a "something" must be a thing, place, or idea. So guess what? The subject is usually a noun, because a noun is a person, place, thing, or idea. I say *usually* because sometimes the subject is a pronoun — a word that substitutes for a noun — *he, they, it,* and so forth. (For more on pronouns, see Chapter 10.)

Teaming up: Subject and verb pairs

Another way to think about the subject is to say that the subject is the "who" or "what" part of the subject–verb pair. The subject–verb pair is the main idea of the sentence, stripped to essentials. A few sentences:

> *Jasper gasped* at the mummy's sudden movement.

In this sentence, *Jasper gasped* is the main idea; it's also the subject–verb pair. (This subject–verb pair is also really hard to say four times fast.)

> *Justicia will judge* the beauty contest only if the *warthog competes*.

You should spot two subject–verb pairs in this sentence: *Justicia will judge* and *warthog competes*.

Now try a sentence without action. This one describes a state of being, so it uses a linking verb:

> *Jackhammer has* always *been* an extremely noisy worker.

The subject–verb pair is *Jackhammer has been*. Did you notice that *Jackhammer has been* sounds incomplete? *Has been* is a linking verb, and linking verbs always need something after the verb to complete the idea. I give you more links in the verb chain in Chapter 2; now back to the *subject* at hand. (Uh, sorry about that one.) The subject–verb pair in action-verb sentences may usually stand alone, but the subject–verb pair in linking verb sentences may not.

Compound subjects and verbs: Two for the price of one

Subjects and verbs pair off, but sometimes you get two (or more) for the price of one. For example:

> Warthog *burped* and *cried* after the contest.

You've got two actions *(burped, cried)* and one person doing both *(Warthog)*. *Warthog* is the subject of both *burped* and *cried*.

Some additional samples of double verbs, which in grammatical terms are called *compound verbs*:

> Lochness *snatched* the atomic secret and quickly *stashed* it in his navel. *(snatched, stashed* = verbs)

Ludmilla *ranted* for hours about Ludwig's refusal to hold an engagement party and then *crept* home. (*ranted, crept* = verbs)

Eggworthy *came* out of his shell last winter but *didn't stay* there. (*came, did stay* = verbs)

You can also have two subjects (or more) and one verb. The multiple subjects are called *compound subjects*. Here's an example:

Warthog and *Justicia* went home in defeat.

Here you notice one action *(went)* and two people *(Warthog, Justicia)* doing the action, if you count Warthog as a person. So the verb *went* has two subjects.

Now take a look at some additional examples:

Lola and *Lulu* ganged up on Legghorn yesterday to his dismay and defeat. (*Lola, Lulu* = subjects)

The *omelet* and *fries* revolted Eggworthy. (*omelet, fries* = subjects)

Snort and *Squirm* were the only two dwarves expelled from Snow White's band. (*Snort, Squirm* = subjects)

Pop the Question: Locating the Subject–Verb Pair

Allow me to let you in on a little trick for pinpointing the subject–verb pair of a sentence: Pop the question! (No, I'm not asking you to propose.) Pop the question tells you what to ask in order to find out what you want to know. The correct question is all important in the search for information, as all parents know:

WRONG QUESTION FROM PARENT: What did you do last night?

TEENAGER'S ANSWER: Nothing.

RIGHT QUESTION FROM PARENT: When you came in at 2 a.m., were you hoping that I'd ignore the fact that you went to the China Club?

TEENAGER'S ANSWER: I didn't go to the China Club! I went to Moomba.

PARENT: Aha! You went to a club on a school night. You're grounded.

In Chapter 2, I explain that the first question to ask is not "Is this going to be on the test?" but "What's the verb?" (To find the verb, ask *what's happening?*

or *what is?*) After you uncover the verb, put "who" or "what" in front of it to form a question. The answer is the subject!

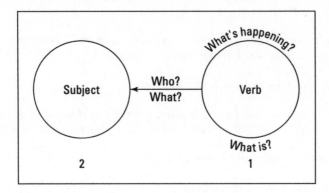

Try one:

Jackknife sharpens his dives during hours of practice.

1. Pop the question: What's happening? Answer: *sharpens. Sharpens* is the verb.
2. Pop the question: Who or what *sharpens?* Answer: *Jackknife sharpens. Jackknife* is the subject.

A pop quiz on popping the question. What are the subject and verb in the following sentence?

Jolly Roger will soon be smiling because of all the treasure in his ship.

Answer: The verb is *will be smiling* and the subject is *Jolly Roger.* Try one more. Identify the subject and verb.

No matter what the weather, Ratrug never even considers wearing a hat.

Answer: The verb is *considers* and the subject is *Ratrug.*

What's a Nice Subject Like You Doing in a Place Like This?: Unusual Word Order

In this chapter, all the sample sentences up to this point are in the normal subject–verb order, which is (gasp) subject–verb. In other words, the subject usually comes before the verb. Not every sentence follows that order, though most do. Sometimes a subject hides out at the end of the sentence or in some other weird place. (Hey, even a subject needs a break sometime. Don't you like a change of scenery once in a while?)

If you pop the question and answer it according to the meaning of the sentence — not according to the word order — you'll be fine. The key is to put the subject questions (who? what?) in front of the verb. Then think about what the sentence is actually saying and answer the questions. And voilà! Your subject will appear.

Try this one:

> Up the avenue and around the park trudged Godzilla on his way to tea with the Loch Ness Monster.

1. Pop the question: What's happening? What is? Answer: *trudged. Trudged* is the verb.
2. Pop the question: Who *trudged?* What *trudged?* Answer: *Godzilla. Godzilla* is the subject. (I'll let you decide if Godzilla is a who or a what.)

If you were answering by word order, you'd say *park.* But the *park* did not *trudge, Godzilla trudged.* Pay attention to meaning, not to placement in the sentence, and you can't go wrong.

What are the subjects and verbs in the following sentences?

A. Alas, what a woefully inadequate grammarian am I.
B. Across the river and through the woods to the grammarian's house go Ludmilla and Ludwig.

Answers: In sentence A, *am* is the verb and *I* is the subject. In sentence B, the verb is *go* and the subjects are *Ludmilla* and *Ludwig.*

Always find the verb first. Then look for the subject.

Find That Subject! Detecting You-Understood

> "Cross on the green, not in between."

> "Eat your vegetables."

> "Don't leave your chewing gum on the bedpost overnight."

Me, myself, and I

You can use *I* as a subject, but not *me* or *myself.*

> Wrong: Bill and me are going to rob that bank. Bill and myself will soon be in jail.

> Right: Bill and I are going to rob that bank. Bill and I will soon be in jail.

> Wrong: Lola and myself plan to stage the musical version of Legghorn's next play. Legghorn and me are writing the music.

> Right: Lola and I plan to stage the musical version of Legghorn's next play. Legghorn and I are writing the music.

Me doesn't perform actions; it receives actions. To put this rule another way: *me* is an object of some action or form of attention:

> He gave it to *me.*

Lulu's offer was far more profitable for *me* than Lochness's.

Myself is appropriate only for actions that double back on the person performing the action:

> I told *myself* not to be such a nerd!

> Because no one else did, I paid *myself* a compliment.

Myself may also be used for emphasis, along with the word *I.*

> *I myself* will disclose the secret to the tabloid offering the most bucks.

> Murgatroyd and *I myself* wrote that screenplay, so don't you dare criticize it.

What do these sentences have in common? Yes, they're all nagging comments you've heard all your life. More importantly, they're all commands. The verbs give orders: *cross, eat, don't leave.* So where's the subject in these sentences?

If you pop the question, here's what happens:

1. Pop the question: What's happening? What is? Answer: *cross, eat, don't leave.*

2. Pop the question: *Who cross, eat, don't leave?* Answer: Uh. . . .

The second question appears to have no answer, but appearances can be deceiving. The answer is *you. You* cross at the green, not in between. *You* eat your vegetables. *You* don't leave your chewing gum on the bedpost overnight. What's that you say? *You* is not in the sentence? True. *You* is not written, but it's implied. And when your mom says, "Eat your vegetables," you understand that she means *you.* So grammarians say that the subject is *you-understood.* The subject is *you,* even though *you* isn't in the sentence and even though *you* don't intend to eat those horrible lima beans.

Pop the questions and find the subject–verb pairs in these three sentences.

A. Ludmilla, dancing the cha-cha, forgot to watch her feet.

B. Stop, Ludmilla!

C. Over the bandleader and across five violin stands fell Ludmilla, heavily.

Answers: In sentence A, *forgot* is the verb and *Ludmilla* is the subject. *Dancing* is a fake verb. (I discuss finding fake verbs and subjects later in this chapter.) In sentence B, *stop* is the verb and *you-understood* is the subject. The remark is addressed to *Ludmilla,* but *you-understood* is still the subject. In sentence C, *fell* is the verb and *Ludmilla* is the subject.

Don't Get Faked Out: Avoiding Fake Verbs and Subjects

As I walk through New York City, I often see "genuine" Rolex watches (retail $10,000 or so) for sale from street peddlers for "$15 — special today only!" You need to guard against fakes when you're on the city streets (no surprise there). Also (and this may be a surprise), you need to guard against fakes when you're finding subject–verb pairs.

Finding fake verbs

Verbs in English grammar can be a little sneaky sometimes. You may ask *who?* or *what?* in front of a verb and get no answer or at least no answer that makes sense. When this happens, you may gather that you haven't really found a verb. You've probably stumbled upon a lookalike, or, as I like to call it, a "fake verb." Here's an example:

> Wiping his tears dramatically, Grumpus pleaded with the teacher to forgive his lack of homework.

Suppose you pop the verb question *(What's happening? What is?)* and get *wiping* for an answer. A reasonable guess. But now pop the subject question: *Who wiping? What wiping?* The questions don't sound right, and that's your first hint that you haven't found a real verb. But the question is not important. The answer, however, is! And there is no real answer in the sentence. You may try *Grumpus,* but when you put him with the "verb," it doesn't match: *Grumpus wiping.* (*Grumpus is wiping* would be okay, but that's not what the sentence says.) So now you know for sure that your first "verb" isn't really a verb. Put it aside and keep looking. What's the real verb? *Pleaded.*

Who made these rules anyway? Old guys in America?

When English settlers crossed the ocean and landed in America, they found themselves submerged in a stew of languages. Colonists from France, Spain, the Netherlands, and other European countries were around, and so were Native Americans speaking hundreds of different tongues. The English language immediately began to pick up words from all these sources. And of course, the language itself, cut off from the mother country by a months-long journey, began to follow its own path.

Almost as soon as America became a country, schools began to teach English grammar. (This practice was a major break from the British, who were still teaching Latin grammar in their schools and hoping that something good would rub off onto their students' English skills.) But once again the old guys weighed in with a strong tsk-tsk, this time worrying that the teachers themselves didn't know the rules. W B. Fowle, nineteenth-century author of a popular grammar textbook, complained that grammarians (and grammar teachers) "have generally been unable to write or speak pure English."

All of those complaining grammarians spent a lot of time writing books that a) attacked all the previous grammar texts and b) claimed that their own books were more fun. Samuel Kirkham in his 1825 *English Grammar in Familiar Lectures,* for example, said that *his* text made "interesting and delightful" a subject that was, until then, "tedious, dry, and irksome." Joseph Neef, my favorite nineteenth-century grammarian, paused for a moment in his list of rules to admit that "the education of children and the rearing of vegetables are the only occupations for which I feel any aptitude."

To sum up: Lots of words in the sentence express action or being, but only some of these words are verbs. (Most are what grammarians call verbals; check out Chapter 24 for more on verbals.) At any rate, if you get no answer to your pop-the-subject question, just ignore the "verb" you think you found and look for the real verb.

Watching out for here and there and other fake subjects

Someone comes up to you and says, "Here is one million dollars." What's the first question that comes into your mind? I know, good grammarian that you are, that your question is *What's the subject of that sentence?* Well, try to answer your question in the usual way, by popping the question.

Here is one million dollars.

1. Pop the question: What's happening? What is? Answer: *is.*

2. Pop the question: Who *is?* What *is?* Answer: ?

What did you say? *Here is?* Wrong. *Here* can't be a subject. Neither can *there.* Both of these words are fake subjects. (*Here* and *there* are adverbs, not nouns.) What's the real answer to the question *What is? One million dollars.* Here and there are fill-ins, place markers; they aren't what you're talking about. *One million dollars* — that's what you're talking about!

Although they sometimes try to disguise themselves as nouns, *here* and *there* are actually adverbs. Adverbs modify verbs, adjectives, other adverbs. They are busy little words. (For more on adverbs, see Chapter 8.)

The moral of my story: Avoid *here* and *there* when searching for the subject of a sentence.

Choosing the correct verb for here and there sentences

If you write *here* and *there* sentences, be sure to choose the correct verb. Because *here* and *there* are never subjects, you must always look *after* the verb for the real subject. When you match a subject to a verb (something I discuss in detail in Chapter 11), be sure to use the real subject, not *here* or *there.* Example:

> Here are ten anteaters.

NOT

> Here is ten anteaters.
>
> *anteaters* = subject

Another example:

> There are a pen and a pencil in Mr. Nerd's plastic pocket protector.

NOT

> There is a pen and a pencil in Mr. Nerd's plastic pocket protector.
>
> *pen, pencil* = subject (compound)

One last example:

> There were far too many pimples on Murgatroyd's face.

NOT

> There was far too many pimples on Murgatroyd's face.
>
> *pimples* = subject

If you want to check your choice of verb, try reversing the sentence. In the sample sentences above, say *ten anteaters is/are, a pen and pencil is/are, far too many pimples was/were*. Chances are your "ear" will tell you that you want *ten anteaters are, a pen and pencil are, far too many pimples were*.

Which sentence is correct?

    A. There are 50 reasons for my complete lack of homework.

    B. There's 50 reasons for my complete lack of homework.

Answer: Sentence A is correct. In sentence B, *there's* is short for *there is,* but *reasons,* the plural subject, takes a plural verb.

Subjects Aren't Just a Singular Sensation: Forming the Plural of Nouns

Distinguishing between singular and plural subjects is a really big deal, and I go into it in detail in Chapter 11. But before I go any further, I want to explain how to form the plural of nouns (words that name persons, places, or things) because most subjects are nouns. If you learn how to form plurals, you'll also be able to recognize them.

Regular plurals

Plain old garden-variety nouns form plurals by adding the letter *s*. Check out Table 4-1 for some examples.

Table 4-1	Examples of Regular Plurals
Singular	*Plural*
xylophone	xylophones
quintuplet	quintuplets
worrywart	worrywarts
nerd	nerds
lollipop	lollipops
eyebrow	eyebrows

Singular nouns that end in *s* already, as well as singular nouns ending in *sh, ch,* and *x* form plurals by adding *es.* Some examples are shown in Table 4-2.

Table 4-2	Examples of Regular Plurals Ending in S and CH
Singular	*Plural*
grinch	grinches
box	boxes
kiss	kisses
George Bush	both George Bushes
mess	messes
catch	catches

The IES and YS have it

If a noun ends in the letter *y,* and the letter before the *y* is a vowel (a, e, i, o, u), just add *s.* For examples, see Table 4-3.

Table 4-3	Examples of Regular Plurals Ending in a Vowel Plus Y
Singular	*Plural*
monkey	monkeys
turkey	turkeys
day	days
boy	boys
honey	honeys
bay	bays

If the noun ends in *y* but the letter before the *y* is not a vowel, form the plural by changing the *y* to *i* and adding *es.* For examples, see Table 4-4.

Table 4-4 Examples of Regular Plurals Ending in a Consonant Plus Y	
Singular	*Plural*
sob story	sob stories
unsolvable mystery	unsolvable mysteries
a cute little ditty (it means *song*)	cute little ditties
pinky	pinkies
bat-filled belfry	bat-filled belfries
tabby	tabbies

No knifes here: Irregular plurals

This topic wouldn't be any fun without irregulars, now would it? Okay, you're right. Irregulars are always a pain. However, they're also always around. Table 4-5 gives you examples of irregular plurals.

Table 4-5	Examples of Irregular Plurals
Singular	*Plural*
knife	knives
sheep	sheep
man	men
woman	women
child	children
hanky-panky	hanky-panky

Listing all the irregular plurals is an impossible task. Check the dictionary for any noun plural that puzzles you.

The brother-in-law rule: Hyphenated plurals

If you intend to insult your relatives, you may as well do so with the correct plural form. Remember: Form the plural of hyphenated nouns by adding *s* or *es* to the important word, not to the add-ons. These words are all plurals:

- ✔ mothers-in-law
- ✔ brothers-in-law
- ✔ vice-presidents
- ✔ secretaries-general
- ✔ dogcatchers-in-chief

When the Subject Is a Number

Numbers are sometimes the subject of a sentence. Check out this example: You're a star pitcher and your agent tells you that your favorite team has made an offer. You add up the numbers and send off an e-mail. What do you say?

> $10,000,000 is not enough.

No, that's not what you say. Why? Leaving aside the fact that $10,000,000 is more than enough for any human being's work, even work as crucial to the future of civilization as hurling a ball past a batter, your answer has a more important problem. It's not grammatically correct. Here's the rule: Always begin a sentence with a capital letter. Don't begin a sentence with a number, because you can't capitalize numbers, and to repeat, you must begin every sentence with a capital letter. If need be, reword the sentence or write out the number. So what do you, the star pitcher, write?

> A mere $10,000,000 a year is not enough.

or you can write out the amount that you're negotiating:

> Ten million dollars a year is not enough.

Here are yet more examples:

> WRONG: 1966 was a very good year.
>
> RIGHT BUT CLUMSY: Nineteen sixty-six was a very good year.
>
> ALSO RIGHT: The year 1966 was a good one.
>
> ALSO RIGHT: I had a good time in 1966, as least what I remember of it.

Are you affected? Or effected?

Has the study of grammar *affected* or *effected* your brain? Should you *set* or *sit* on the porch to think about this sentence? These two pairs of words are a complete annoyance, but once you learn them, you're all set. (And I do mean *set*.) Here are the definitions:

Affect versus *effect*: *Affect* is a verb. It means to influence. *Effect* is a noun meaning result. Hence

> Sunlight *affects* Ludwig's appetite; he never eats during the day.

> Ludmilla thinks that her vegetarian pizza will *affect* Ludwig's dietary regimen, but I think the *effect* will be disastrous.

Special note: *Affect* may also be a noun meaning "the way one relates to and shows emotions." *Effect* may act as a verb meaning "to cause a complete change." However, you rarely need these secondary meanings.

Sit versus *set*: *Sit* is a verb meaning "to plop yourself down on a chair, to take a load off your feet." *Set* means "to put something else down, to place something in a particular spot." Thus

> Ratrug seldom *sits* for more than two minutes.

> I'd like to *sit* down while I speak, but only if you promise not to *set* that plate of pickled fish eyeballs in front of me.

Chapter 5

Having It All: The Complete Sentence

. . . .

In This Chapter

▶ Distinguishing between complete sentences and sentence fragments

▶ Understanding when complete sentences are necessary

▶ Deciding when sentence fragments are acceptable

▶ Learning how to punctuate sentences correctly

. . . .

Everyone knows the most important rule of English grammar: All sentences must be complete.

But everyone breaks the rule. I just did! *But everyone breaks the rule* is not a complete sentence. And you understood me, didn't you? (Another half sentence.) Because what I was trying to say was quite clear. (One more.) In this chapter, I explain how to decide whether your sentence is complete. I show you how to identify partial sentences, or *fragments*. I tell you when fragments are acceptable and when they send you to the grammar penitentiary. I also provide everything you need to know about endmarks, the punctuation that separates one sentence from another.

Completing Sentences: The Essential Subjects and Verbs

What is a complete sentence, anyway? First of all, a complete sentence has at least one subject–verb pair; they're a pair because they match. That is, the subject and verb go together. You may think about a subject–verb pair this way: The sentence must include one element expressing action or being, and one element that you're talking about in relation to the acting or being. (For more information on verbs, see Chapters 2 and 3; for more information on subjects, see Chapter 4.) A few subject–verb pairs that match are

Eggworthy scrambled

Ms. Drydock repairs

The little engine will be repaired

Murgatroyd had repelled

Ratrug will have screeched

Just for comparison, here is one mismatch:

Eggworthy scrambling

You may find some mismatches in your sentences when you go subject–verb hunting. Mismatches are not necessarily wrong; they're simply not subject–verb pairs. Take a look at the preceding mismatch, this time inside its sentence:

Eggworthy, scrambling for a seat on the plane, knocked over the omelet plate.

When you're checking a sentence for completeness, ignore the mismatches. Keep looking until you find a subject–verb pair that matches. If you can't find one, you don't have a complete sentence. (For more information, see Chapter 4.) Complete sentences may also include more than one subject–verb pair:

Dillbly fiddled while Elmira burned. (*Dillbly* = subject of the verb *fiddled*, *Elmira* = subject of the verb *burned*)

Because Lester jumped on the trampoline, the earth shook. (*Lester* = subject of the verb *jumped, earth* = subject of the verb *shook*)

Not only did Lochness swim, but he also drank. (*Lochness* = subject of the verb *did swim, he* = subject of the verb *drank*)

Complete sentences may also match one subject with more than one verb, and vice versa:

The animated pumpkin appeared in three commercials but sang in only two. (*pumpkin* = subject of verbs *appeared, sang*)

Alice and Archie will fight endlessly over a single birdseed. (*Alice, Archie* = subjects of the verb *will fight*)

Ratrug and I put crayons on the radiator. (*Ratrug, I* = subjects of the verb *put*)

Complete sentences that give commands may match an understood subject (you) with the verb:

Give a coupon to whoever needs a new tire. (*you-understood* = subject of the verb *give, whoever* = subject of the verb *needs*)

Visit Grandma, you little creep! (*you-understood* = subject of the verb *visit*)

Murder Murgatroyd, please. (*you-understood* = subject of the verb *murder*)

To find the subject–verb pair, start with the verb. Pop the verb question: *What's happening?* or *What is?* The answer is the verb. Then pop the subject question: Ask *who?* or *what?* in front of the verb. The answer is the subject. (For a more complete explanation, see Chapter 4.)

The sentence below contains one true subject–verb pair and one mismatch. Can you find the subject–verb pair?

The angry ant caught in a blob of glue vowed never to build a model airplane again.

Answer: The subject–verb pair is *ant vowed*. The mismatch is *ant caught*. The sentence isn't saying that the *ant caught* something, so *ant caught* is not a match.

In the preceding pop quiz, *to build* is not the verb. *To build* is an infinitive, the basic form from which verbs are made. Infinitives are never used as verbs in a sentence. (See Chapter 2 for more information on infinitives.)

Complete Thoughts, Complete Sentences

What's an incomplete sentence? It's the moment in the television show just before the last commercial. You know what I mean. *The hero slowly edges the door open a few inches, peeks in, gasps, and . . . FADE TO DANCING DETERGENT BOTTLE.* You were planning to change the channel, but instead you wait to see if the villain's cobra really didn't die and is now going to bite the hero's nose. You haven't gotten to the end. You don't know what's happening. You stick it out. A complete sentence is the opposite of that moment in a television show. You have gotten to the end, you do know what's happening, and you have stuck it out. In other words, a complete sentence must express a complete thought. (You've probably noticed that grammar terminology is not terribly original; in fact, it's terribly obvious.)

Check out these complete sentences. Notice how they express complete thoughts:

Despite Eggworthy's fragile appearance, he proved to be a tough opponent.

Ms. Drydock will sail solo around the world, as soon as her boat is sound again.

I can't imagine why anyone would want to ride on top of a Zamboni.

Ludwig bought a genuine Zamboni just for that purpose.

Ludmilla melted the ice on purpose.

Here are a few incomplete thoughts, just for comparison:

The reason I wanted a divorce was.

Because I said so.

I can guess what you're thinking. Both of those incomplete thoughts may be part of a longer conversation. Yes, in context those incomplete thoughts may indeed express a complete thought:

Sydney: So the topic of conversation was the Rangers' season opener?

Alice: No! "The reason I wanted a divorce" was!

and

Sydney: Why do I have to do this dumb homework?

Alice: Because I said so.

Fair enough. You can pull a complete thought out of the examples. However, the context of a conversation is not enough to satisfy the complete thought/complete sentence rule. To be legal, your sentence must express a complete thought.

Check out these examples:

What we talked about was the reason I wanted a divorce, even though his real interest was the Rangers' season opener.

You have to do this dumb homework because I said so.

Final answer: Every complete sentence has at least one subject–verb pair and must express a complete thought.

In deciding whether you have a complete sentence or not, you may be led astray by words that resemble questions. Consider these three words: *who knits well*. A complete thought? Maybe yes, maybe no. Suppose those three words form a question:

Who knits well?

This question is understandable and its thought is complete. Verdict: legal. Suppose these three words form a statement:

Who knits well.

Now they don't make sense. This incomplete sentence needs more words to make a complete thought:

The honor of making the Chihuahua's sweater will go to the person who knits well.

The moral of the story? Don't change the meaning of what you're saying when deciding whether a thought is complete. If you're *questioning,* consider your sentence as a *question.* If you're *stating,* consider your sentence as a *statement.*

Which sentence is complete?

   A. Martin sings.

   B. Martin, who hopes to sing professionally some day but can't get beyond the do-re-mi level.

Answer: Even though it is short, sentence A is correct. *Martin sings* is a complete idea and includes the necessary subject–verb pair. In sentence B, one subject is paired with two verbs *(who + hopes, can get),* but no complete thought is stated.

Taking an Incomplete: Fragment Sentences

I use incomplete sentences, or fragments, here and there throughout this book, and (I hope) these incomplete sentences aren't confusing. Especially now in the MTV-Internet Age, quick cuts and quick comments are the rule. Everyone today, particularly young people, is much more comfortable with half-sentences than our elderly relatives were. (I have to point out that the entire older generation, no matter how fanatically correct in grammar, loves one incomplete sentence: *Because I said so.*)

The most common type of fragment uses the words *and, or, but,* and *nor.* These words are called *conjunctions,* and they work like rubber bands; they bind things together. (For more information on conjunctions, see Chapter 6.) Frequently these words are used to combine two complete sentences (with two complete thoughts) into one longer sentence:

> Eggworthy went to his doctor for a cholesterol check, *and* then he scrambled home.

> Ratrug will rule the roost, *or* he will die trying.

> President Drinkwater was extremely thirsty, *but* he was not fond of chamomile tea.

> Ludwig did not want to clean the Zamboni, *nor* did Ludmilla want to drive it away.

Whether or if it rains

Whether and *if* both connect one idea to another in the sentence, but each is used in a different situation. Are you choosing between two alternatives? Select *whether,* as in *whether or not.* Look at the following examples:

Lochness is not sure *whether* he should activate the wind machine. (He has two choices — to activate or not to activate.)

Whether I go or stay is completely irrelevant to me. (Two choices — going and staying.)

If, on the other hand, describes a possibility. Check out these examples:

Lulu will reach the top of Mount Everest *if* the sunny weather continues. (The sentence talks about the possibility of sunny weather.)

If I have my way, the Grammarians' Ball will be held in the Participle Club. (The sentence talks about the possibility of my having what I want.)

In the first sample sentence, *and* is a rubber band joining

Eggworthy went to his doctor for a cholesterol check

to

then he scrambled home.

In the second sentence, the rubber band is *or,* which joins

Ratrug will rule the roost

to

he will die trying.

The next pair of complete sentences (1. *President Drinkwater was extremely thirsty.* 2. *He was not fond of chamomile tea.*) is joined by *but.* In the last sample sentence, *nor* joins the two complete sentences (1. *Ludwig did not want to clean the Zamboni.* 2. *Ludmilla did want to drive it away.*).

Note that the word *nor* changes the meaning of the second sentence from positive *(Ludmilla did want)* to negative *(Ludmilla did not want).*

Nowadays, more and more writers begin sentences with *and, or, but,* and *nor,* even in formal writing. For example, the previous sentences may be turned into

Eggworthy went to his doctor for a cholesterol check. And then he scrambled home.

Ratrug will rule the roost. Or he will die trying.

President Drinkwater was extremely thirsty. But he was not fond of chamomile tea.

Ludwig did not want to clean the Zamboni. Nor did Ludmilla want to drive it away.

The rubber bands — *and, or, but,* and *nor* in these sentences — are still there. However, they aren't connecting two or more complete thoughts in *single* sentences. Logically, of course, the conjunctions are connecting the thoughts in both sentences.

Beginning sentences with *and, but, or,* and *nor* is still not quite acceptable in formal English grammar. (I wouldn't suggest using these incomplete sentences in school essays or professional reports, for example.) In most instances, however, you probably won't go to the grammar penitentiary if you begin a sentence with one of these words. Consider your audience and then make your choice.

Oh, Mama, Could This Really Be the End? Understanding Endmarks

When you speak, your body language, silences, and tone act as punctuation marks. You wriggle your eyebrows, stop at significant moments, and raise your tone when you ask a question.

When you write, you can't raise an eyebrow or stop for a dramatic moment. No one hears your tone of voice. That's why grammar uses endmarks. The endmarks take the place of live communication and tell your reader how to "hear" the words correctly. Plus, you need endmarks to close your sentences legally. Your choices include the period (.), question mark (?), exclamation point (!), or ellipsis (. . .). The following examples show how to use endmarks correctly.

The period is for ordinary statements, declarations, and commands:

I can't do my homework.

I refuse to do my homework.

I will never do homework again.

The question mark is for questions:

Why are you torturing me with this homework?

Is there no justice in the world of homework?

Does no one know the trouble I've seen in my assignment pad?

Why clarity is important

One of my favorite moments in teaching came on a snowy January day. A student named Danny ran into the lunchroom, clearly bursting with news. "Guess what?" he shouted triumphantly to his friends. "A kid on my bus's mother had a baby last night!"

This situation wasn't critical. After all, the baby had already been born. But imagine if Danny had been greeting an ambulance with "Quick! Over here! A kid on my bus's mother is having a baby!" I think everyone agrees that the best reaction from an emergency medical technician isn't "Huh?"

Being clear is probably the first rule of English grammar, and that rule wins a fight with any other rule. Faced with a choice between confusion and incomplete sentences, for example, incomplete sentences should win. In other words, here's the news Danny should have spread that cold January day:

> This kid on my bus? His mother had a baby last night.

Of course, he could also have told his story correctly by saying:

> The mother of a kid on my bus had a baby last night.

Either way, everyone would've yawned, eaten another bite of mystery meat, and filed out to math class. Hearing either of these statements, the students would've understood what Danny was trying to say.

So remember: First comes meaning. Second comes everything else.

The exclamation point adds a little drama to sentences that would otherwise end in periods:

> I can't do my homework!
>
> I absolutely positively refuse to do it!
>
> Oh, the agony of homework I've seen!

An ellipsis (three dots) signals that something has been left out of a sentence. When missing words occur at the end of a sentence, use four dots (three for the missing words and one for the end of the sentence):

> Murgatroyd choked, "I can't do my. . . ."
>
> Ratrug complained, "If you don't shut up, I. . . ."

Don't put more than one endmark at the end of a sentence, unless you're trying to create a comic effect:

> He said my cooking tasted like what?!?!?!

Don't put any endmarks in the middle of a sentence. You may find a period inside a sentence as part of an abbreviation; in this case, the period is not considered an endmark. If the sentence ends with an abbreviation, let the period after the abbreviation do double duty. Don't add another period:

WRONG: When Griselda woke me, it was six a.m..

RIGHT: When Griselda woke me, it was six a.m.

WRONG: Lulu prefers to buy artifacts made before 700 B.C..

RIGHT: Lulu prefers to buy artifacts made before 700 B.C.

Can you punctuate this example correctly?

Who's there Archie I think there is someone at the door Archie it's a murderer Archie he's going to

Answer: Who's there? Archie, I think there is someone at the door. Archie, it's a murderer! (A period is acceptable here also.) Archie, he's going to. . . .

Who made these rules anyway? You do

Listen to yourself talk. What you hear is grammar. You may not be hearing correct grammar, but if enough people talk the way you do, you are hearing *grammar in the making* — at least according to some grammarians.

There are two schools of thought on grammar: In one, teachers and other so-called experts give you a list of rules and tell you to follow them. In another, grammarians listen and describe what they hear. Once enough people speak a certain way, the expression becomes part of standard English. Or, as a grammarian named Lathan said in 1848, "In Language, whatever is, is right."

Take the word *hopefully,* for example. This word originally meant *with hope* and was used to describe the feelings accompanying a specific action:

Griselda wrote *hopefully,* her mind filled with thoughts of a rosy future with Grimface and their dot com start-up.

Some time ago, people began to use *hopefully* in a different way, to mean, *it is hoped that.*

Hopefully Griselda won't decide to redecorate Grimface's castle in post-modern style.

English teachers sometimes frowned on the use of *hopefully* in the second sentence, but most people ignored those frowns quite successfully. The result? *Hopefully* now means *it is hoped that* in normal speech (though not on English tests and not in all dictionaries). Who made the new rule? You did. The *you* above is a collective *you,* not an individual *you.* Don't assume that you can say anything you want and be correct! First a critical mass of speakers (think millions, not you and a bunch of your friends) must accept a new usage before grammarians take notice. And even then, some will still frown. Know your audience, and be careful in your speech and writing when you are dealing with a known frowner or an unknown audience.

Chapter 6

Handling Complements

· ·

In This Chapter
▶ Recognizing complements
▶ Understanding how a complement adds to the meaning of a sentence
▶ Distinguishing between linking-verb and action-verb complements
▶ Placing complements after linking verbs and action verbs
▶ Using the correct pronouns as complements

· ·

Speeding down the grammar highway, the sentence is a flatbed truck carrying meaning to the reader. The verbs are the wheels and the subject is the driver. Complements are the common, not-always-essential parts of the truck — perhaps the odometer or the turn signals. These words are a little more important than those fuzzy dice some people hang from their rearview mirrors or bumper stickers declaring *I stop at railroad tracks.* (What do they think the rest of us do? Leap over the train?) You can sometimes create a sentence without complements, but their presence is generally part of the driving — sorry, I mean *communicating* — experience.

You can find four kinds of complements in sentences: direct objects, indirect objects, objective complements, and subject complements. The first three types of complements are related to the *object* of a sentence (notice that the word *object* is part of the name), and the fourth type of complement is related to the *subject* of a sentence (notice the word *subject* is part of its name). Knowing the difference between these two groups is helpful. In this chapter, I discuss the complements in two sections. The first section explains objects, which follow action verbs. The next section tackles the subject complement, which follows linking verbs.

Before I go any further, it's time to straighten out the compliment/complement divide. The one with an "i" is not a grammatical term; *compliment* is just a word meaning "praise." *Complement* with an "e" is a grammatical term. A complement adds meaning to the idea that the subject and verb express. That is, a complement completes the idea that the subject and verb begin.

Getting to the Action: Action Verb Complements

Action verbs express — surprise! — action. No action verb needs a complement to be grammatically legal. But an action-verb sentence without a complement may sound bare, stripped down to the bone. The complements that follow action verbs — the direct object, indirect object, and objective complement — enhance the meaning of the subject-verb pair.

Receiving the action: Direct objects

Imagine that you're fourteen. You're holding the baseball, ready to throw it to a buddy in your yard. But in your imagination, you're facing Mark McGuire, the home-run champ. You go into your windup and pitch a 99-mile-an-hour fastball. (Okay, a 40-mile-an-hour curve.) The ball arcs gracefully against the clear blue sky — and crashes right through the picture window in your living room.

You broke the picture window!

Before you can retrieve your ball, the phone rings. It's your mom, who has radar for situations like this. *What's going on?* she asks. You mutter something containing the word *broke*. (There's the verb.) *Broke? Who broke something?* she demands. You concede that *you* did. (There's the subject.) *What did you break?* You hesitate. You consider a couple of possible answers: *a bad habit, the world's record for the hundred-meter dash.* Finally you confess: *the picture window.* (There's the complement.)

Here's another way to think about the situation (and the sentence). *Broke* is an action verb because it tells you what happened. The action came from the subject *(you)* and went to an object *(the window)*. As some grammarians phrase it, *the window* receives the action expressed by the verb *broke*. Conclusion? *Window* is a *direct object* because it receives the action directly from the verb.

Try another.

With the force of 1,000 hurricanes, you pitch the baseball.

Pitch is an action verb because it expresses what is happening in the sentence. The action goes from the subject *(you,* the pitcher) to the object *(the baseball).* In other words, *baseball* receives the action of *pitching.* Thus, baseball is the *direct object* of the verb *pitch.*

Here are a few examples of sentences with action verbs. The direct objects are italicized.

> The defective X-ray machine took strange *pictures* of the giant frog. (*took* = verb, *X-ray machine* = subject)
>
> Legghorn hissed the secret *word* in the middle of the graduation ceremony. (*hissed* = verb, *Legghorn* = subject)
>
> Green marking pens draw naturally beautiful *lines*. (*draw* = verb, *pens* = subject)
>
> Griselda kissed the giant *frog*. (*kissed* = verb, *Griselda* = subject)
>
> Leroy's laser printer spurted *ink* all over his favorite shirt. (spurted = *verb*, printer = *subject*)

You may be able to recognize direct objects more easily if you think of them as part of a pattern in the sentence structure: subject (S) – action verb (AV) – direct object (DO). This S–AV–DO pattern is one of the most common in the English language; it may even be the most common (I don't know if anyone has actually counted all the sentences and figured it out!). At any rate, think of the parts of the sentence in threes, in the S–AV–DO pattern:

> machine took pictures
>
> Legghorn hissed word
>
> pens draw lines
>
> Griselda kissed frog
>
> printer spurted ink

Of course, just to make your life a little bit harder, a sentence can have more than one DO. Check out these examples:

> Algernon autographed *posters* and *books* for his many admirers.
>
> Ratrug will buy a dozen *doughnuts* and a few *slabs* of cheesecake for breakfast.
>
> The new president of the Heart Society immediately phoned *Eggworthy* and his *brother*.
>
> Lochness sent *spitballs* and old *socks* flying across the room.
>
> Ludmilla bought *orange juice, tuna, aspirin,* and a *coffee table*.

Some sentences have no DO. Take a look at this example:

> Throughout the endless afternoon and into the lonely night, Allegheny sighed sadly.

No one or nothing receives the sighs, so the sentence has no direct object. Perhaps that's why Allegheny is lonely.

The grammar point: This sentence doesn't have a direct object, though it is powered by a verb and expresses a complete thought.

Rare, but sometimes there: Indirect objects

Another type of object is the indirect object. This one is called *indirect* because the action doesn't flow directly to it. The *indirect object,* affectionately known as the IO, is an intermediate stop along the way between the action verb and the direct object. Read this sentence, in which the indirect object is italicized:

> Knowing that I'm on a diet, my former friend sent *me* six dozen chocolates.

The action is *sent.* My former *friend* performed the action, so *friend* is the subject. What received the action? Six dozen *chocolates. Chocolates* is the direct object. That's what was sent, what received the action of the verb directly. But *me* also received the action, indirectly. *Me* received the sending of the boxes of chocolate. *Me* is called the indirect object.

The sentence pattern for indirect objects is subject (S) – action verb (AV) – indirect object (IO) – direct object (DO). Notice that the indirect object always precedes the direct object: S–AV–IO–DO. Here are a few sentences with the indirect objects italicized:

> Grunhilda will tell *me* the whole story tomorrow. (*will tell* = verb, *Grunhilda* = subject, *story* = direct object)
>
> Murgatroyd promises *Lulu* everything. (*promises* = verb, *Murgatroyd* = subject, *everything* = direct object)
>
> As a grammarian, I should have given *you* better sample sentences. (*should have given* = verb, *I* = subject, *sentences* = direct object)
>
> Ludmilla radioed *Ludwig* a tart message. (*radioed* = verb, *Ludmilla* = subject, *message* = direct object)
>
> The crooked politician offered *Agnes* a bribe for dropping out of the senate race. (*offered* = verb, *politician* = subject, *bribe* = direct object)

Like clerks in a shoe store, indirect objects don't appear very often. When indirect objects do arrive, they're always in partnership with a direct object. You probably don't need to worry about knowing the difference between direct and indirect objects (unless you're an English teacher). As long as you understand that these words are objects, completing the meaning of an action verb, you recognize the basic composition of a sentence.

A fight about indirect objects is tearing apart the world of grammar. (Did you gasp — or was that a yawn?) Read these two sentences:

Archie gave me a bit of birdseed.

Archie gave a bit of birdseed to me.

According to one school of thought, the first sentence has an indirect object *(me),* and the second sentence doesn't. This thinking assumes that because *to* is present in the second sentence, *me* isn't an indirect object. (If you're into labels, *to me* is a prepositional phrase.) According to another group of grammarians, both sentences have indirect objects *(me),* because in both sentences, *me* receives the action of the verb indirectly; the presence of the word *to* is irrelevant. What's really irrelevant is this discussion. You may side with either camp, or, more wisely, ignore the whole thing.

No bias here: Objective complements

Finally, a grammar rule that's hard to bungle. Here's the deal: sometimes a direct object doesn't get the whole job done. A little more information is needed (or just desired), and the writer doesn't want to bother adding a whole new subject–verb pair. The solution? An *objective complement* — an added fact about the direct object.

The *objective complement* (italicized in the following sentences) may be a person, place, or thing. In other words, the objective complement may be a noun:

Eggworthy named Lester *copy chief* of the Heart Society Bulletin. (*named* = verb, *Eggworthy* = subject, *Lester* = direct object)

Grunhilda and others with her world view elected Ratrug *president.* (*elected* = verb, *Grunhilda and others* = subject, *Ratrug* = direct object)

Allegheny called his dog *Allegheny Too.* (*called* = verb, *Allegheny* = subject, *dog* = direct object)

The objective complement may also be a word that describes a noun. (A word that describes a noun is called an *adjective;* see Chapter 8 for more information.) Take a peek at some sample sentences:

Nimby considered her *hazy* at best. (*considered* = verb, *Nimby* = subject, *her* = direct object)

Lochness dubbed Allegheny Too *ridiculous.* (*dubbed* = verb, *Lochness* = subject, *Allegheny Too* = direct object)

Ratrug called Lochness *heartless.* (*called* = verb, *Ratrug* = subject, *Lochness* = direct object)

As you see, the objective complements in each of the sample sentences give the sentence an extra jolt — not lightning, but a double-espresso sort of jolt. You know more with it than you do without it, but the objective complement is not a major player in the sentence.

Finishing the Equation: Linking Verb Complements

Linking verb complements are major players in sentences. A *linking verb* begins a word equation; it expresses a state of being, linking two ideas. The complement completes the equation. Because a complement following a linking verb expresses something about the *subject* of the sentence, it is called a *subject complement.* In each of the following sentences, the first idea is the subject, and the second idea (italicized) is the complement:

> Nerdo is *upset* by the bankruptcy of the pocket-protector manufacturer. *(Nerdo = upset)*

> Grunhilda was a *cheerleader* before the dog bite incident. *(Grunhilda = cheerleader)*

> Nasalhoff should have been *head* of the allergy committee. *(Nasalhoff = head)*

> The little orange book will be *sufficient* for all your firework information needs. *(book = sufficient)*

> It is *I,* the master of the universe. *(It = I)*

Subject complements can take on several forms. Sometimes the subject complement is a descriptive word (an *adjective,* for those of you who like the correct terminology). Sometimes the subject complement is a *noun* (person, place, thing, or idea) or a *pronoun* (a word that substitutes for a noun). The first sample sentence equates *Nerdo* with a description (the adjective *upset*). The second equates *Grunhilda* with a position (the noun *cheerleader*). *Nasalhoff,* in the third sentence, is linked with a title (the noun *head*). In the fourth sample sentence, the subject *book* is described by the adjective *sufficient.* The last sentence equates the subject *it* with the pronoun *I.* Don't worry about these distinctions. They don't matter! As long as you can find the subject complement, you're grasping the sentence structure.

The linking verbs that I mentioned in the previous paragraph are forms of the verb "to be." Other verbs that give sensory information (*feel, sound, taste, smell,* and so on) may also be linking verbs. Likewise, *appear* and *seem* are linking verbs. (For more information on linking verbs, see Chapter 2.) Here are a couple of sentences with sensory linking verbs. The complements are italicized:

Ludwig sounds *grouchier* than usual today. *(Ludwig = grouchier)*

At the end of each algebra proof, Analivia feels strangely *depressed*. *(Analivia = depressed)*

Don't mix types of subject complements in the same sentence, completing the meaning of the same verb. Use all descriptions (adjectives) or all nouns and pronouns. Take a look at these examples:

WRONG: Grumpus is grouchy and a patron of the arts.

RIGHT: Grumpus is a grouch and a patron of the arts.

ALSO RIGHT: Grumpus is grouchy and arty.

WRONG: Lester's pet tarantula will be annoying and a real danger.

RIGHT: Lester's pet tarantula will be an annoyance and a danger.

ALSO RIGHT: Lester's pet tarantula will be annoying and dangerous.

Pop the Question: Locating the Complement

In Chapter 2, I explain how to locate the verb by asking the right questions. *(What's happening? What is?)* In Chapter 4, I show you how to pop the question for the subject. *(Who? What?* before the verb). Now it's time to pop the question to find the complements. You ask the complement questions after both the verb and subject have been identified. The complement questions are

Who or whom?

What?

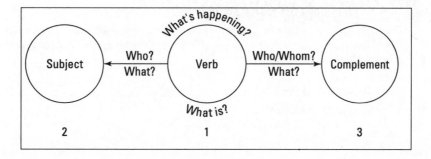

Try popping the questions in a couple of sentences:

Flossie maintains the cleanest teeth in Texas.

1. Pop the verb question: What's happening? Answer: *maintains. Maintains* is the action verb.

2. Pop the subject question: Who or what *maintains?* Answer: *Flossie maintains. Flossie* is the subject.

3. Pop the complement question: *Flossie maintains* who/whom? No answer. *Flossie maintains* what? Answer: Flossie maintains *the cleanest teeth in Texas (teeth* for short). *Teeth* is the direct object.

Remember that objects (direct or indirect) follow action verbs.

Time for you to try another:

The ancient lawn gnome appeared tired and worn.

1. Pop the verb question: What's happening? No answer. What is? Answer: *Appeared. Appeared* is the linking verb.

2. Pop the subject question: Who or what *appeared?* Answer: *Gnome appeared. Gnome* is the subject.

3. Pop the complement question: *Gnome appeared* who? No answer. *Gnome appeared* what? Answer: *Tired* and *worn. Tired* and *worn* are the subject complements.

Remember that subject complements follow linking verbs.

Pop the Question: Finding the Indirect Object

Though indirect objects seldom appear, you can check for them with another "pop the question." After you locate the action verb, the subject, and the direct object, ask

To whom? For whom?

To what? For what?

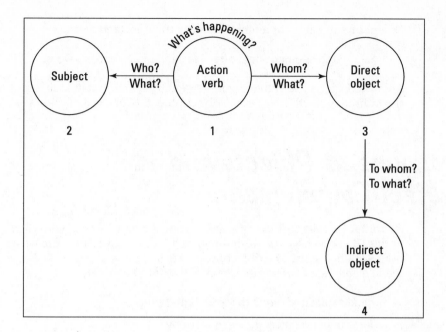

If you get an answer, it should reveal an indirect object. Here's an example:

Mildred will tell me the secret shortly.

1. Pop the verb question: What's happening? Answer: *will tell. Will tell* is an action verb.

2. Pop the subject question: Who will tell? Answer: *Mildred. Mildred* is the subject.

3a. Pop the DO question: *Mildred will tell* whom? or what? Answer: *Mildred will tell the secret. Secret* is the direct object.

3b. Pop the IO question: *Mildred will tell the secret* to whom? Answer: to *me. Me* is the indirect object.

You may come up with a different answer when you pop the DO question in number 3a (*Mildred will tell* whom? or what?). You can answer *Mildred will tell me*. True. The only problem is that the sentence then has *secret* flapping around with no label. So, your attempt to determine the sentence structure has reached a dead end. As long as you understand that both *me* and *secret* are objects, let the I-have-no-life grammarians worry about which one is direct and which one is indirect.

Object or subject complement? Identify the italicized words.

Sasquatch seemed *soggy* after his semi-final swim, so we gave *him* a *towel.*

Answer: *Soggy* is the subject complement. (*Seemed* is a linking verb.) *Him* is the indirect object. *Towel* is the direct object. (*Gave* is an action verb.)

Pronouns as Objects and Subject Complements

He told I? He told me? Me, of course. Your ear usually tells you which pronouns to use as objects (both direct and indirect), because the wrong pronouns sound funny. The object pronouns include *me, you, him, her, it, us, them, whom,* and *whomever.* Check them out in context:

Rickie splashed *her* with icy water.

The anaconda hissed *them* a warning.

The babbling burglar told *her* everything.

Your ear may not tell you the correct pronoun to use after a linking verb. That's where you want a *subject* pronoun, not an *object* pronoun. (Just for the record, the subject pronouns include *I, you, he, she, it, we, they, who,* and *whoever.*) Why do you need a subject pronoun after a linking verb? Remember the equation: What's before the verb should be equal to what's after the verb (S = SC). You put subject pronouns before the verb as subjects, so you put subject pronouns after the verb, as subject complements. (For more information, see Chapter 2.)

Which sentence is correct?

A. According to the witness, the burglar is her, the one with the bright orange eyes!

B. According to the witness, the burglar is she, the one with the bright orange eyes!

Answer: Sentence B is correct if you're writing formally. *Is* is a linking verb and must be followed by a subject pronoun, *she.* Sentence A is acceptable in conversation.

DEMONS

You gotta problem with grammar?

Do you possess an "ear" for grammar? Do you recognize proper English, distinguishing it from the way everyone else around you speaks? If so, you probably don't say *gotta, gonna, gotcha,* or *hisself.* You never use *done* all by itself as the verb in the sentence. These expressions come from various regional accents and customs (similar to the one that makes New Yorkers shop at a store on *Toidy-toid and Toid* — Thirty-third and Third, for those of you from other parts of the world). Although saying *gotta* when you're chatting with a friend is perfectly okay, it isn't okay when you're speaking to a teacher, a boss, a television interviewer, the supreme ruler of the universe, and anyone else in authority. Thus,

> WRONG: Allegheny: You *gonna* wait for Cedric? He bought *hisself* a new car and he might give us a ride.

RIGHT: Allegheny: *Are* you *going* to wait for Cedric? He bought a new car for himself, and he might give us a ride.

WRONG: Basil: No, I *gotta* go.

RIGHT: Basil: No, I *have to* go.

WRONG: Allegheny: We *done* nothing today! I'm not coming anymore. All we do is talk.

RIGHT: Allegheny: We *have done* nothing today! (or, We haven't done anything today!) I'm not coming anymore. All we do is talk.

WRONG: Basil: *Gotcha.* Next week we'll go bowling.

RIGHT: Basil: *I understand.* Next week we'll go bowling.

I'd add another sample conversation, but it's almost time for lunch. I gotta go.

Part II
Avoiding Common Errors

The 5th Wave   By Rich Tennant

"Before we continue with the interview, I think we should establish the difference between the words 'further' and 'farther.'"

In this part . . .

Want to build a castle? You can build one using only chunky squares, but how much more interesting it is to throw in cones, arches, and a banner or two! Communication is the same way. To express yourself with any flair, you want to add descriptions, joining words, and an occasional exclamation to your sentences. In this part, I explain a few more parts of speech — conjunctions, adjectives, adverbs, prepositions, and interjections. This part also contains a field guide to the pronoun, a useful little part of speech that resembles a World War II minefield when it comes to error possibilities. Finally, I delve a little further into the complexities of subject–verb agreement, also a minefield. Never fear: I provide a flak jacket's worth of tricks for understanding these grammar rules.

Chapter 7

Getting Hitched: Marrying Sentences

*H*aving come of age in the Sixties, I learned a special meaning of the word *together*. To us flower children (yes, I got married with daisies in my hair), *together* meant more than just two or more things mixed into one batch. *Together* had a cosmic sense to it, a feeling of harmony. If you were *together*, your life flowed along in a peaceful, wise, balanced way. People wanted to get their heads *together*, but the task was difficult.

Your sentences have a much easier time of it. A *together* sentence, to borrow the Sixties term, flows well; it simply sounds good. How do you go about getting your sentences together? Read on.

Matchmaking: Combining Sentences Legally

Listen to the nearest toddler and you may hear something like "I played with the clay and I went to the zoo and Mommy said I had to take a nap and. . . ." and so forth. Monotonous, yes. But — surprise, surprise — grammatically correct. Take a look at how the information would sound if that one sentence turned into three: *I played with the clay. I went to the zoo. Mommy said I had to take a nap.* The information sounds choppy. When the sentences are combined, the information flows more smoothly. Granted, joining everything with *and* is not a great idea. Read on for better ways of gluing one sentence to another.

Although combining sentences may improve your writing, it can be dangerous. You may easily end up with a *run-on sentence*, which is two or more complete sentences faultily run together. A run-on (a grammatical felony, by the way) is like a dinner speaker who's supposed to entertain the guests during the appetizer but instead talks right through the entrée, the dessert, and the kitchen cleanup. You don't want run-ons in your writing! The best way to avoid these sentences is to figure out how to connect sentences legally.

Connecting with coordinate conjunctions

The words used to join clauses are called *conjunctions*. You're familiar with these common words: *for, but, yet, so, nor, and,* and *or.* (*And* is the most popular, for those of you keeping track.) These little powerhouses, which are called *coordinate conjunctions,* eat their spinach and lift weights every day. They're strong enough to join complete sentences. They may use their strength to join all sorts of equal grammatical elements. Here they are in action joining equal clauses:

> The rain pelted Abernathy's gray hair, *and* his green velvet shoes were completely ruined.

> The CEO told Agwam to call all the numbers on the Rolodex, *but* Agwam had no idea what a Rolodex was.

> You can take a hike, *or* you can jump off a cliff.

> Blathersby did not know how to shoe a horse, *nor* did he understand equine psychology.

> The town lined the streets, *for* they had heard a rumor about Lady Godiva.

The coordinate conjunctions give equal emphasis to the elements they join. In the preceding sentences, the ideas on one side of the conjunction have no more importance than the ideas on the other side of the conjunction.

Pausing to place commas

In the sample sentences in the previous section, all the conjunctions have commas in front of them. A few special rules govern the use of commas in joined sentences:

- ✔ When you join two complete sentences, always put a comma in front of the conjunction.

- ✔ These same conjunctions — *and, but, or, nor, for, yet, so* — may also unite other things. For example, these words may join two nouns (*Mac and Agnes*) or two verbs (*sing or dance*) and so forth. Use the comma only when joining two complete sentences. Here are a few examples:

WRONG: Little Jack Horner sat in the corner, and then pulled a plum out of his pie.

WHY IT IS WRONG: *And* joins two verbs, *sat* and *pulled*.

RIGHT: Little Jack Horner sat in the corner and then pulled a plum out of his pie.

Take a look at another set:

WRONG: The head of the Committee on Punishment for Grammatical Crimes, and Abernathy propose exile for misuse of comma, first degree.

WHY IT IS WRONG: *And* joins two nouns, *head* and *Abernathy*

RIGHT: The head of the Committee on Punishment for Grammatical Crimes and Abernathy propose exile for misuse of comma, first degree.

And just to make sure you're with me on this point:

WRONG: Blind mice seem to spend a lot of time running up clocks, and singing nursery rhymes.

WHY IT IS WRONG: *And* joins two descriptions, *running* and *singing*.

RIGHT: Blind mice seem to spend a lot of time running up clocks and singing nursery rhymes.

✔ Don't send a comma out all by itself when you want to join two complete sentences. Commas are too weak to glue one sentence to another. Despite the fact that these puny little punctuation marks can't hold anything together, every single day people try to use commas for just that purpose. So many people, in fact, that this sort of error actually has a name: a *comma splice*. (You know a grammar error has made it to the major leagues when the error has its very own name.) Here are some comma splices and their corrections:

WRONG: Glue sticks fascinate Lola, glitter attracts Lulu.

WHY IT IS WRONG: The comma joins two complete thoughts.

RIGHT: Although glue sticks fascinate Lola, glitter attracts Lulu.

ALSO RIGHT: Glue sticks fascinate Lola, but glitter attracts Lulu.

RIGHT AGAIN: Glue sticks fascinate Lola; glitter attracts Lulu.

Another example for you to consider:

WRONG: As usual, Ludwig dove off the board without looking, Ratrug hopes to convince him of the value of caution.

WHY IT IS WRONG: The comma joins two complete thoughts.

RIGHT: Although Ludwig as usual dove off the board without looking, Ratrug hopes to convince him of the value of caution.

ALSO RIGHT: As usual, Ludwig dove off the board without looking, and Ratrug hopes to convince him of the value of caution.

RIGHT AGAIN: As usual, Ludwig dove off the board without looking. Ratrug hopes to convince him of the value of caution.

Now you're getting the hang of these:

WRONG: The monkeys see, the monkeys do.

WHY IT IS WRONG: Though short, each statement about the monkeys is a complete thought.

RIGHT: The monkeys see, and the monkeys do.

ALSO RIGHT: The monkeys see and the monkeys do.

WHY IT IS ALSO RIGHT: When the sentences you are joining are very short, you may omit the comma before the conjunction.

RIGHT AGAIN: Primates imitate.

Which sentence is correct?

A. The professor sits sedately on his sofa sniffing sweet scents, but no one else takes a moment to smell the flowers.

B. The professor sits sedately on his sofa sniffing sweet scents but no one else takes a moment to smell the flowers.

C. The professor sits sedately on his sofa sniffing sweet scents, no one else takes a moment to smell the flowers.

D. The professor sits sedately on his sofa sniffing sweet scents. But no one else takes a moment to smell the flowers.

Answer: Sentence A is correct because two complete thoughts are joined by the word *but,* which is preceded by a comma. Sentence B is incorrect, because the comma is missing. Sentence C is a comma splice; you can't join two complete thoughts only by a comma. Sentence D is incorrect in formal English because the second part begins with *but,* technically an error. See the following paragraph for a more complete explanation of sentence D.

Beginning a sentence with a word that joins equals (particularly *and* and *but*) is increasingly popular. This practice is perfectly acceptable in conversational English and in informal writing (which is the sort you're reading in this book). In formal English, beginning a sentence with a conjunction may still be considered incorrect. Be careful! (For more on sentence fragments, see Chapter 5.)

Attaching thoughts: Semi-colons

The semi-colon is a funny little punctuation mark; it gets its name from another punctuation mark, the colon. (These days, the colon is frequently used to create smiley faces in e-mail messages.) The semi-colon is no less important or no less powerful than its relative. This punctuation mark is strong enough to attach one complete sentence to another, and it has some other useful abilities in lists. (See Chapter 15 for more information on lists.)

The thing about semi-colons is that some people express strong feelings about them. I've seen writing manuals that proclaim, "Never use semi-colons!" with the same intensity of feeling as, say, "Don't blow up the world with that nuclear missile." Other people can't get enough of them, sprinkling them like confetti on New Year's. As far as I'm concerned, use them if you like them. Ignore them if you don't.

If you do put a semi-colon in your sentence, follow two general guidelines. First, attach equals — that is, two complete sentences — with a semi-colon. Don't use the semi-colon to join nouns. (except in lists — see Chapter 15.) Second, use the semi-colon only to attach related ideas. When your reader encounters a semi-colon, he or she pauses a bit, but not for long. The semi-colon says, "More information coming." So the reader has a right to expect a logical train of thought — not something completely new. Here's an example:

> RIGHT: Grover was born in Delaware; he moved to Virginia when he was four.

> WRONG: I put nonfat yogurt into that soup; I like Stephen King's books.

In the first example, both parts of the sentence are about Grover's living arrangements. In the second, those two ideas are, to put it mildly, not in the same universe. (At least not until Stephen King writes a book about a killer container of yogurt. It could happen.)

Some logical semi-colon sentences, just to give you some role models:

> Lulu visits that tattoo parlor regularly; when she retires she plans to start a second career as a tattoo designer.

> Griselda mowed the lawn yesterday; she cut the electric cord in half at least twice.

> Cedric thinks that iced tea is best when it tastes like battery acid; no one drinks anything at Cedric's house anymore.

> Lucilla detests purple pens; she's just torn up her vocabulary quiz because the teacher graded it in a lovely shade of lilac.

> The pearl box is harder to open than an oyster; here's a pair of pliers for the job.

Punctuate the following, adding or subtracting words as needed:

Abner will clip the thorns from that rose stem he is afraid of scratching himself.

Answer: Many combinations are possible:

Abner will clip the thorns from that rose stem. He is afraid of scratching himself.

Abner will clip the thorns from that rose stem; he is afraid of scratching himself.

Abner will clip the thorns from that rose stem even though he is afraid of scratching himself.

Abner will clip the thorns from that rose stem, but he is afraid of scratching himself.

Boss and Employee: Joining Ideas of Unequal Ranks

In the average company, the boss runs the show. The boss has subordinates who play two important roles. They must do at least some work. They must also make the boss feel like the center of the universe. Leave the boss alone in the office, and everything's fine. Leave the employees alone in the office, and pretty soon someone is swinging from the chandelier.

Some sentences resemble companies. The "boss" part of a sentence is all right by itself; it expresses a complete thought *(independent clause)*. The "employee" can't stand alone; it's an incomplete thought (also known as a fragment or *subordinate clause*). For more information on independent and subordinate clauses see chapter 24. Together, the "boss" and the "employee" create a more powerful sentence. Check out some examples:

BOSS: Mugwump ate the bagel.

EMPLOYEE: After he had picked out all the raisins.

JOINING 1: Mugwump ate the bagel after he had picked out all the raisins.

JOINING 2: After he had picked out all the raisins, Mugwump ate the bagel.

Try these on for size:

BOSS: Lochness developed the secret microfilm.

EMPLOYEE: Because he felt traitorous.

JOINING 1: Lochness developed the secret microfilm because he felt traitorous.

JOINING 2: Because he felt traitorous, Lochness developed the secret microfilm.

Here's another:

BOSS: Lulu will be screaming at exactly six o'clock.

EMPLOYEE: Although she often argues for a quiet environment.

JOINING 1: Lulu will be screaming at exactly six o'clock, although she often argues for a quiet environment.

JOINING 2: Although she often argues for a quiet environment, Lulu will be screaming at exactly six o'clock.

And another example:

BOSS: The book bag is in the dragon's cave.

EMPLOYEE: that Ludwig lost

JOINING: The book bag that Ludwig lost is in the dragon's cave.

The joined example sentences are all grammatically legal because they all contain at least one complete thought (the boss, also known as an independent clause). In several of the sample sentences, the less important idea is connected to the rest of the sentence by a subordinate conjunction, indicating that the ideas are not of equal importance. See the next section for more information on subordinate conjunctions.

Choosing subordinate conjunctions

The conjunctions in the boss–employee type of sentence do double duty. These conjunctions emphasize that one idea ("boss" or independent clause) is more important than the other ("employee" or subordinate clause), and they also give some information about the relationship between the two ideas. These conjunctions are called *subordinate conjunctions*. Here are some common subordinate conjunctions: *while, because, although, though, since, when, where, if, whether, before, until, than, as, as if, in order that, so that, whenever,* and *wherever.* (Whew!)

Check out how subordinate conjunctions are used in these examples:

Sentence 1: Michael was shaving. (not a very important activity)

Sentence 2: The earthquake destroyed the city. (a rather important event)

Avoiding false joiners

Some words appear to be strong enough to join sentences, but in reality they're just a bunch of 98-pound weaklings. Think of these words as guys who stuff socks in their sleeves, creating biceps without all the hassle of going to the gym. These fellows may look good, but the minute you need them to pick up a truck or something, they're history. False joiners include *however, consequently, therefore, moreover, also,* and *furthermore.* Use these words to add meaning to your sentences but not to glue the sentences together. For more information on the proper placement and punctuation associated with these false joiners, see Chapter 15.

If these two sentences are joined as equals, the writer emphasizes both events:

> Michael was shaving, *and* the earthquake destroyed the city.

Grammatically, the sentence is legal. Morally, this statement poses a problem. Do you really think that Michael's avoidance of five-o'clock shadow is equal in importance to an earthquake that measures seven on the Richter scale? Better to join these clauses as unequals, making the main idea about the earthquake the boss:

> *While* Michael was shaving, the earthquake destroyed the city.

or

> The earthquake destroyed the city *while* Michael was shaving.

The *while* gives you *time* information, attaches the employee sentence to the boss sentence, and shows the greater importance of the earthquake. Not bad for five letters.

Here's another:

> Sentence 1: Esther must do her homework now.

> Sentence 2: Mom is on the warpath.

In combining these two ideas, you have a few decisions to make. First of all, if you put them together as equals, the reader will wonder why you're mentioning both statements at the same time:

> Esther must do her homework now, *but* Mom is on the warpath.

This joining may mean that Mom is running around the house screaming at the top of her lungs. Although Esther has often managed to concentrate on her history homework while blasting Smashing Pumpkins tapes at mirror-shattering levels, she finds that concentrating is impossible during Mom's tantrums. Esther won't get anything done until Mom settles down with a cup of tea. That's one possible meaning of this joined sentence. But why leave your reader guessing? Try another joining:

> Esther must do her homework now *because* Mom is on the warpath.

This sentence is much clearer: Esther's mother got one of those little pink notes from the teacher *(Number of missing homeworks: 323)*. Esther knows that if she wants to survive through high-school graduation, she'd better get to work now. One more joining to check:

> Mom is on the warpath *because* Esther must do her homework now.

Okay, in this version Esther's mother has asked her daughter to clean the garage. She's been asking Esther every day for the last two years. Now the health inspector is due and Mom's really worried. But Esther told her that she couldn't clean up now because she had to do her homework. World War III erupted immediately.

Do you see the power of these joining words? These subordinate conjunctions strongly influence the meanings of the sentences.

Steering clear of fragments

Remember: Don't write a sentence without a "boss" or independent clause, the section that can stand alone as a complete sentence. If you leave an "employee" all by itself, you've got trouble. An "employee" all by itself is called a sentence fragment. A *sentence fragment* is any set of words that doesn't fit the definition of a complete sentence. Like run-on sentences, sentence fragments are felonies in formal English. Don't let the number of words in sentence fragments fool you. Not all sentence fragments are short, though some are. Decide by meaning, not by length.

Here are some fragments, so you know what to avoid:

> When it rained pennies from heaven

> As if he were king of the world

> After the ball was over but before it was time to begin the first day of the rest of your life and all those other cliches that you hear every day in the subway on your way to work

> Whether Algernon likes it or not

Because I said so

Whether you like it or not, and despite the fact that you don't like it, although I am really sorry that you are upset

If hell freezes over

and so on.

Which is a sentence fragment? Which is a complete sentence? Which is a comma splice (a run-on)?

A. Cedric sneezed.

B. Because Cedric sneezed in the middle of the opera, just when the main character removed that helmet with the little horns from on top of her head.

C. Cedric sneezed, I pulled out a handkerchief.

Answers: Sentence A is complete. Sentence B is not really a sentence; it's a fragment with no complete idea. Sentence C is a comma splice because it contains two complete thoughts joined only by a comma.

Employing Pronouns to Combine Sentences

A useful trick for combining short sentences legally is "the pronoun connection." (A *pronoun* substitutes for a noun, which is a word for a person, place, thing, or idea. See Chapter 10 for more information.) Check out these combinations:

Sentence 1: Amy read the book.

Sentence 2: The book had a thousand pictures in it.

Joining: Amy read the book *that* had a thousand pictures in it.

Sentence 1: The paper map stuck to Wilbur's shoe.

Sentence 2: We plan to use the map to take over the world.

Joining: The paper map, *which* we plan to use to take over the world, stuck to Wilbur's shoe.

Sentence 1: Margaret wants to hire a carpenter.

Sentence 2: The carpenter will build a new ant farm for her pets.

Joining: Margaret wants to hire a carpenter *who* will build a new ant farm for her pets.

Being that I like grammar

Many people say *being that* to introduce a reason. Unfortunately, *being that* is a grammatical felony in the first degree (if there are degrees of grammatical felonies — I'm a grammarian, not a lawyer). Here's the issue: People use *being that* as a subordinate conjunction, but *being that* is not acceptable, at least in formal English usage. Try *because*. For example:

WRONG: *Being that* it was Thanksgiving, Mugwump bought a turkey.

RIGHT: *Because* it was Thanksgiving, Mugwump bought a turkey.

WRONG: The turkey shed a tear or two, *being that* it was Thanksgiving.

RIGHT: The turkey shed a tear or two, *because* it was Thanksgiving.

You may like the sound of *since* in the sample sentences. Increasingly, *since* is a synonym for *because,* and so far civilization as we know it hasn't crumbled. The grammarians who like to predict the end of the world because of such issues have a problem with the *since/because* connection. They prefer to use *since* for time statements:

I haven't seen the turkey *since* the ax came out of the box.

Since you've been gone, I've begun an affair with Bill Bailey.

Another grammatical no-no is *irregardless.* I think *irregardless* is popular because it's a long word that feels good when you say it. Those *r's* just roll right off the tongue. Sadly, *irregardless* is not a conjunction. It's not even a word, according to the rules of formal English. Use *regardless* (not nearly so much fun to pronounce) or *despite the fact that.*

WRONG: Irregardless, we are going to eat you, you turkey!

RIGHT: Regardless, we are going to eat you, you turkey!

ALSO RIGHT: Despite the fact that you are a tough old bird, we are going to eat you, you turkey!

Sentence 1: Ludwig wants to marry Ludmilla.

Sentence 2: He's been singing under her window.

Joining: Ludwig, *who* has been singing under her window, wants to marry Ludmilla.

Sentence 1: The tax bill was passed yesterday.

Sentence 2: The tax bill will lower taxes for the top .00009% income bracket.

Joining: The tax bill *that* was passed yesterday will lower taxes for the top .00009% income bracket.

Alternate joining: The tax bill that was passed yesterday will lower taxes for Bill Gates. (Okay, I interpreted a little.)

That, which, and *who* are pronouns. In the combined sentences, each takes the place of a noun. *(That* replaces *book, which* replaces *map, who* replaces *carpenter, who* replaces *Ludwig, that* replaces *tax bill.)* These pronouns serve as thumbtacks, attaching a subordinate or less important idea to the main body of the sentence.

That, which, and *who* (as well as *whom* and *whose*) are pronouns that may relate one idea to another. When they do that job, they are called relative pronouns. Relative pronouns often serve as subjects or objects of the subordinate or dependent clause. For more information on clauses see Chapter 24.

Combine these sentences with a pronoun.

> Sentence 1: Cedric slowly tiptoed toward the poisonous snakes.

> Sentence 2: The snakes soon bit Cedric right on the tip of his long red nose.

Answer: Cedric slowly tiptoed toward the poisonous snakes, *which* soon bit Cedric right on the tip of his long red nose. The pronoun *which* replaces *snakes* in sentence 2.

Combine these sentences so that they flow smoothly.

> Sentence 1: Lochness slipped the microfilm into the heel of his shoe.

> Sentence 2: The shoe had been shined just yesterday by the superspy.

> Sentence 3: The superspy pretends to work at a shoeshine stand.

> Sentence 4: The superspy's name is unknown.

> Sentence 5: The superspy's code number is –4.

> Sentence 6: Lochness is terrified of the superspy.

Answer: Dozens of joinings are possible. Here are two:

Lochness slipped the microfilm into the heel of his shoe, which had been shined just yesterday by the superpy. The superspy, whose name is unknown but whose code number is –4, pretends to work at a shoeshine stand and terrifies Lochness.

or

After the shoe had been shined by the superspy, who pretends to work at a shoeshine stand, Lochness slipped the microfilm into the heel. Lochness is terrified by the superspy, whose name is unknown and whose code number is –4.

Chapter 8

Do You Feel Bad or Badly? The Lowdown on Adjectives and Adverbs

● ●

In This Chapter

▶ Identifying adjectives and adverbs

▶ Deciding whether an adjective or an adverb is appropriate

▶ Understanding why double negatives are wrong

▶ Placing descriptive words so that the sentence means what you intend

● ●

*W*ith the right nouns (names of persons, places, things, or ideas) and verbs (action or being words) you can build a pretty solid foundation in a sentence. The key to expressing your precise thoughts is to choose the correct descriptive words to enhance your sentence's meaning. In this chapter I explain the two basic types of descriptive words of the English language — *adjectives* and *adverbs*. I also show you how to use each correctly to add meaning to your sentence.

In case you doubt the significance of descriptive words, take a look at this sentence:

> Grunhilda sauntered past Lord and Taylor's when the sight of a Ferragamo Paradiso Pump paralyzed her.

Will the reader fully comprehend the meaning of this sentence? What must the reader know in order to understand this sentence? Here's a list:

✔ The reader should know that Lord and Taylor's is a department store.

✔ The reader should be able to identify Ferragamo as an upscale shoe label.

✔ The reader should be familiar with a Paradiso Pump (a shoe style I made up).

✔ A good vocabulary — one that includes *saunter* and *paralyze* — is helpful.

✔ A nice plus is some knowledge of Grunhilda and her obsession with the latest fashion in shoes.

If all of those pieces are in place, or if the reader has a good imagination and the ability to use context clues in reading comprehension, your message will be understood. But sometimes you can't trust the reader to understand the specifics of what you're trying to say. In that case, descriptions are quite useful. Here's Grunhilda, version 2:

> Grunhilda walked *slowly* past the *stately* Lord and Taylor's *department* store when the sight of a *fashionable, green, low-heeled dress* shoe with the *ultra-chic Ferragamo* label paralyzed her.

Okay, I overloaded the sentence a bit, but you get the point. The descriptive words help clarify the meaning of the sentence, particularly for the fashion-challenged.

Now that I've driven home the point that descriptions are essential to the meaning of your sentence, I know you're dying to learn more. Read on.

Adding Adjectives

An *adjective* is a descriptive word that changes the meaning of a noun or a pronoun. An adjective adds information on number, color, type, and other qualities to your sentence

Where do you find adjectives? In the adjective aisle of the supermarket. Okay, you don't. Most of the time you find them in front of a noun or pronoun — the one the adjective is describing. Keep in mind that adjectives can also roam around a bit. Here's an example:

> Legghorn, *sore* and *tired,* pleaded with Lulu to release him from the head-lock she had placed on him when he called her *"fragile."*

Sore and *tired* tells you about *Legghorn. Fragile* tells you about *her.* (Well, *fragile* tells you what Legghorn thinks of *her.* Lulu actually works out with free weights every day and is anything but fragile.) As you can see, these descriptions come after the words they describe, not before.

Adjectives describing nouns

The most common job for an adjective is describing a noun. Consider the adjectives *poisonous, angry,* and *rubber* in these sentences. Then decide which sentence would you like to hear as you walk through the jungle.

There is a *poisonous* snake on your shoulder.

There is an *angry poisonous* snake on your shoulder.

There is a *rubber* snake on your shoulder.

The last one, right? In these three sentences, those little descriptive words certainly make a difference. *Angry, poisonous,* and *rubber* all describe *snake,* and all of these descriptions give you information that you would really like to have. See how diverse and powerful adjectives can be?

Find the adjectives in this sentence.

With a sharp ax, the faithful troll parted the greasy hair of the seven ugly ogres.

Answer: *sharp* (describing *ax*), *faithful* (describing *troll*), *greasy* (describing *hair*), *seven* and *ugly* (describing *ogres*).

Adjectives describing pronouns

Adjectives can also describe *pronouns* (words that substitute for nouns):

There's something *strange* on your shoulder. (The adjective *strange* describes the pronoun *something.*)

Everyone *conscious* at the end of Legghorn's play made a quick exit. (The adjective *conscious* describes the pronoun *everyone.*)

Anyone *free* should report to the meeting room immediately! (The adjective *free* describes the pronoun *anyone.*)

Attaching adjectives to linking verbs

Adjectives may also follow linking verbs, in which case they describe the subject of the sentence. To find an adjective after a linking verb, ask the question *what.* See Chapter 6 for more information.

Just to review for a moment: *Linking verbs* join two ideas, associating one with the other. These verbs are like giant equal signs, equating the subject — which comes before the verb — with another idea after the verb. (See Chapter 2 for a full discussion of linking verbs.)

Sometimes a linking verb joins an adjective (or a couple of adjectives) and a noun:

Lulu's favorite dress is *orange* and *purple.* (The adjectives *orange* and *purple* describe the noun *dress.*)

The afternoon appears *gray* because of the nuclear fallout from Ratrug's cigar. (The adjective *gray* describes the noun *afternoon*.)

Legghorn's latest jazz composition sounds *great*. (The adjective *great* describes the noun *composition*.)

Pop the question: Identifying adjectives

To find adjectives, go to the words they describe — nouns and pronouns. Start with the noun and ask it three questions. (Not "What's the next hot dot-com?" or "Will you marry me?" This is grammar, not life.) Here are the three questions:

- ✔ How many?
- ✔ Which one?
- ✔ What kind?

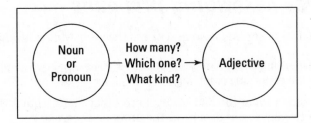

Take a look at this sentence:

Lochness placed three stolen atomic secrets inside his cheese burrito.

You see three nouns: *Lochness, secrets,* and *burrito.* Lochness has led a colorful life, but you can't find the answer to the following questions: How many *Lochnesses?* Which *Lochness?* What kind of *Lochness?* No words in the sentence provide that information, so no adjectives describe *Lochness.*

But try these three questions on *secrets* and *burrito* and you do come up with something: How many *secrets?* Answer: *three. Three* is an adjective. Which *secrets?* What kind of *secrets?* Answer: *stolen* and *atomic. Stolen* and *atomic* are adjectives. The same goes for *burrito:* What kind? Answer: *cheese. Cheese* is an adjective.

His answers one of the questions. (Which *burrito?* Answer: *his burrito.*) *His* is working as an adjective, but *his* is also a pronoun. Don't worry about the distinction, unless you're goal is to be an authority on the subject (sure to get you some laughs at parties). Some English textbooks call *his* a pronoun, and others call *his* an adjective. Whatever you want to call it, *his* functions in the same way in the sentence. This kind of completely irrelevant discussion gives English teachers a bad reputation.

Look at another sentence:

> The agonized glance thrilled Lochness's rotten, little, hard heart.

This sentence has three nouns. One *(Lochness's)* is possessive. If you ask how many *Lochness's,* which *Lochness's,* or what kind of *Lochness's,* you get no answer. The other two nouns, *glance* and *heart,* do yield an answer. What kind of *glance? Agonized glance.* What kind of *heart? Rotten, little, hard heart.* So *agonized, rotten, little,* and *hard* are all adjectives.

You may notice that a word changes its part of speech depending upon how it's used in the sentence. In the last sample sentence, *glance* is a noun, because *glance* is clearly a thing. Compare that sentence to this one:

> Lochness and Ludwig *glance* casually at the giant television screen.

Here *glance* is not a thing; it is an action that Lochness and Ludwig are performing. In this example sentence, *glance* is a verb. The moral of the story? Read the sentence, see what the word is doing, and then — if you like — give it a name.

Stalking the Common Adverb

Adjectives aren't the only descriptive words. Adverbs — words that alter the meaning of a verb, an adjective, or another adverb — are another type of description. Check these out:

> The boss *regretfully* said no to Philpot's request for a raise.

> The boss *furiously* said no to Philpot's request for a raise.

> The boss *never* said no to Philpot's request for a raise.

If you're Philpot, you care whether the words *regretfully, furiously,* or *never* are in the sentence. (Of course, if you're the boss, you don't care at all. You do a Nancy Reagan and "just say no.") *Regretfully, furiously,* and *never* are all adverbs. Notice how adverbs add meaning in these sentences:

Cedric *sadly* sang Legghorn's latest song. (Perhaps Cedric is in a bad mood.)

Cedric sang Legghorn's latest song *reluctantly*. (Cedric doesn't want to sing.)

Cedric *hoarsely* sang Legghorn's latest song. (Cedric has a cold.)

Cedric sang Legghorn's latest song *quickly*. (Cedric is in a hurry.)

Cedric sang even Legghorn's latest song. (Cedric sang everything, and with Legghorn's latest, he hit the bottom of the barrel.)

Pop the question: Finding the adverb

Adverbs mostly describe verbs, giving more information about an action. Nearly all adverbs — enough so that you don't have to worry about the ones that fall through the cracks — answer one of these four questions:

- ✔ How?
- ✔ When?
- ✔ Where?
- ✔ Why?

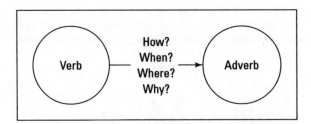

To find the adverb, go to the verb and pop the question. (See Chapter 2 for information on finding the verbs.) Look at this sentence:

Ludmilla secretly swiped the Sacred Slipper of the Potomac Princess yesterday and then happily went home.

You note two verbs: *swiped* and *went*. Take each one separately. *Swiped* how? Answer: *swiped secretly*. *Secretly* is an adverb. *Swiped* when? Answer: *swiped yesterday*. *Yesterday* is an adverb. *Swiped* where? No answer. *Swiped* why? Knowing Ludmilla, I'd say she stole for the fun of it, but you find no answer in the sentence.

Go on to the second verb in the sentence. *Went* how? Answer: *went happily*. *Happily* is an adverb. *Went* when? Answer: *went then*. *Then* is an adverb. *Went* where? Answer: *went home. Home* is an adverb. *Went* why? Probably to drink champagne out of the slipper, but again, you find no answer in the sentence.

Here's another example:

Eggworthy soon softly snored and delicately slipped away.

You identify two verbs again: *snored* and *slipped.* First one up: *snored. Snored* how? Answer: *snored softly. Softly* is an adverb. *Snored* when? Answer: *snored soon. Soon* is an adverb. *Snored* where? No answer. *Snored* why? No answer again. Now for *slipped. Slipped* how? Answer: *slipped delicately. Delicately* is an adverb. *Slipped* where? Answer: *slipped away. Away* is an adverb. *Slipped* when? No answer. *Slipped* why? No answer. The adverbs are *soon, delicately,* and *away.*

Adverbs can be lots of places in a sentence. If you're trying to find them, rely on the questions *how, when, where,* and *why,* not the location. Similarly, a word may be an adverb in one sentence and something else in another sentence. Check out this example:

Griselda went *home* in a huff because of that slammed door.

Home is where the heart is, unless you are in Lochness's cabin.

Home plate is cleaned by the umpire.

In the first example, *home* tells you where Griselda went, so *home* is an adverb in that sentence. In the second example, *home* is a place, so *home* is a noun in that sentence. In the third example, *home* is an adjective, telling you what kind of *plate.*

Final answer: pop the question and see if you reveal an adverb, adjective, or another part of speech.

Adverbs describing adjectives and other adverbs

Adverbs also describe other descriptions, usually making the description more or less intense. (A description describing a description? Give me a break! But it's true.) Here's an example:

An extremely unhappy Ludwig flipped when his pet frog learned to talk.

How *unhappy?* Answer: *extremely unhappy. Extremely* is an adverb describing the adjective *unhappy.*

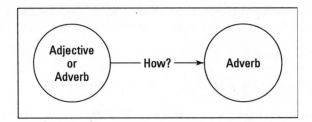

 Sometimes the questions you pose to locate adjectives and adverbs are answered by more than one word in a sentence. In the previous example sentence, if you ask, "*Seemed* when?" the answer is *when his pet frog learned to talk*. Don't panic. These longer answers are just different forms of adjectives and adverbs. For more information, see Chapters 9 and 24.

Now back to work. Here's another example:

> Once he began to speak, Ludwig's very talkative pet frog *wouldn't stop*.

How *talkative?* Answer: *very talkative*. *Very* is an adverb describing the adjective *talkative*.

And another:

> Ludwig's frog croaked *quite hoarsely*.

This time an adverb is describing another adverb. *Hoarsely* is an adverb because it explains how the frog *croaked*. In other words, *hoarsely* describes the verb *croaked*. How *hoarsely?* Answer: *quite hoarsely*. *Quite* is an adverb describing the adverb *hoarsely*, which in turn describes the verb *croaked*.

In general, you don't need to worry too much about adverbs that describe adjectives or other adverbs; only a few errors are associated with this type of description. See "Sorting out adjective/adverb pairs" later in this chapter for some tips.

Distinguishing Between Adjectives and Adverbs

Does it matter whether a word is an adjective or an adverb? Some of the time, no. You've been talking and writing happily for years, and you've spent very little time worrying about this issue. In your crib, you demanded, "I want a bottle NOW, Mama." You didn't know you were adding an adverb to your sentence. For that matter, you didn't know you were making a sentence. You were just hungry. But some of the time knowing the difference is helpful. In this section I tell you how to apply the *-ly* test to sort adjectives from adverbs and how to decide between some commonly confused pairs of adjectives and adverbs.

Sorting adjectives from adverbs: The -ly test

Strictly is an adverb, and *strict* is an adjective. *Nicely* is an adverb, and *nice* is an adjective. *Generally* is an adverb, and *general* is an adjective. *Lovely* is a . . . gotcha! You were going to say *adverb*, right? Wrong. *Lovely* is an adjective. But you can use the *-ly* test for many adverbs. Just keep in mind that *soon, now, home, fast,* and many other words that don't end in *-ly* are adverbs too. The best way to tell if a word is an adverb is to ask the four adverb questions: *how, when, where,* and *why.* If the word answers one of those questions, it's an adverb.

As Wayne from the movie *Wayne's World* would say, "One of the most common adverbs ends in *ly* — NOT." *Not* is an adverb because it reverses the meaning of the verb from positive to negative. While I'm speaking of not, I should remind you to avoid double negatives. In many languages (Spanish, for example), doubling or tripling the negative adjectives and adverbs or throwing in a negative pronoun or two simply makes your denial stronger. In Spanish, saying "I did not kill no victim" is okay. In English, however, that sentence is a confession. English grammar, supremely irrational in a million ways (see Chapter 3 on irregular verbs!) decides that strict logic is best in sentences with negatives. If you *did not* kill *no* victim, you killed at least *one* victim. In other words, two negatives equal a positive. You can put a lot of negatives together; just don't put them in the same sentence. (Other types of double negatives may trip you up. See Chapter 22 for more information.)

Identify the adjectives and adverbs in the following sentences.

A. Thank you for the presents you gave us yesterday.

B. The lovely presents you gave us smell like old socks.

C. The presents you kindly gave us are very rotten.

Answers: In sentence A, *yesterday* is an adverb, describing when *you gave* the presents. In sentence B, *lovely* is an adjective describing the noun *presents.* *Old* is an adjective describing *socks;* sentence B has no adverbs. In sentence C, the adverb is *kindly* and it describes the verb *gave.* Also in sentence C, the adverb *very* describes the adjective *rotten.* *Rotten* is an adjective describing *presents.*

Try one more. Find the adjectives and adverbs.

> The carefully decorated purse that Legghorn knitted is quickly fraying around the edges.

Answers: The adverb *carefully* describes the adjective *decorated*. The verb *is fraying* is described by the adverb *quickly*.

Sorting out adjective/adverb pairs

Time for some practice in choosing between adjectives and adverbs. First I show you some easy pairs, ones that allow you to apply the *-ly* test. Then I look at some irregular pairs.

The most common adjective/adverb pairs are distinguished by the letters *-ly*. Sneak a peek at these examples:

> WRONG: Abernathy stopped *sudden* when the stop sign loomed.
>
> RIGHT: Abernathy stopped *suddenly* when the stop sign loomed.
>
> WHY IT IS RIGHT: The adverb *suddenly* describes how Abernathy *stopped*.

Here's more:

> WRONG: Legghorn will grin *casual* when he swoops down on the nest of spies.
>
> RIGHT: Legghorn will grin *casually* when he swoops down on the nest of spies.
>
> WHY IT IS RIGHT: The adverb *casually* describes how Legghorn *will grin*.
>
> ALSO RIGHT: Legghorn's *casual* grin is deceiving.
>
> WHY IT IS ALSO RIGHT: The adjective *casual* describes the noun *grin*.

Don't stop now; check these examples:

> WRONG: The syrup tasted *sweetly* when Eggworthy sipped it.
>
> RIGHT: The syrup tasted *sweet* when Eggworthy sipped it.
>
> WHY IT IS RIGHT: The adjective *sweet* describes the noun *syrup. Tasted* is a linking verb, so the adjective that follows the verb describes the subject.
>
> ALSO RIGHT: Eggworthy drowns his pancakes in *sweet* syrup.
>
> WHY IT IS ALSO RIGHT: The adjective *sweet* describes the noun *syrup*.

And one last set:

> WRONG: Legghorn, unlike Lochness, plays clean on the football field.
>
> RIGHT: Legghorn, unlike Lochness, plays cleanly on the football field.
>
> WHY IT IS RIGHT: The adverb *cleanly* describes how Legghorn *plays*.

Remember: Adjectives describe nouns or pronouns, and adverbs describe verbs, adjectives, or other adverbs.

Choosing between adjectives and adverbs — some tough pairs

The sentences in the preceding section were easy. Your "ear" for good English probably told you the proper word choice. However, at times, your ear may not automatically tell you which word is correct. In this section I show you some confusing pairs, including good/well, bad/badly, and continual/continuous.

Choosing between good and well

If I am ever elected president of the universe, one of the first things I'm going to do (after I get rid of apostrophes — see Chapter 12) is to drop all irregular forms. Until then, you may want to read about *good* and *well.*

Good is an adjective, and *well* is an adverb, except when you're talking about your health:

> I am *good.*

Good is an adjective here. The sentence means *I have the qualities of goodness* or *I am in a good mood.* Or the sentence is a really bad pickup line.

> I am *well.*

Well is an adjective here. The sentence means *I am not sick.*

> I play the piano *well.*

This time *well* is an adverb. It describes how I play. In other words, the adverb well describes the verb *play.* The sentence means that I don't have to practice anymore.

Which sentence is correct?

A. When asked how he was feeling, Ludwig smiled at his ex-girlfriends and replied, "Not well."

B. When asked how he was feeling, Ludwig smiled at his ex-girlfriends and replied, "Not good."

Answer: Sentence A is correct because Ludwig's ex-girlfriends are inquiring about his health.

Try one more. Which sentence is correct?

A. Eggworthy did not perform good on the crash test.

B. Eggworthy did not perform well on the crash test.

Answer: Sentence B is correct because the adverb *well* describes the verb *did perform*. *Did perform* how? Answer: *did perform well.*

Choosing between bad and badly

Bad is a bad word, at least in terms of grammar. Confusing *bad* and *badly* is one of the most common errors. Check out these examples:

I felt badly.

I felt bad.

Badly is an adverb (Remember the *-ly* test mentioned earlier in this chapter?), and *bad* is an adjective. Which one should you use? Well, what are you trying to say? In the first sentence, you went to the park with your mittens on. The bench had a sign on it: "WET PAINT." The sign looked old, so you decided to check. You put your hand on the bench, but the mittens were in the way. You felt *badly* — that is, not very accurately. In the second sentence, you sat on the bench, messing up the back of your coat with dark green stripes. When you saw the stripes, you felt *bad* — that is, you were sad. In everyday speech, of course, you're not likely to express much about *feeling badly*. Not that many people walk around testing benches, and not that many people talk about their ability to feel. So 99.99 percent of the time you feel *bad* — unless you're in a good mood.

Choosing between continuous and continual

Another pair that may confuse you is *continuous* and *continual*. Read this paragraph:

The continual interruptions are driving me crazy. Every ten minutes someone barges in and asks me where the coffee machine is. Do I look like a coffeehouse? I've been working *continuously* for seven hours, and my feet are now numb. Perhaps I'll stop for a while and find that coffee machine.

Continual refers to events that happen over and over again, but with breaks in between each instance. *Continuous* means without stopping. *Continuous* noise is steady, uninterrupted, like the drone of the electric generator in your local power plant. *Continual* noise is what you hear when I go bowling. You hear silence (that's when I stare at the pins), a little noise (that's when the ball rolls down the alley), and silence again (that's when the ball hits the gutter). After an hour you hear noise (that's when I finally hit something). Here are some examples:

> WRONG: Ratrug screamed *continually* until Lulu stuffed rags in his mouth.
>
> WHY IT IS WRONG: Ratrug's screams don't come and go. When he's upset, he's really upset, and nothing shuts him up except force.
>
> RIGHT: Ratrug screamed *continuously* until Lulu stuffed rags in his mouth.
>
> WHY IT IS RIGHT: In this version, he takes no breaks.

Check out another set of examples:

> WRONG: Ludmilla's *continuous* attempts to impress Ludwig were fruitless, including the fruit basket she sent him on Monday and the piranha she Fed-Exed on Tuesday.
>
> WHY IT IS WRONG: Ludmilla's attempts stop and start. She does one thing on Monday, rests up, and then does another on Tuesday.
>
> RIGHT: Ludmilla's *continual* attempts to impress Ludwig were fruitless, including the fruit basket she sent him on Monday and the piranha she Fed-Exed on Tuesday.
>
> WHY IT IS RIGHT: Now the sentence expresses a recurring action.

Adjectives and adverbs that look the same

Odd words here and there (and they are odd) do double duty as both adjectives and adverbs. They look exactly the same, but they take their identity as adjectives or adverbs from the way that they function in the sentence. Take a look at these examples:

> Upon seeing the stop sign, Abernathy stopped *short.* (adverb)
>
> Abernathy did not notice the sign until the last minute because he is too *short* to see over the steering wheel. (adjective)
>
> Lola's advice is *right:* Abernathy should not drive. (adjective)
>
> Abernathy turned *right* after his last-minute stop. (adverb)
>
> Abernathy came to a *hard* decision when he turned in his license. (adjective)
>
> Lola tries *hard* to schedule some time for Abernathy, now that he is carless. (adverb)

The English language has too many adjectives and adverbs to list here. If you're unsure about a particular word, check the dictionary for the correct form.

Which sentence is correct?

    A. It was real nice of you to send me that bouquet of poison ivy.

    B. It was really nice of you to send me that bouquet of poison ivy.

Answer: B. How *nice? Really nice. Real* is an adjective and *really* is an adverb. Adverbs answer the question *how.*

Avoiding Common Mistakes with Adjectives and Adverbs

A few words — *even, almost, only, and others* — often end up in the wrong spots. If these words aren't placed correctly, your sentence may say something that you didn't intend.

Placing even

Even is one of the sneaky modifiers that can land any place in a sentence — and change the meaning of what you're saying. Take a look at this example:

> It's two hours before the grand opening of the school show. Lulu and Legghorn have been rehearsing for weeks. They know all the dances, and Lulu has only one faint bruise left from Legghorn's tricky elbow maneuver. Suddenly, Legghorn's evil twin Lochness, mad with jealousy, "accidentally" places his foot in Legghorn's path. Legghorn's down! His ankle is sprained! What will happen to the show?

- Possibility 1: Lulu shouts, "We can still go on! *Even Lester* knows the dances."

- Possibility 2: Lulu shouts, "We can still go on! Lester *even knows* the dances."

- Possibility 3: Lulu shouts, "We can still go on! Lester knows *even the dances.*"

What's going on here? These three statements look almost the same, but they aren't. Here's what each one means:

- Possibility 1: Lulu surveys the fifteen boys gathered around Legghorn. She knows that any one of them could step in at a moment's notice. After all, the dances are very easy. *Even Lester,* the clumsiest boy in the class, knows the dances. If *even Lester* can perform the role, it will be a piece of cake for everyone else.

✔ Possibility 2: Lulu surveys the fifteen boys gathered around Legghorn. It doesn't look good. Most of them would be willing, but they've been busy learning other parts. There's no time to teach them Legghorn's role. Then she spies Lester. With a gasp, she realizes that Lester has been watching Legghorn every minute of rehearsal. Although the curtain will go up very soon, the show can still be saved. Lester doesn't have to practice; he doesn't have to learn something new. Lester *even knows* the dances.

✔ Possibility 3: The whole group looks at Lester almost as soon as Legghorn hits the floor. Yes, Lester knows the words. He's been reciting Legghorn's lines for weeks now, helping Legghorn learn the part. Yes, Lester can sing; everyone's heard him. But what about the dances? There's no time to teach him. Just then, Lester begins to twirl around the stage. Lulu sighs with relief. Lester knows *even the dances.* The show will go on!

Got it? *Even* is a description; *even* describes the words that follow it. To put it another way, *even* begins a comparison:

✔ Possibility 1: *even* Lester (as well as everyone else)

✔ Possibility 2: *even* knows (doesn't have to learn)

✔ Possibility 3: *even* the dances (as well as the songs and words).

So here's the rule. Put *even* at the beginning of the comparison implied in the sentence.

Placing almost

Almost is another tricky little modifier to place. Here's an example:

Last night Lulu wrote for *almost* an hour and then went rollerblading.

and

Last night Lulu *almost* wrote for an hour and then went rollerblading.

In the first sentence, Lulu wrote for 55 minutes and then stopped. In the second sentence, Lulu intended to write, but every time she sat down at the computer, she remembered that she hadn't watered the plants, called her best friend Lola, made a sandwich, and so forth. After an hour of wasted time and without one word on the screen, she grabbed her rollerblades and left.

Almost begins the comparison. Lulu *almost wrote,* but she didn't. Or Lulu wrote for *almost an hour,* but not for a *whole hour.* In deciding where to put these words, add the missing words and see whether the position of the word makes sense. (I discuss comparisons further in Chapter 17.)

The farther of our country: Farther and further

Farther refers to distance. If you need to travel *farther,* you have more miles to cover. *Further* also has a sense of *more* in it, but not more distance. Instead, *further* means additional. *Further* is for time, ideas, activities, and lots more. Some examples:

Abernathy needs *further* work on his teeth before the studio will approve a five-picture deal. (additional work)

Murgatroyd flew *farther* than anyone else who had been kicked by the same bull. (longer distance)

Grunhilda thinks *further* discussion will be fruitless, as the pineapple conglomerate

has already decided to breed orange and purple plants. (additional discussion)

The *farther* he walks, the more Legghorn's toenails hurt. (extra distance)

The loneliness of the short-distance runner does not impress Lochness, because everyone he knows travels *farther* than the runner. (more distance)

Further planning is planned for that plan, the brainchild of the new Planning Commission on the Elimination of Redundant Language. (extra planning)

Placing only

If only the word *only* were simpler to understand! Like the other tricky words in this section, *only* changes the meaning of the sentence every time its position is altered. For example:

Only Lochness went to Iceland last summer. (No one else went.)

Lochness *only* went to Iceland last summer. (He didn't do anything else.)

Lochness went *only* to Iceland last summer. (He skipped Antarctica.)

Lochness went to Iceland *only* last summer. (Two possible meanings: 1) He didn't go three years ago or at any other time — just last summer. 2) The word *only* may mean *just,* as in *recently.*)

Chapter 9

Prepositions and Interjections and Articles, Oh My! Other Parts of Speech

*H*ow does the proverb go? Little things mean a lot? Whoever said that was probably talking about prepositions. Some of the shortest words in the language — at least most of them — these little guys pack a punch in your sentences. All the more reason to use them correctly. In this chapter, I explain everything you always wanted to know about prepositions but hoped you wouldn't have to ask. I also give you the basics on interjections (the rarest parts of speech) and articles (the most common words in the language).

Proposing Relationships: Prepositions

Imagine that you encounter two nouns: *aardvark* and *book*. (A *noun* is a word for a person, place, thing, or idea.) How many ways can you connect the two nouns to express different ideas?

the book *about* the aardvark

the book *by* the aardvark

the book *behind* the aardvark

the book *in front of* the aardvark

the book *near* the aardvark

the book *under* the aardvark

The italicized words relate two nouns to each other. These relationship words are called prepositions. *Prepositions* may be defined as any word or group of words that relates a noun or a pronoun to another word in the sentence.

Sometime during the last millennium when I was in grammar school, I had to memorize a list of prepositions. (How quaint, right? We had inkwells, too.) I was so terrified of Sister Saint Vincent, my seventh grade teacher, that not only did I learn the list, I made it part of my being. In fact, I can still recite it. I don't think memorizing prepositions is worth the time, but a familiarity would be nice. In other words, don't marry the preposition list. Just date it a few times. Take a look at Table 9-1 for a list of some common prepositions:

Table 9-1	Common Prepositions		
about	above	according to	across
after	against	along	amid
among	around	at	before
behind	below	beside	besides
between	beyond	by	concerning
down	during	except	for
from	in	into	like
of	off	on	over
past	since	through	toward
underneath	until	up	upon
with	within	without	

The objects of my affection: Prepositional phrases and their objects

Prepositions never travel alone; they're always with an object. In the examples in the previous section, the object of each preposition is *aardvark*. Just to get all the annoying terminology over with at once, a *prepositional phrase* consists of a preposition and an object. The object of a preposition is always a noun or a pronoun, or perhaps one or two of each. (A *pronoun* is a word that takes the place of a noun, like *he* for *Eggworthy* and so forth.)

Here's an example:

In the afternoon, the snow pelted Eggworthy on his little bald head.

This sentence has two prepositions: *in* and *on. Afternoon* is the object of the preposition *in,* and *head* is the object of the preposition *on.*

Why, you may ask, is the object *head* and not *little* or *bald?* Sigh. I was hoping you wouldn't notice. Okay, here's the explanation. You can throw a few other things inside a prepositional phrase — mainly descriptive words. Check out these variations on the plain phrase *of the aardvark:*

of the *apologetic* aardvark

of the *always apoplectic* aardvark

of the *antagonizingly argumentative* aardvark

Despite the different descriptions, each phrase is still basically talking about an *aardvark.* Also, *aardvark* is a noun, and only nouns and pronouns are allowed to be objects of the preposition. So in the *Eggworthy* sentence, you need to choose the most important word as the object of the preposition. Also, you need to choose a noun, not an adjective. Examine *his little bald head* (the words, not Eggworthy's actual head, which is better seen from a distance). *Head* is clearly the important concept, and *head* is a noun. Thus *head* is the object of the preposition.

Pop the question: Questions that identify the objects of the prepositions

All objects — of a verb or of a preposition — answer the questions *whom?* or *what?* To find the object of a preposition, ask *whom?* or *what?* after the preposition.

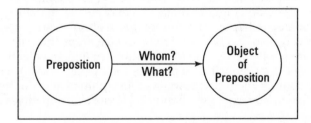

In this sentence you see two prepositional phrases:

Marilyn thought that the election of the aardvark to the senate was quite unfair.

In the group: Between/Among

Between and *among* are two tricky prepositions that are often used incorrectly. To choose the appropriate preposition, decide how many people or things you're talking about. If the answer is two, you want *between:* Lola was completely unable to choose *between* the biker magazine and *Poetry for Weightlifters.* (two magazines only)

If you're talking about more than two, *among* is the appropriate word: Lola strolled *among* the

parked motorcycles, reading poetry aloud. (more than two motorcycles)

One exception: Treaties are made *between* nations, even if more than two countries sign: The treaty to outlaw bubble gum was negotiated *between* Libya, the United States, Russia, and Ecuador.

The first preposition is *of. Of* what? *Of the aardvark. Aardvark* is the object of the preposition *of.* The second preposition is *to. To* what? To the senate. *Senate* is the object of the preposition *to.*

What is the object of the preposition in this sentence?

> The heroic teacher pounded the grammar rules into her students' tired brains.

Answer: *Brains* is the object of the preposition *into.* When you pop the question — *into* whom? or what? — the answer is *her students' tired brains.* The most important word is *brains,* which is a noun.

Why do I need to know this?

When you're checking subject–verb pairs, you need to identify and then ignore the prepositional phrases. Why? Because the prepositional phrases are distractions. If you don't ignore them, you may end up matching the verb to the wrong word. See Chapter 11 for more information on subject–verb agreement. You may also find it helpful to recognize prepositional phrases because sometimes, when you "pop the question" to find an adjective or an adverb, the answer is a prepositional phrase. Don't panic. You haven't done anything wrong. Simply know that a prepositional phrase may do the same job as an adjective or adverb. (See Chapter 8 for more on adjectives and adverbs.)

Prepositional phrases fall into two large categories — *adjectival phrases* and *adverbial phrases.* You don't have any reason at all to know this fact, so forget it immediately, unless you're set on being an English know-it-all.

You should pay attention to prepositions because choosing the wrong one may be embarrassing:

>   Person 1: May I sit *next* to you?
>
>   Person 2: (smiling) Certainly.
>
>   Person 1: May I sit *under* you?
>
>   Person 2: (sound of slap) Help! Police!

Are you talking to 1? Prepositions and pronouns

A big preposition pitfall is pronouns. (Can you say that three times fast — without spitting?) A *pronoun* is a word that substitutes for a noun. The problem with pronouns is that only some pronouns are allowed to act as objects of prepositions; they're called *object pronouns*. (See Chapters 10 and 17 for details on pronoun rules.) Use the wrong pronoun — a non-object pronoun — and the grammar cops will be after you.

The object pronouns, cleared to act as objects of the preposition, are *me, you, him, her, it, us, them, whom,* and *whomever.*

Take a look at some sentences with *pronouns* as objects of the prepositions:

>   Among Bilbo, Harry, and *me* there is no contest. (*Me* is one of the objects of the preposition *among.*)
>
>   Without *them,* the bridge will fall out of Cedric's mouth. (*Them* is the object of the preposition *without* — also, in case you're wondering, it's a dental bridge, not the Golden Gate.)
>
>   Legghorn added an amendment to the bill concerning us, but the bill did not pass. (*Us* is the object of the preposition *concerning.*)

What is one of the most common errors in the use of object pronouns? Is the correct prepositional phrase *between you and I* or *between you and me?* Answer: The correct expression is *between you and me. Between* = the preposition. *You and me* = the objects of the preposition. *Me* is an object pronoun. (*I* is a subject pronoun.) The next time you hear someone say *between you and I,* I expect you to recite the rule.

Which sentence is correct?

A. According to Elberg and she, the aardvark's nose is simply too long.

B. According to Elberg and her, the aardvark's nose is simply too long.

Answer: Sentence B is correct. *According to* is the preposition. The object of the preposition is *Elberg and her. Her* is an object pronoun. (*She* is a subject pronoun.)

Most of the tough pronoun choices come when the sentence has more than one object of the preposition (*Elberg and her,* for example, in the pop quiz). Your "ear" for grammar will probably tell you the correct pronoun when the sentence has a single pronoun object. You probably wouldn't say *according to she* because it sounds funny (to use a technical term).

If the sentence has more than one object of the preposition, try this rule of thumb — and I really mean thumb, at least when you're writing. Take your thumb and cover one of the objects. Say the sentence. Does it sound right?

> According to Elberg

Okay so far. Now take your thumb and cover the other object. Say the sentence. Does it sound right?

> According to she

Now do you hear the problem? Make the change:

> According to her

Now put the two back together:

> According to Elberg and her

This method is not foolproof, but chances are good that you'll get a clue to the correct pronoun choices if you check the objects one by one.

A good part of speech to end a sentence with?

As I write this paragraph, global warming is increasing, the stock market is sending out mixed signals, and the Yankees' pitching staff is in deep trouble. In the midst of all these earth-shattering events, some people still walk around worrying about where to put a preposition. Specifically, they (okay, I must admit that sometimes I, too) worry about whether or not ending a sentence with a preposition is acceptable. Let me illustrate the problem:

> Tell me whom he spoke *about.*

> Tell me *about* whom he spoke.

Here's the verdict: Both sentences are correct, at least for most people and even for most grammarians. But not, I must warn you, for all. You know the kind of person who insisted on ignoring the celebrations at midnight on January 1, 2000, because technically the millennium didn't really start until January 1, 2001? The kind of person who is right, but completely out of step with the rest of the culture? Well, those people still tsk-tsk when they hear a sentence that ends with a preposition. The rest of us have gotten over it. Unless you're writing something for that kind of person, put the preposition wherever you like, including at the end of a sentence.

Interjections Are Easy!

Yes! An English topic that is foolproof. *Interjections* are exclamations that often express intense emotion. These words or phrases aren't connected grammatically to the rest of the sentence. Check out these examples:

> *Ouch!* I caught my finger in the hatch of that submersible oceanographic vessel.

> *Curses,* foiled again.

> *Yes!* We've finally gotten to a topic that is foolproof.

Interjections may be followed by commas, but sometimes they're followed by exclamation points or periods. The separation by punctuation shows the reader that the interjection is a comment on the sentence, not a part of it. (Of course, in the case of the exclamation point or period, the punctuation mark also indicates that the interjection is not a part of the sentence at all.)

You can't do anything wrong with interjections, except perhaps overuse them. Interjections are like salt. A little salt sprinkled on dinner perks up the taste buds; too much sends you to the telephone to order take-out.

Articles: Not Just for Magazines Anymore

Another topic, this time almost foolproof. Articles are those little words — *a, an, the* — that sit in front of nouns. In meaning, *the* is usually more specific than *an* or *a.*

> Sentence 1: Melanie wants *the* answer, and you'd better be quick about it.

This statement means that Melanie is stuck on problem 12, and her mother won't let her go out until her homework is finished. A really good movie is playing at the cineplex, and now she's on the phone, demanding *the* answer to number 12.

Sentence 2: Melanie wants *an* answer, and you'd better be quick about it.

This statement means that Melanie simply has to have a date for the prom. She asked you a week ago, but if you're not going to be her escort, she'll ask someone else. She's lost patience, and she doesn't even care anymore whether you go or not. She just wants *an* answer.

To sum up: Use *the* when you're speaking specifically and *an* or *a* when you're speaking more generally.

The is called a definite article. *A* and *an* are called indefinite articles.

A apple? An book? A precedes words that begin with consonant sounds (all the letters except *a, e, i, o,* and *u*). *An* precedes words beginning with the vowel sounds *a, e, i,* and *o.* The letter *u* is a special case. If the word sounds like *you,* choose *a.* If the word sounds like someone kicked you in the stomach — *uh* — choose *an.* Another special case is the letter *h.* If the word starts with a hard *h* sound, as in *horse,* choose *a.* If the word starts with a silent letter *h,* as in *herb,* choose *an.* Here are some examples:

> an aardvark (a = vowel)
>
> a belly (b = consonant)
>
> an egg (e = vowel)
>
> a UFO (*U* sounds like *you*)
>
> an unidentified flying object (*u* sounds like *uh*)
>
> a helmet (hard *h*)
>
> an hour (silent *h*)

Special note: Sticklers-for-rules say *an historic event.* The rest of us say *a historic event.*

Chapter 10

Everyone Brought Their Homework: Pronoun Errors

*P*ronouns are words that substitute for nouns. Even though they're useful, pronouns can also be pesky. You see, English has many different types of pronouns, each governed by its own set of rules. (See Chapters 4 and 6 for information on subject and object pronouns.)

The whole topic of pronouns is enough to give you a headache, so get out your aspirin. In this chapter, I concentrate on how to avoid the most common errors associated with this part of speech.

Pairing Pronouns with Nouns

To get started on everything you need to know about pronouns, take a close look at how pronouns are paired with nouns. A pronoun's meaning can vary from sentence to sentence. Think of pronouns as the ultimate substitute teachers. One day they're solving quadratic equations, and the next they're doing push-ups in the gym. Such versatility comes from the fact that pronouns don't have identities of their own; instead, they stand in for nouns. In a few very weird situations, pronouns stand in for other pronouns. I discuss pronoun–pronoun pairs later in this chapter.

To choose the appropriate pronoun, you must consider the word that the pronoun is replacing. The word that the pronoun replaces is called the pronoun's *antecedent.*

Identifying the pronoun–antecedent pair is really a matter of reading comprehension. If the sentence (or in some cases, the paragraph) doesn't make the pronoun–antecedent connection clear, the writing is faulty. Time to edit! But in most cases the meaning of the pronoun leaps off the page. Take a look at some examples:

Hasenfeff stated *his* goals clearly: *He* wanted to take over the world. (The pronouns *his* and *he* refer to the noun *Hasenfeff.*)

The lion with a thorn in *her* paw decided to wear sneakers the next time *she* went for a walk in the jungle. (The pronouns *her* and *she* in this sentence refer to the noun *lion.*)

Our cause is just! Down with sugarless gum! *We* demand that all bubble gum be loaded with sugar! (The pronouns *our* and *we* refer to the speakers, who aren't named.)

Tattered books will not be accepted because *they* are impossible to resell. (The pronoun *they* refers to the noun *books.*)

Ludwig, *who* types five or six words a minute, is writing a new encyclopedia. (The pronoun *who* refers to *Ludwig.*)

Ameba and *I* demand that the microscope be cleaned before *we* begin the exam. (The pronoun *I* refers to the speaker. The pronoun *we* refers to *Ameba and I.*)

When analyzing a sentence, you seldom find a noun that's been replaced by the pronouns *I* and *we.* The pronoun *I* always refers to the speaker and *we* refers to the speaker and someone else.

Similarly, the pronoun *it* sometimes has no antecedent:

It is raining.

It is obvious that Smyrna has not won the card-flipping contest.

In the above sentences, *it* is just a place-filler, setting up the sentence for the true expression of meaning (First sample sentence: Take your umbrella and cancel the picnic. Second sample sentence: Smyrna's flipping hand is broken and she has lost all her baseball cards.)

Sometimes the meaning of the pronoun is explained in a previous sentence:

Thistle's ice cream *cone* is cracked. I don't want *it.* (The pronoun *it* refers to the noun *cone.*)

Don't confuse *its* and *it's.* One is a possessive pronoun *(its),* and the other is a contraction *(it's)* meaning "it is." For more information on *its* and *it's,* see the discussion later in this chapter.

Identify the pronouns and their antecedents in this paragraph:

> Cedric arrived at his mother's charity ball, although it was snowing and no taxis had stopped to pick him up. Once inside the ballroom, he glimpsed Lulu and her boyfriend dancing the tango. Their steps were strange indeed, for the orchestra was actually playing a waltz. As she sailed across the floor — her boyfriend had lost his grip — Lulu cried, "Help me!"

Answer: Cedric arrived at *his (Cedric's)* mother's charity ball, although *it* (no antecedent) was snowing and no taxis had stopped to pick *him (Cedric)* up. Once inside the ballroom, *he (Cedric)* glimpsed Lulu and *her (Lulu's)* boyfriend dancing the tango. *Their (Lulu and boyfriend's)* steps were strange indeed, for the orchestra was actually playing a waltz. As *she (Lulu)* sailed across the floor — *her (Lulu's)* boyfriend had lost *his (boyfriend's)* grip — Lulu cried, "Help *me!" (Lulu).*

Deciding between Singular and Plural Pronouns

All pronouns are either singular or plural. Singular pronouns replace singular nouns, which are those that name *one* person, place, thing, or idea. Plural pronouns replace plural nouns — those that name *more than one* person, place, thing, or idea. (Grammar terminology has flair, doesn't it?) A few pronouns replace other pronouns; in those situations, singular pronouns replace other singular pronouns, and plurals replace plurals. You need to understand pronoun number — singulars and plurals — before you place them in sentences. Take a look at Table 10-1 for a list of some common singular and plural pronouns.

Table 10-1	Common Singular and Plural Pronouns
Singular	*Plural*
I	We
Me	Us
Myself	Ourselves

(continued)

Table 10-1 *(continued)*

Singular	Plural
You	You
Yourself	Yourselves
He/She/It	They/Them
Himself/Herself/Itself	Themselves
Who	Who
Which	Which
That	That

Notice that some of the pronouns in Table 10-1 do double duty; they take the place of both singular and plural nouns or pronouns. (You think this double duty is a good idea? Hah! Wait until you get to the next chapter when you have to match singular and plural subjects with their verbs.)

Most of the time choosing between singular and plural pronouns is easy. You're not likely to say

> Ludmilla tried to pick up the ski poles, but it was too heavy.

because *ski poles* (plural) and *it* (singular) don't match. Automatically you say

> Ludmilla tried to pick up the ski poles, but they were too heavy.

Matching *ski poles* with *they* should please your ear.

Goldilocks and the three there's

They're putting all *their* bets on the horse over *there.* In other words, *there* is a place. *Their* shows ownership. *They're* is short for *they are.* Some examples:

RIGHT: "*They're* too short," muttered Eggworthy as he eyed the strips of bacon.

WHY IT IS RIGHT: *They're* means *they are.*

RIGHT: "Why don't you take some longer strips from *their* plates," suggested Lola.

WHY IT IS RIGHT: The plates belong to *them* — expressed by the possessive pronoun *their.*

RIGHT: "My arm is not long enough to reach over *there,*" sighed Eggworthy.

WHY IT IS RIGHT: *There* is a place (a place Eggworthy can't reach).

If you're learning English as a second language, your ear for the language is still in training. Put it on an exercise regimen of at least an hour a day of careful listening. A radio station or a television show in which reasonably educated people are speaking will help you to train your ear. You'll soon become comfortable hearing and choosing the proper pronouns.

Using Singular and Plural Possessive Pronouns

Possessive pronouns — those all-important words that indicate who owns what — also have singular and plural forms. You need to keep them straight. Table 10-2 helps you identify each type.

Table 10-2	Singular and Plural Possessive Pronouns
Singular	*Plural*
my	our
mine	ours
your	your
yours	yours
his	their/theirs
her	their
hers	theirs
its	their
whose	whose

Do you have an *its* problem? I'm not talking about a poison ivy rash that you need to scratch all the time. I'm talking about a possessive pronoun and a *contraction* (a shortened word in which an apostrophe substitutes one or more letters). In other words, do you know the difference between *its* and *it's?*

Its shows possession:

>   The computer has exploded, and *its* screen is now decorating the ceiling.

It's means it is:

>   *It's* raining cats and dogs, but I don't see any alligators.

An act of parliament

For centuries the words *they* and *their* were allowed to refer to both singular and plural words. Such usage meant that the writer or speaker didn't have to make a gender choice because *their* didn't refer specifically to either men or women.

But the fact that *their* could be both singular and plural bothered grammarian John Kirby, who declared in 1746 that the male gender was more universal than the female gender. Kirby made up a new rule saying that male terms should always be understood to include the female. (In other words, when you want to talk about someone in a mixed-gender group, *he* and *his* are the words you need.)

Enter Parliament, the chief law-making body of the mighty British Empire. In 1850, Parliament passed a law stating that masculine terms were always to be read as including females. Parliament actually enacted an official grammar rule! (If they had time for grammar, I wonder what they were neglecting.) Now if I could just get the misuse of *whom* declared a felony. . . .

So *it's* nice to know that grammar has *its* own rules. By the way, one of those rules is that *no possessive pronoun ever has an apostrophe.* Ever. Never. Never ever. Remember: If *it* owns something, dump the apostrophe. Here are some additional examples:

WRONG: *Its* a rainy day, and Lochness's dog is getting tired of plopping *it's* paws into puddles.

WHY IT IS WRONG: The first *its* should be *It's* because *it is* a rainy day. The second *its* shouldn't have an apostrophe because no possessive pronoun ever has an apostrophe.

RIGHT: *It's* a rainy day, and Lochness's dog is getting tired of plopping *its* paws into puddles.

ALSO RIGHT: *It's* a rainy day, and Lochness's dog is getting tired of plopping *his* paws into puddles.

WHY THE "ALSO RIGHT" SENTENCE IS ALSO RIGHT: *It* and *its* may refer to animals, but many people prefer to use *he, she, his,* and *her* for pets. Of course, Lochness's pet scares just about everyone, and because of all the animal hair, no one knows whether *it* is a *he* or a *she.* Personally, I'm going with *it* and *its.*

WRONG: *Its* paws wrapped in towels, Lochness's dog seems to be thinking that *its* time for a new bone.

WHY IT IS WRONG: The first *its* is okay because the paws belong to the dog. The second *its* needs an apostrophe because *it is* time.

RIGHT: *Its* paws wrapped in towels, Lochness's dog seems to be thinking that *it's* time for a new bone.

Positioning Pronoun–Antecedent Pairs

Keep the pronoun and its antecedent near each other. Often, but not always, they appear in the same sentence. Sometimes they're in different sentences. Either way, the idea is the same: If the antecedent of the pronoun is too far away, the reader or listener may become confused. Check out this example:

> Bogsroyal picked up the discarded *paper.* Enemy ships were all around, and the periscope's lenses were blurry. The sonar pings sounded like a Mozart sonata, and the captain's hangnails were acting up again. Yet even in the midst of such troubles, Bogsroyal was neat. *It* made the deck look messy.

It? What's the meaning of *it?* You almost have to be an FBI decoder to find the partner of *it (paper).* Try the paragraph again.

> Enemy ships were all around, and the periscope's lenses were blurry. The sonar pings sounded like a Mozart sonata, and the captain's hangnails were acting up again. Yet even in the midst of such troubles, Bogsroyal was neat. He picked up the discarded *paper. It* made the deck look messy.

Now the antecedent and pronoun are next to each other. Much better!

Rewrite these sentences, moving the pronoun and antecedent closer together.

> Bogsroyal pulled out his handkerchief, given to him by Loella, the love of his life. He sniffed. His sinuses were acting up again. The air in the submarine was stale. He blew his nose. She was a treasure.

Answer: Several possibilities exist. The most important correction involves *Loella* and *she,* now too far apart. Here is one answer:

> Bogsroyal pulled out his handkerchief, given to him by Loella, the love of his life. She was a treasure. He sniffed. His sinuses were acting up again. The air in the submarine was stale. He blew his nose.

Some believe that position alone is enough to explain a pronoun–antecedent pairing. It's true that a pronoun is more likely to be understood if it's placed near the word it represents. In fact, you should form your sentences so that the pairs are neighbors. However, position isn't always enough to clarify the meaning of a pronoun. The best way to clarify the meaning of a pronoun is to make sure that only one easily identifiable antecedent may be represented by each pronoun. If your sentence is about two females, don't use *she.* Provide an extra noun to clarify your meaning.

Look at this sentence:

Hortensia told her mother that she was out of cash.

Who is out of cash? The sentence has one pronoun — *she* — and two females (*Hortensia*, Hortensia's *mother*). *She* could refer to either of the two nouns.

The rule here is simple: Be sure that your sentence has a clear, understandable pronoun–antecedent pair. If you can interpret the sentence in more than one way, rewrite it, using one or more sentences until your meaning is clear:

Hortensia said, "*Mom*, can I have your ATM card? I looked in the cookie jar and *you're* out of cash."

or

Hortensia saw that her mother was out of cash and told her so.

What does this sentence mean?

Alexander and his brother went to Arthur's birthday party, but he didn't have a good time.

A. Alexander didn't have a good time.

B. Alexander's brother didn't have a good time.

C. Arthur didn't have a good time.

Answer: Who knows? Rewrite the sentence, unless you're talking to someone who was actually at the party and knows that Arthur got dumped by his girlfriend just before his chickenpox rash erupted and the cops arrived. If your listener knows all that, the sentence is fine. If not, here are a few possible rewrites:

Alexander and his brother went to Arthur's party. Arthur didn't have a good time.

or

Arthur didn't have a good time at his own birthday party, even though Alexander and his brother attended.

or

Alexander and his brother went to Arthur's party, but Arthur didn't have a good time.

Avoiding Common Pronoun Errors

Most of the time, determining whether a pronoun should be singular or plural is easy. Just check the noun that acts as the antecedent, and bingo, you're done. But sometimes a pronoun takes the place of another pronoun. The pronouns being replaced are particularly confusing because they're singular, even though they look plural. In this section I tackle the hard cases, showing you how to handle these tricky pronouns. I also show you how to avoid sexist pronoun usage.

Using troublesome singular pronouns properly

Everybody, somebody, and *no one* (not to mention *nothing* and *everyone*): These words should be barred from the English language. Why? Because matching these pronouns to other pronouns is a problem. If you match correctly, your choices sound wrong. But if you match incorrectly, you sound right. Sigh. Here's the deal. All of these pronouns are singular:

- The "ones": one, everyone, someone, anyone, no one.
- The "things": everything, something, anything, nothing.
- The "bodies": everybody, somebody, anybody, nobody.
- And a few more: each, either, neither.

These pronouns don't sound singular. *Everybody* and *everyone* sound like a crowd. If you didn't leave anyone out, if you included *everyone* or *everybody,* how can you be talking about a singular word? Well, you are. The logic (yes, logic applies, even though English grammar rules don't always bother with logic) is that *everyone* talks about the members of a group one by one. You follow this logic, probably unconsciously, when you choose a verb. You don't say

> Everyone are here. Let the party begin!

You do say

> Everyone is here. Let the party begin!

Picking the correct verb comes naturally, but picking the correct pronoun doesn't. Check out this pair:

> Everyone was asked to bring their bubble gum to the bubble-popping contest.

Everyone was asked to bring his or her bubble gum to the bubble-popping contest.

Which one sounds right? The first one, I bet. Unfortunately, the second one is correct, formal English.

The bottom line: When you need to refer to "ones," "things," "bodies," and so on in formal English, choose singular pronouns to match (*he/she, his/her*) and avoid using "*their.*"

Which sentence is correct?

A. Matilda the lifeguard says that nobody should wear their earplugs in the pool in case shark warnings are broadcast.

B. Matilda the lifeguard says that nobody should wear his or her earplugs in the pool in case shark warnings are broadcast.

Answer: Sentence B is correct. *Nobody* is singular. *His or her* is singular. *Their* is plural. I know, I know, the sentence sounds horrible.

Once upon a time, sentence A would've been accepted, even by authors that English teachers love, such as Shakespeare and Jane Austen. A little more than 100 years ago, however, sentence A was arrested by the grammar police. Now B is correct and A is not. (In conversational English, sentence A abounds. Actually, it abounds in formal English also; it's wrong in both.)

Try another. Which sentence is correct?

A. Each of the computers popped its disk drive when the doughnut cream dripped in.

B. Each of the computers popped their disk drives when the doughnut cream dripped in.

Answer: Sentence A is correct. The pronoun *its* refers to *each of the computers. Each* is singular, all the time. Think of *each* as converting a group of computers into *one computer,* followed by another, then another, and so on. *Each* makes you consider the computers one by one. Thus *its* — the singular pronoun — is correct.

Try one more. Which sentence is correct?

A. I'm sorry that somebody lost their bookbag, but I've lost my mind!

B. I'm sorry that somebody lost his or her bookbag, but I've lost my mind!

Answer: Sentence B is correct in formal English because *somebody* is singular and should be matched with a singular pronoun *(his or her),* not with a plural pronoun *(their).*

Sex or gender?

The word *gender* used to refer only to words. For example, the gender of *his* is male, and the gender of *her* is female. The word that describes male or female identity — the *It's a boy! It's a girl!* birth announcements sort of identity — is *sex*. But as everyone over the age of two minutes knows (okay, maybe not two minutes, but at a very young age) *sex* may also refer to an activity that greatly interests the human race.

In the late twentieth century, feminists and others began to analyze the way men and women were treated by society, the way men and women related to each other, and many similar topics. To speak of *sex* in reference to these topics was correct according to the dictionary definition of *sex*. Naturally, the word *sex* sometimes caused participants in those very serious discussions to stop thinking about societal roles and start thinking about, well, sex.

A new word was clearly needed — one that distinguished between boy/girl identity and what they start thinking about when they reach puberty. Enter *gender*. The word already signified the difference between *his* and *hers,* but it had the advantage of being separate from physical pleasure.

At least once a month for a few years, every article on feminism in my local newspaper *(The New York Times)* was followed by a letter from an outraged grammarian. The letters would say something like "You advocate *gender equality* but the word *gender* is an attribute of a word, not of a paycheck. You should advocate *sexual equality.*" After a few more tsk-tsks, the writer would cite the dictionary and sign off.

Despite all of those outraged grammarians (or perhaps because of them), the word *gender* left the dictionary and settled comfortably into its new meaning. *Gender* is now accepted as a grammar term, designating male and female. *Gender* is also accepted when it sorts people, societal roles, and anything else into male and female categories.

Steering clear of sexist pronouns

In preparing to write this section, I typed "pronoun + gender" into a Web search engine and then clicked "search." I wanted a tidbit or two from the Internet about the use of non-sexist language. I got more than a tidbit. In fact, I got over 700,000 hits. I can't believe that so many people are talking about pronouns! Actually, *talking* is not quite the appropriate word. *Arguing, warring, facing off, cursing,* and a few other less polite terms come to mind. Here's the problem. For many years, the official rule was that masculine terms (those that refer to men) could refer to men only or could be *universal,* referring to both men and women. This rule is referred to as the *masculine universal.* Here's an example. In an all-female gym class the teacher would say:

Everyone must bring *her* gym shorts tomorrow.

and in an all-male gym class, the teacher would say,

Everyone must bring *his* gym shorts tomorrow.

Employing the masculine universal, in a mixed male and female gym class, the teacher would say,

> Everyone must bring *his* gym shorts tomorrow.

Judging by the Internet, the battles over this pronoun issue aren't likely to be over in the near future. My advice? I think you should say *he or she* and *his or her* when grammar requires such terms. The masculine universal excludes females and may offend your audience.

However, you may say,

> Everyone must bring *his or her* gym shorts.

or

> Everyone must bring *his* gym shorts.

or

> All the students must bring *their* gym shorts.

or

> Bring *your* gym shorts, *you* little creeps!

All of these example sentences are grammatically correct.

Chapter 11

Just Nod Your Head: About Agreement

*H*ollywood filmmakers and about a million songwriters have tried to convince the public that opposites attract. Grammarians have clearly not gotten that message! Instead of opposites, the English language prefers matching pairs. Matching, in grammar terminology, is called *agreement*. In this chapter, I explain agreement in *number* — the singular or plural quality of a word. Here's the rule: You must match singular elements with other singular elements, and you must pair plurals with other plurals. In this chapter, I show you how to make subjects and verbs agree. I tackle this issue in a couple of tenses and in questions, and then I show you some special cases — treacherous nouns and pronouns that are often mismatched.

Writing Singular and Plural Verbs

If you're a native speaker of English, you correctly match singular and plural subjects and verbs most of the time. Your ear for proper language effortlessly creates these subject–verb pairs. Helping you along with this task is the fact that in most tenses, you use exactly the same form for both singular and plural verbs. In this section I show you the forms that don't change and the ones that do.

The unchangeables

When you're writing or speaking regular verbs in simple past, simple future, past perfect, and future perfect tense, this topic is almost a free pass. (Some of the progressive forms change; see the next section for more detail.) The non-progressive forms of these verbs don't change. Here are some samples, all with the regular verb *to snore,* of tenses that use the same form for both singular and plural subjects.

> Ludwig *snored* constantly, but his cousins *snored* only on national holidays. (The simple past tense verb *snored* matches both the singular subject *Ludwig* and the plural subject *cousins.*)

> Ludmilla *will snore* if she eats cheese before bedtime, but her bridesmaids *will snore* only after a meal containing sardines. (The simple future tense verb *will snore* matches both the singular subject *Ludmilla* and the plural subject *bridesmaids.*)

> Cedric *had snored* long before his tonsils were removed by that saber-toothed tiger. The tigers *had snored* nightly before they met Cedric. (The past perfect verb *had snored* matches both the singular subject *Cedric* and the plural subject *tigers.*)

> By the time this chapter is over, Lola *will have snored* for at least an hour, and her friends *will have snored* for an even longer period. (The future perfect verb *will have snored* matches both the singular subject *Lola* and the plural subject *friends.*)

For more information on verb tenses, see Chapter 3.

The changeables

Have you just resolved to speak only in those unchanging tenses? Sorry! You won't be able to keep to that resolution. The other tenses are crucial to your communication skills. But take heart. You need to know only a few principles to identify singular and plural verbs.

Simple present tenses

In simple present tense, nearly all the regular verb forms are the same for both singular and plural. If the subject of the sentence is *I, we,* or *you,* don't worry. They all use the same verb, and number isn't an issue. (*I snore, we snore, you snore.*)

In choosing simple present tense verbs, you do have to be careful when the subject is a singular noun (*Lola, tribe, motorcycle, loyalty,* and so on) or a plural noun (*planes, trains, automobiles,* and so on). You also have to be on your toes when the subject is a pronoun that replaces a singular noun (*he, she, it, another, someone,* and so on). Finally, you have to take care when the subject is a pronoun that replaces a plural noun (*they, both, several,* and so on). To boil all this down to a simpler rule: Be careful when your sentence is talking *about* someone or something. You don't need to worry about subject–verb agreement in sentences in which the subject is *I, you,* or *we.*

For sentences that talk about someone or something, here's how to tell the difference between the singular and plural forms of a regular verb: The singular verb ends in *s* and the plural form doesn't. Here are some examples of simple present tense regular verbs:

Singular	*Plural*
the tiger *bites*	the tigers *bite*
Lulu *rides*	they *ride*
she *screams*	the boys *scream*
Lochness *burps*	both *burp*

When in Rome and Greece: Classical plurals

Granted, the Coliseum is a magnificent sight, and the Greek myths are pretty cool. But those languages! Thanks to the ancient Romans and Greeks, a number of English words form their plurals in a strange way. Here are some singular/plural pairs:

✔ **Alumnus/alumni:** The singular, *alumnus,* is a masculine term. The plural may refer to groups of males, or, if you accept the masculine term as universal, *alumni* may refer to both males and females. (See Chapter 10.)

✔ **Alumna/alumnae:** The singular, *alumna,* is a feminine term. The plural refers to groups of females, though some speakers protest the masculine universal by using *alumnae* for both males and females.

✔ **Analysis/analyses:** *Analysis* is the singular, meaning "a course of psychological therapy" or, more generally, "a serious investigation or examination." The plural changes the *i* to *e*.

✔ **Parenthesis/parentheses:** (This sentence is in *parenthesis,* but I try not to write with too many *parentheses* because readers find more than three *parentheses* confusing.)

✔ **Datum/data:** Technically, *data* is the plural of *datum* and takes a plural verb *(the data are clear).* However, more and more people are matching *data* with a singular verb *(the data is clear).* To be correct and to impress all your grammarian friends, match *data* with a plural verb.

✔ **Phenomenon/phenomena:** The singular term is *phenomenon,* a noun meaning "a marvel, a special occurrence or event." The plural term is *phenomena,* correct but so obscure nowadays that my computer thesaurus keeps trying to change it to *phenomenon.*

You guys understand, don't you?

You may have noticed that the word *you* is both singular and plural. I can say,

> You are crazy.

to Eggworthy when he is dancing around wearing only blue dye. I can also say,

> You are crazy.

to all those people who think Martians constructed the pyramids. In either case, I use the plural form of the verb *(are)*. The fact that *you* is both singular and plural may be responsible for the popularity of such terms as *you all, y'all,* *youse* (very big in New York City), *you guys* (ditto), *and you people*. These terms are colorful but not correct in formal English. Use *you* for both singular and plural subjects, and if you care enough, make the meaning clear with context clues:

> Today you must all wear clothes to the Introduction to Nudism class because the heat is broken.

> "I must have you and only you!" cried Ludwig to his soon-to-be sixth wife.

Progressive tenses

Progressive tenses — those that contain an *-ing* verb form — may also cause singular/plural problems. These tenses rely on the verb *to be*, a grammatical weirdo that changes drastically depending on its subject. Just be sure to match the subject to the correct form of the verb *to be*. (See Chapter 3 for all the forms of *to be*.) Check out these examples of progressive verbs:

- **Singular present progressive:** I *am biting*, you *are biting*, Agwamp *is biting*, no one *is biting*

- **Plural present progressive:** We *are biting*, you *are biting*, the tigers *are biting*, they *are biting*.

- **Singular past progressive:** I *was biting*, you *were biting*, Agwamp *was biting*, no one *was biting*.

- **Plural past progressive:** We *were biting*, you *were biting*, the tigers *were biting*, both *were biting*.

In case you're wondering about the future progressive, I'll mention the good news: This one never changes! Singular and plural forms are the same (I *will be biting*, we *will be biting*, and so on). No problems here.

Present perfect and future perfect tenses

The present perfect and future perfect tenses (both progressive and non-progressive) contain forms of the verb *to have*. Use *have* when the subject is *I*, *you*, or a plural noun or pronoun. Use *has* when you're talking about a singular noun or pronoun that may replace the singular noun. Some examples:

✔ **Singular present perfect:** I *have bitten,* I *have been biting,* you *have bitten,* you *have been biting,* Agwamp *has bitten,* Lola *has been biting,* she *has bitten,* everyone *has been biting.*

✔ **Plural present perfect:** We *have bitten,* we *have been biting,* you *have bitten,* you *have been biting,* the tigers *have bitten,* the tigers *have been biting,* several *have bitten,* they *have been biting.*

Easier Than Marriage Counseling: Making Subjects and Verbs Agree

Once you're able to tell a singular from a plural verb (see previous section), you can concentrate on matchmaking. Remember that you must always pair singular subjects with singular verbs, and plural subjects with plural verbs. No mixing allowed.

Notice how in these sample sentences, singular subjects are matched with singular verbs, and plural subjects are matched with plural verbs:

The ugly lawn gnome loves the lovely plastic elf. (*gnome* = singular subject, *loves* = singular verb)

The lovely plastic elf is pining after the ugly lawn gnome. (*elf* = singular subject, *is pining* = singular verb)

The weeds are a problem to this unhappy couple. (*weeds* = plural subject, *are* = plural verb)

The hedge clippers are their only hope! (*clippers* = plural subject, *are* = plural verb)

We plan to start clipping on St. Valentine's Day. (*we* = plural subject, *plan* = plural verb)

How did I know that the subject–verb pairs were either singular or plural? I determined the number of subjects performing the action and then matched the verbs.

Here are some steps to take in order to make sure that your subjects and verbs agree:

1. Pop the question to find the verb. (See Chapter 2.)

2. Pop the question to find the subject. (See Chapter 4.)

3. Determine whether the subject is singular or plural.

4. Match the appropriate verb: singular verb to singular subject, plural verb to plural subject.

Time isn't money, but in grammar, they're both singular

Time and money are the same, at least in grammar. In grammar, you count them as one single quantity, not as separate units. Thus,

> Fifty minutes *is* not enough for a television news show about Lochness.

> A hundred dollars *was* a powerful temptation to Analivia, and she decided to allow the giant computer company to use her latest equation.

One exception to the rule occurs when you talk about money as a physical thing — pieces of paper or metal. For example,

> Fifty dollars *are* taped to the wall behind Lochness's cash register because he thinks that such a display is "classy."

> One hundred francs *were* dropped, one by one and with great ceremony, into the child's piggybank.

Choosing Verbs for Two Subjects

Sentences with two subjects joined by *and* take a plural verb, even if each of the two subjects is singular. (Think of math: one + one = two. One subject + one subject = plural subject.)

Here are some sample sentences with subjects joined by the word *and:*

> The lawnmower and the hedge clipper are their salvation. (*lawnmower + clipper* = plural subject, *are* = plural verb)

> The ugly lawn gnome and the lovely plastic elf belong together. (*gnome + elf* = plural subject, *belong* = plural verb)

> Romance and lawn care do not mix well. (*romance + lawn care* = plural subject, *do mix* = plural verb)

Subjects joined by *or*, like subjects joined by *either/or*, may take either a singular or a plural verb. See Chapter 21.

Which sentence is correct?

A. Lubdub and his co-conspirator plan to steal the lawn ornament.

B. Lubdub and his co-conspirator plans to steal the lawn ornament.

Answer: Sentence A is correct. The subject is *Lubdub and his co-conspirator*, a plural subject. The plural verb *plan* is needed.

Try one more. Which sentence is correct?

A. Lubdub and his co-conspirator have had no mercy for the gnome.

B. Lubdub and his co-conspirator has had no mercy for the gnome.

Answer: Sentence A is correct. The subject is still plural *(Lubdub and his co-conspirator)* so it needs a plural verb. The verb in sentence A is *have had,* which is also plural. In sentence B the verb *(has had)* is singular.

The Question of Questions

Just to make subject–verb agreement even more complicated, English grammar shuffles a sentence around to form questions and often throws in a helping verb or two. (See Chapter 2 for more information on helping verbs.) Adding insult to injury, questions are formed differently in different tenses. In this section, I show you how to form singular and plural questions in each tense.

Present tense questions

Check out the italicized subjects and verbs in these questions:

Do the *holes* from Lulu's pierced eyebrows *fill* with water when it rains? (*holes* = plural subject, *do fill* = plural verb)

Does the *ring* in Lulu's navel *rust* when she showers? (*ring* = singular subject, *does rust* = singular verb)

Do Ludwig and *Ludmilla need* a good divorce lawyer? (*Ludwig + Ludmilla* = plural subject, *do need* = plural verb)

Does Eggworthy like artichoke omelets? (*Eggworthy* = singular subject, *does like* = singular verb)

You've probably figured out that the verbs are formed by adding *do* or *does* to the main verb. *Do* matches all plurals as well as the singular subjects *I* and *you. Does* is for all other singular subjects. That's the system for most present tense questions. (Questions formed with the verb *to be* don't need *do* or *does.*) When *do* or *does* is used to form a question, the main verb doesn't change. So when checking subject–verb agreement in present-tense questions, be sure to note the helping verb — *do* or *does.*

Just for comparison, here are a couple of questions with the verb *to be:*

Is Lola in style right now? (*Lola* = singular subject, *is* = singular verb)

Am I a good grammarian? (*I* = singular subject, *am* = singular verb)

Are the *grammarians analyzing* that sentence? (*grammarians* = plural subject, *are analyzing* = plural verb)

Is Lochness spying again? (*Lochness* = singular subject, *is spying* = singular verb)

Change this statement into a question:

Ludmilla meets Ludwig's parents today.

Answer: *Does* Ludmilla *meet* Ludwig's parents today? To form the question, add the helping verb *does*.

Past tense questions

Past tense questions make use of the helping verb *did*. I imagine you'll cheer when you hear that *did* forms both singular and plural questions. Questions with the verb *to be* (always a maverick) don't need helping verbs, but the order changes. Here are some examples of past tense questions:

Did Felonia play the same song for eight hours? (*Felonia* = singular subject, *did play* = singular past tense verb)

Did the *grammarians complain* about that question? (*grammarians* = plural subject, *did complain* = plural past tense verb)

Was Lola on the Committee to Combat Body Piercing? (*Lola* = singular subject, *was* = singular past tense verb)

Were the villagers angry about the new tax? (*villagers* = plural subject, *were* = plural verb)

Was I talking too fast? (*I* = singular subject, *was talking* = singular verb)

Were the lions roaring? (*lions* = plural subject, *were roaring* = plural verb)

Change this statement into a question.

Ludmilla and Ludwig *had* the invitations.

Answer: *Did* Ludmilla and Ludwig *have* the invitations? To form the past tense question, add the helping verb *did*.

Future tense questions

Once again, this topic is a free pass when it comes to singular and plural questions. The future tenses already have helping verbs, so no additions are necessary. Here's the best part: The helping verbs are the same for both singular and plural subjects. Read these sample future tense questions:

Will Cedric and *Blathersby see* that movie about the exploding doughnut? (*Cedric* + *Blathersby* = plural subject, *will see* = plural future tense verb)

Will Lola ever *see* the error of her ways? (*Lola* = singular subject, *will see* = plural future tense verb)

Will Legghorn be screening his new movie tonight? (*Legghorn* = singular subject, *will be screening* = plural future tense verb)

Will both of you *be ordering* another dessert? (*both* = plural subject, *will be ordering* = plural future tense verb)

Negative Statements and Subject–Verb Agreement

Some present-tense negative statements are also formed by adding *do* or *does,* along with the word *not,* to a main verb. Remember that *does* is always singular. The helping verb *do* may be paired with the singular subjects *I* and *you. Do* is also used with all plural subjects. Here are some examples:

Ludwig does not *drive* a sports car because he wants to project a whole-some image. (*Ludwig* = singular subject, *does drive* = singular present tense verb)

The killer *bees do* not *chase* Lochness, because they are afraid of him. (*bees* = plural subject, *do chase* = plural present tense verb)

I do not *want* to learn anything else about verbs ever again. (*I* = singular subject, *do want* = singular present tense verb)

You do not *dance* on your elbows in this club! (*You* = singular or plural subject, *do dance* = singular or plural present tense verb.)

One more joyous thought: To form past and future tense questions, you don't need additional helping verbs, and the helping verbs are the same for both singular and plural. Don't worry about these tenses!

Change this statement into a negative (opposite).

Legghorn gave me help for the grammar test.

Answer: Legghorn *did* not *give* me help for the grammar test. You form the negative with the helping verb *did.*

Questions and negative statements in many foreign languages are formed in a different way. In Spanish, for example, all you have to do is raise the tone of your voice or add question marks to statements to indicate that you're asking a question. A Spanish-speaking questioner need only say the equivalent of "He sings?" or "He not sings." In English, however, the helping verb is necessary for those statements.

The Distractions: Prepositional Phrases and Other Irrelevant Words

Subjects and their verbs are like nannies and babies on a stroll through the park; they always travel together. From time to time, a passerby leans into the carriage and makes funny faces or plays peek-a-boo. The passerby is a distraction, irrelevant to the nanny and, after a few moments of wriggling and cooing, to the baby as well.

The sentence world has lots of distracting peek-a-boo players. These players show up, slip between a subject and its verb, and distract you from the important stuff. The best strategy is to ignore these distractions. Identify them and then cross them out (at least mentally) to get to the bare bones of the sentence — the subject–verb pair.

The most common interrupters, but not the only ones, are prepositional phrases. A *prepositional phrase* contains a preposition (*on, to, for, by,* and so on) and an object of the preposition (a noun or pronoun). These phrases may contain some descriptive words as well. (For a full discussion of prepositional phrases, see Chapter 9.)

In addition to prepositional phrases, the "distractions" may be clauses or participles. For more information on clauses and participles, see Chapter 24.

In the following sentences, I added some camouflage. The interrupters (not all prepositional phrases) are italicized.

> The ugly lawn gnome *with 10,000 eyes and only five toes* loves the lovely plastic elf. (*gnome* = subject, *loves* = verb)

In this sentence, *gnome* is the subject. *Gnome* is singular. If you pay attention to the prepositional phrase, you may incorrectly focus on *eyes* and *toes* as the subject — both plural words.

> The lovely plastic elf, *fascinated with folktales,* is pining after the ugly lawn gnome. (*elf* = subject, *is pining* = verb)

By ignoring the distracting interrupter phrase in this sentence, you can easily pick out the subject–verb pair.

> The weeds, *not the edge of the lawn,* are a problem to this unhappy couple. (*weeds* = subject, *are* = verb)

In this sentence, *weeds* is the subject. If you go for the interrupter, you may incorrectly match your verb to *edge* or *lawn,* both of which are singular.

Final answer: Ignore all distracting phrases and find the true subject–verb pair.

Which sentence is correct?

A. The boy in the first row, along with all the hedgehogs under his desk, is ignoring the teacher.

B. The boy in the first row, along with all the hedgehogs under his desk, are ignoring the teacher.

Answer: Sentence A is correct. The subject is *boy.* The boy *is ignoring. Along with all the hedgehogs under his desk* is an interrupter (in this case, a prepositional phrase).

Another: Which sentence is correct?

A. The girl in the last row, but not the trolls standing on the coat rack, are firing spitballs at the teacher.

B. The girl in the last row, but not the trolls standing on the coat rack, is firing spitballs at the teacher.

Answer: Sentence B is correct. The subject is *girl.* The verb must therefore be singular *(is firing).* The interrupters (both prepositional phrases) are *in the last* row and *but not the trolls standing on the coat rack.*

Sentences with unusual word order or with the words *here* and *there* often cause confusion. See Chapter 4 for tips on matching subjects and verbs in these situations.

Can't We All Just Get Along? Agreement with Difficult Subjects

Every family has a problem child, or at least a problem cousin. Every topic in English grammar has at least one problem child, including the topic of subject–verb agreement. In this section, I take you through several scenarios, each featuring a difficult subject.

Five puzzling pronouns as subjects

Earlier in this chapter I told you to ignore prepositional phrases. Now I must confess that this rule has one small exception — well, five small exceptions.

Five pronouns — five little words that just have to stir up trouble — change from singular to plural because of the prepositional phrases that follow them. The five troublemaking pronouns are as follows:

- ✔ any
- ✔ all
- ✔ most
- ✔ none
- ✔ some

A good way to remember these five important words is with this nonsense sentence. (What? You say all the sentences in *English Grammar For Dummies* are nonsense sentences? Thanks for the compliment.) Anyway, remember these pronouns, if you like, with this sentence:

Amy Aardvark makes nice salads. (*Amy* = any, *Aardvark* = all, *makes* = most, *nice* = none, *salads* = some)

Here they are with some prepositional phrases and verbs. Notice how the prepositional phrase affects the verb number.

Singular	*Plural*
any of the book is	*any* of the magazines are
all of the pie is	*all* of the shoes are
most of the city is	*most* of the pencils are
none of the pollution is	*none* of the toenails are
some of the speech is	*some* of the politicians are

See the pattern? For these five words, the prepositional phrase is the determining factor. If the phrase refers to a plural idea, the verb is plural. If the phrase refers to a singular idea, the verb is singular.

So remember *Amy Aardvark makes nice salads,* check the prepositional phrase, and determine whether the verb should be singular or plural. Easy, right? You got it!

Here and there you find problems

A variation on unusual word order is a sentence beginning with *here* or *there.* In the examples below, the subject–verb pairs are italicized:

Here *is* the ugly lawn *gnome* with his new love, a ceramic deer.

There *are* many *problems* in every lawn-ornament relationship.

Here, for example, *are* a *frog* and a *birdbath*.

There *is* no *privacy* in lawn-ornament romances.

As you see, the words *here* and *there* aren't italicized. These words are never subjects! The true subject in this type of sentence comes after the verb, not before. For more examples of *here* and *there* sentences, see Chapter 4.

The Ones, the Things, and the Bodies

The *Ones,* the *Things,* and the *Bodies* are not the names of families on your block; you won't find the *Ones,* the *Things,* and the *Bodies* in the phone book (unless some folks in your town have really weird names). The *Ones,* the *Things,* and the *Bodies* are families of pronouns that delight in mischief-making. Here's the family tree:

The Ones: *one, everyone, someone, anyone, no one*

The Things: *everything, something, anything, nothing*

The Bodies: *everybody, somebody, anybody, nobody*

These pronouns are always singular, even if they're surrounded by prepositional phrases that express plurals. These pronouns must be matched with singular verbs. Take a look at these examples:

So everybody *is* happy because *no one has caused* any trouble, and *anything goes.*

Anyone in the pool of candidates for dogcatcher *speaks* better than Lulu.

One of the million reasons why I hate you *is* your tendency to use bad grammar.

Not *one* out of a million spies *creates* as much distraction as Lochness.

You must also match the *Ones,* the *Things,* and the *Bodies* with singular pronouns. (See Chapter 10 for more information on pronoun agreement.) For now, just remember that the *Ones,* the *Things,* and the *Bodies* are singular all the time.

Each and every mistake is painful

Each and *every* are very powerful words; they're strong enough to change whatever follows them in the sentence — no matter what — into a singular idea. Sneak a peek at these examples:

Each shoe and sock *is* in need of mending, but Ludwig refuses to pick up a needle and thread.

Every dress and skirt in that store *is* on sale, and Lulu's in a spending mood.

Each of those Halloween pumpkins *was* fairly rotten by December, although Lola made pies out of them anyway.

Every one of the atomic secrets *has been eaten* by Lochness in an attempt to avoid capture.

Do these sentences look wrong to you? Each has some expression of a plural in it: two things *(shoe and sock)* in sentence one, another two things *(dress and skirt)* in sentence two, *pumpkins* in sentence three, and *secrets* in sentence four. Because the sentences are about groups, they call for plural verbs. Right?

Wrong. The logic is that when *each* or *every* is placed in front of a group, you take the items in the group one by one — one at a time. In the first sample sentence, the subject consists of one *shoe,* one *sock,* another *shoe,* another *sock,* and so on. Therefore, the sentence needs a singular verb to match the singular subject. So in the sample sentences, singular verbs match with the subjects that are made singular by the magic words, *each* and *every:*

Each shoe and sock is

Every dress and skirt is

Each of those Halloween pumpkins was

Every one of the atomic secrets has been eaten

Remember: *Each* mistaken subject and verb *is* a problem, and *every* grammar rule and example *is* important.

I want to be alone: Either and neither without their partners

Either often hangs out with its partner *or,* just as *neither* spends a lot of time with *nor.* (For information on matching verbs to subjects in sentences with *either/or* and *neither/nor* pairs, see Chapter 21.) But each of these words does a Garbo from time to time, saying, "I want to be alone." When they're alone, *either* and *neither* are always singular, even if you insert a huge group (or just a group of two) between them and their verbs. Hence

Either of the two armies *is* strong enough to take over the entire planet.

Neither of the football teams *has shown* any willingness to accept Lola as quarterback.

Either of the dinosaur herds *was* capable of trampling a huge forest of ferns.

Neither of the lawyers *does* anything without billing me.

Because the sample sentences are about armies, teams, herds, and lawyers, you may be tempted to choose plural verbs. Resist the temptation! No matter what the sentence says, if the subject is *either* or *neither,* singular is the correct way to go. Also, any pronouns that refer to *either* or *neither* must also be singular. (See Chapter 10 for more information on pronoun usage.) Take a look at these examples:

WRONG: *Either* of the television stars *are going* to be fired because of *their* connection with Blathersby.

WHY IT IS WRONG: *Either* is singular, so it's mismatched with the plurals *are going* (verb) and *their* (pronoun).

RIGHT: Either of the television stars *is going* to be fired because of *his* connection with Blathersby.

WHY IT IS RIGHT: Now everything is singular: *either, is going, his.*

Here are a few more examples:

WRONG: *Neither* of the candidates *are going* to agree to the peace terms.

WHY IT IS WRONG: *Neither* is singular and may not be matched with a plural verb *(are going).*

RIGHT: *Neither* of the candidates *is going* to agree to the peace terms.

WHY IT IS RIGHT: Both are now singular: *neither* and *is going* match.

Final answer: *either* and *neither,* without their partners *or* and *nor,* always indicate singular subjects and always take singular verbs.

Politics, statistics, and other irregular subjects

Besides dirty tricks and spin masters, the problem with politics is number. Specifically, is the word *politics* singular or plural? Surprise! *Politics* is singular and you must match it with a singular verb. Here's an example:

Politics is a dirty sport, very much suited to Ludwig's view of the world.

Politics (singular) is paired with *is* (singular).

And while I'm at it, what about *mathematics, news, economics, measles, mumps,* and *analysis?*

These nouns are all singular as well, even though they end with the letter *s*. Thus, these nouns are paired with singular verbs:

> Ratrug thinks that *mathematics is* overrated. He'd like to see the subject dropped from the school curriculum.

> The *news* about the doughnut *is* not encouraging.

> "*Economics is* my thing," commented Cedric as he stuffed money into his pockets.

> "Do you think that *measles is* a serious disease?" asked Eggworthy as he bought a case of skin lotion. "No, *mumps is* a lot worse," replied Murgatroyd, who was extracting another ice pack from the freezer.

> "Your troubles are all in your mind," said Lola. "*Analysis is* the answer."

Another word — *statistics* — may be either singular or plural. If you're talking about numbers, you may have two *statistics*. For example: *Statistics show* that grammar knowledge is declining. (You may also have one *statistic* when you're using the word to refer to a number: I don't want to become a highway-fatality *statistic*.) If you're talking about a course or a field of study, *statistics* is always singular, as in my study of *statistics*. In my school, *statistics is* a difficult course.

The English language also has words that are always *plural*. Here are a few of them: *pants, trousers,* and *scissors*. (You can't put on *a pant* or *a trouser,* and you can't cut with *a scissor*.) Other common plural-only words are *credentials, acoustics, earnings, headquarters,* and *ceramics*.

When in doubt, check your dictionary and remember to match singular nouns with singular verbs and plural nouns with plural verbs.

Part III

No Garage, but Plenty of Mechanics

The 5th Wave   By Rich Tennant

"It's from the publisher. It says,'Dear Mr. Shakespeare, Your current play is gooder than your last but still not as best as we think you're capable of.'"

In this part . . .

Passed any construction sites lately? If so, you've probably noticed giant piles of lumber, steel, or bricks — all very useful and very noticeable parts of the new building. Off to the side, you've probably seen some of the little things that also make the building possible — the nails, the nuts, the bolts.

In this part, I explain the nails, nuts, and bolts of writing: apostrophes, quotation marks, and other punctuation, as well as the rules for capitalization. By the time you finish reading this part, you'll understand why those little things — what English teachers call *mechanics* — are an essential part of the package that carries your meaning to the reader.

Chapter 12

Punctuation Law That Should Be Repealed: Apostrophes

• •

• •

*I*t happens every time I take a walk. I'm strolling along, thinking all kinds of perfectly grammatical thoughts, when an awning or a window sign catches my eye.

> Bagel's Sold Here
>
> Smiths Furniture — the Best Deals in Town!

I hear a thud as the apostrophe rule bites the dust yet again. Apostrophes are those little curved marks you see hanging from certain letters — as in the *bagels* sign example. Why do those signs upset me? Because in both signs, the apostrophe (or lack thereof) is a problem. The signs should read:

> Bagels Sold Here
>
> Smith's Furniture — the Best Deals in Town!

Why don't they? I don't know. I do know that even very well educated people throw those little squiggles where they don't belong and leave them out where they're needed. So I'm in favor of a change: a repeal of the apostrophe rule. I think we should wipe it off the books. Pry the apostrophe key off computer keyboards. Erase apostrophe from the collective mind of English teachers. Done, over, finito.

Until that happy day when apostrophes disappear, you'll have to learn the rules. In this chapter, I explain how to use apostrophes to show ownership, how to shorten words with apostrophes, and how to form some plurals.

The Pen of My Aunt or My Aunt's Pen? Using Apostrophes to Show Possession

Most other languages are smarter than English. To show possession in French, for example, you say

> the pen of my aunt
>
> the little letters of the lovers
>
> the fine wines of that corner bar

and so on. You can say the same thing in English too, but English has added another option, the apostrophe. Take a look at these same phrases — with the same meaning — using apostrophes:

> my *aunt's* pen
>
> the *lovers'* little letters
>
> that corner *bar's* fine wines

All of these phrases include nouns that express ownership. I like to think of the apostrophe as a little hand, holding on to an *s* to indicate ownership or possession. In these examples, you notice that the apostrophe is used to show that a singular noun owns something *(aunt's pen; bar's fine wines)*. You also see a phrase where the apostrophe indicates that plural nouns own something *(lovers' little letters)*.

Ownership for singles

No, I'm not talking about the ownership of real estate or the singles who sit in bars asking, "What's your sign?" or "Come here often?" I'm talking about using apostrophes to show ownership with singular nouns. Here's the bottom line: To show possession by one owner, add an apostrophe and the letter *s* to the owner:

> the *dragon's* burnt tooth (the burnt tooth belongs to the dragon)
>
> *Lulu's* pierced tooth (the pierced tooth belongs to Lulu)
>
> *Murgatroyd's* gold-filled tooth (the gold-filled tooth belongs to Murgatroyd)

Another way to think about this rule is to see whether the word *of* expresses what you're trying to say. With the *of* method, you note the sharp tooth *of* the crocodile = the *crocodile's* sharp tooth

the peanut-stained tooth *of* the elephant = the *elephant's* peanut-stained tooth

and so on.

Sometimes, no clear owner seems present in the phrase. Such a situation arises mostly when you're talking about time. If you can insert *of* into the sentence, you may need an apostrophe. To give you an idea of how to run the "of test," here are some phrases that express time:

one week's tooth cleaning = one week *of* tooth cleaning

a year's dental care = one year *of* dental care

Here's the bottom line: When you're talking about time, give your sentence the "of test." If it passes, insert an apostrophe.

Which sentence is correct?

A. Lulu told Lola that Lochness needs a years work on his gum disease.

B. Lulu told Lola that Lochness needs a year's work on his gum disease.

Answer. Sentence B is correct because Lochness needs *a year of work* on his mouth. (Actually, he needs false teeth and maybe a nose job, but the year's gum work is a start.)

Because Bill doesn't own everything: Plural possessives

You'd be finished figuring out apostrophes now if everything belonged to only one owner. Bill Gates is close, but even he hasn't taken over everything yet. You still need to deal with plural owners. The plurals of most English nouns — anything greater than one — already end with the letter *s*. To show ownership, all you do is add an apostrophe after the *s*. Take a look at these examples:

ten *gerbils'* tiny teeth (the tiny teeth belong to ten gerbils)

many *dinosaurs'* petrified teeth (the petrified teeth belong to a herd of dinosaurs)

a thousand sword swallowers' sliced teeth (the sliced teeth belong to a thousand sword swallowers)

The owl rule: Who's, whose

Whose shows ownership. It seldom causes any problems, except when it's confused with another word: *who's*. *Who's* is a contraction that is short for *who is*. In other words

The boy *whose* hat was burning was last seen running down the street screaming, "*Who's* in charge of fire fighting in this town?"

and

Whose box of firecrackers is on the radiator? *Who's* going to tell Eggworthy that his living room looks like the Fourth of July?

Here are more correct examples for your consideration:

* *Whose* review will Legghorn read first?

* *Who's* going to tell Legghorn that his play is awful?

The *of* test works for plurals too. If you can rephrase the expression using the word *of,* you may need an apostrophe. Remember to add the apostrophe after the letter *s*.

three *days'* construction work on Legghorn's false teeth = three days *of* construction work

sixteen *years'* neglect on the part of Lulu's dentist = sixteen years *of* neglect

two *centuries'* pain of rotten teeth = two centuries *of* pain

Which is correct?

A. Dentist Roger has only one goal in life: to clean the Yankee's teeth.

B. Dentist Roger has only one goal in life: to clean the Yankees' teeth.

Answer: Sentence A is correct if you're talking about one player. Sentence B is correct if you're talking about 24 sets of teeth, or all the choppers on the team.

Try another. Which sentence is correct?

A. The Halloween decorations are decaying, especially the pumpkins teeth. Cedric carved all ten jack-o-lanterns, and he can't bear to throw them away.

B. The Halloween decorations are decaying, especially the pumpkins' teeth. Cedric carved all ten jack-o-lanterns, and he can't bear to throw them away.

C. The Halloween decorations are decaying, especially the pumpkin's teeth. Cedric carved all ten jack-o-lanterns, and he can't bear to throw them away.

Answer: Sentence B is correct. The context of the sentence *(all ten jack-o-lanterns)* makes clear the fact that more than one pumpkin is rotting away. In sentence B, *pumpkins'* expresses a plural possessive. In sentence A, *pumpkins* has no apostrophe, though it clearly shows possession. In sentence C, the apostrophe is placed before the *s,* showing a single pumpkin.

Irregular plural possessives

In many of my examples in this chapter, I use the word "teeth." (You probably will hear chomping in your sleep.) Hang on for a few more. First, look at the word *teeth.* It is plural, but *teeth* doesn't end with the letter *s.* In other words, *teeth* is an irregular plural. To show ownership for an irregular plural, add an apostrophe and then the letter *s (teeth's).* Check out these examples:

> *teeth's* cavities (The cavities belong to the teeth.)
>
> *children's* erupting teeth (The erupting teeth belong to the children.)
>
> the three blind *mice's* imaginary teeth (The imaginary teeth belong to the three blind mice.)
>
> the *women's* lipstick-stained teeth (The lipstick-stained teeth belong to the women.)
>
> the *mice's* cheesy teeth (The cheesy teeth belong to the mice.)
>
> *geese's* missing teeth (No teeth belong to the geese, because as of course you know, birds have beaks instead.)

Compound plural possessives

What happens when two single people own something? They go to court and fight it out, that's what happens! But forget lawsuits. I'm talking about grammar. The *grammatical* answer is one or two apostrophes, depending upon the type of ownership. If two people own something together, as a couple, use only one apostrophe.

> George and Martha *Washington's* home (The home belongs to the two of them.)
>
> Hillary and Bill *Clinton's* daughter (Chelsea claims both of them as her parents.)
>
> Ludwig and *Ludmilla's* wedding (The wedding was for both the blushing groom and the frightful bride.)
>
> Lulu and *Lola's* new set of nose rings (The set was too expensive for either one alone, so Lulu and Lola each paid half and agreed to an every-other-week wearing schedule.)
>
> Lochness and the superspy's secret (Lochness told it to the superspy, so now they're sharing the secret, which concerns doughnuts and explosives.)

If two people own things separately, as individuals, use two apostrophes:

George's and *Martha's* teeth (He has his set of teeth — false, by the way — and she has her own set.)

Lulu's and *Legghorn's* new shoes. (She wears size 2, and he wears size 12. Hers are lizard skin with four-inch heels. His are plastic with five-inch heels. They definitely own separate pairs.)

Eggworthy's and *Ratrug's* attitudes towards dieting. (Eggworthy doesn't know and doesn't care to know his cholesterol count. Ratrug carries around a nutrition chart and a scale and weighs every scrap of food he eats.)

Lester's and *Archie's* sleeping habits (You don't want to know. I'll just say that Lester sleeps all night, and Archie sleeps all day.)

Cedric's and *Lola's* fingernails. (He has his; she has her own; both sets are polished and quite long.)

Not every plural noun has an apostrophe

Speaking of plurals: Remember that an apostrophe shows ownership. Don't use an apostrophe when you have a plural that is *not* expressing ownership. Here are some examples:

RIGHT: Bagels stick to your teeth.

WRONG: Bagel's stick to your teeth.

ALSO WRONG: Bagels' stick to your teeth.

Look at another set:

RIGHT: The gnus gnashed their teeth when they heard the news.

WRONG: The gnus' gnashed their teeth when they heard the news.

ALSO WRONG: The gnu's gnashed their teeth when they heard the news.

To sum up the rule on plurals and apostrophes: If the plural noun is not showing ownership, *don't* use an apostrophe. If the plural noun shows ownership, *do* add an apostrophe after the *s* (for regular plurals). For irregular plurals showing ownership, add *'s.*

Possession with Proper Nouns

Companies, stores, and organizations also own things, so these proper nouns — singular or plural — also get apostrophes. Put the apostrophe at the end of the name:

Lord & Taylor's finest shoes

Microsoft's finest operating system

Shearson Lehmann's finest money

McGillicuddy, Pinch, and Cinch's finest lawsuit

Grammar, Inc.'s finest apostrophe rule

Special note: Some stores have apostrophes in their names, even without a sense of possession. For example, *Bloomingdale's* is a department store. In the preceding sentence, *Bloomingdale's* is written with an apostrophe, but there's no noun after the store name. Nevertheless, everyone calls the store *Bloomingdale's,* including the store itself. Such names are probably shortened versions of a longer name (perhaps *Bloomingdale's Department Store*).

Place apostrophes where they're needed in this paragraph.

Ratrug went to Macys Department Store to buy a suit for Lolas party. His shopping list also included a heart for the Valentines Day dinner and a card for his brothers next anniversary. Ratrugs shopping spree was successful, in spite of Lulus and Lolas attempts to puncture his tires.

Answer: Ratrug went to *Macy's* Department Store to buy a suit for *Lola's* party. His shopping list also included a heart for the *Valentine's* Day dinner and a card for his *brother's* next anniversary. *Ratrug's* shopping spree was successful, in spite of *Lulu's* and *Lola's* attempts to puncture his tires. (Note: Lulu and Lola made separate stabs at the tires.)

Ownership with Hyphenated Words

Other special cases of possession involve compound words — son-in-law, mother-of-pearl, and all the other words with *hyphens* (those little horizontal lines). The rule is simple: Put the apostrophe at the end of the word. Never put an apostrophe inside a word. Here are some examples of singular compound nouns:

the *secretary-treasurer's* report on teeth (The report belongs to the secretary-treasurer.)

the *dogcatcher-in-chief's* canine teeth (The canine teeth belong to the dogcatcher-in-chief.)

my *mother-in-law's* elderly teeth (The elderly teeth belong to my mother-in-law. Hi, Mom!)

The same rule applies to plural compound nouns that are hyphenated. Take a look at these examples:

the *doctors-of-philosophy's* study lounge (the study lounge is owned by all the doctors-of philosophy)

my *fathers-in-law's* wedding present (the wedding present was from both fathers-in-law)

Possessive Nouns That End in S

Singular nouns that end in *s* present special problems. Let me explain: My last name is Woods. My name is singular, because I am only one person. When students talk about me, they may say,

Ms. Woods's grammar lessons can't be beat.

or

Ms. Woods' grammar lessons can't be beat.

(Okay, they say a lot of other things too, but this is a positive, family-friendly book. I'll leave the other comments out.)

Both of the sentences about me and my grammar lessons (sounds like an old song: "Me and my grammar lessons / down in the good old school / where we learned apostrophes / so we wouldn't drool") are correct. Why are there two options — *Ms. Woods's* and *Ms. Woods'?* The answer has to do with sound. If you say the first sentence above, by the time you get to the word *grammar* you're hissing and spitting all over your listener. Not a good idea. The second sentence sounds better. So the grammar police have given in on this one. If the name of a singular owner ends in the letter *s*, you may add only an apostrophe, not an apostrophe and another *s*. But if you like hissing and spitting, feel free to add an apostrophe *and* an *s*. Both versions are acceptable. Just don't put an apostrophe in the middle of someone's name.

RIGHT: Ms. Woods's hysterically funny jokes

ALSO RIGHT: Ms. Woods' hysterically funny jokes

WRONG: Ms. Wood's hysterically funny jokes.

Which sentence is correct?

A. The walrus' tusk gleamed because the walrus brushed it for ten minutes after every meal.

B. The walrus's tusk gleamed because the walrus brushed it for ten minutes after every meal.

Answer: Both are correct. Sentence B uses up a little more saliva, but it follows the rule. Sentence A breaks the old rule, but nowadays that rule is broken. (Yes, it was a trick question. You know how teachers are.)

Try another set. Which sentence is correct?

A. My whole family got together for Thanksgiving. The Woods' are a large group.

B. My whole family got together for Thanksgiving. The Woodses are a large group.

Answer: Another trick question. Sentence B is correct because Woodses is a plural, not a possessive. In sentence A, the apostrophe is incorrect because plurals shouldn't have apostrophes unless they express ownership.

Common Apostrophe Errors with Pronouns

English also supplies pronouns — words that take the place of a noun — for ownership. Some possessive pronouns are *my, your, his, her, its, our,* and *their.* No possessive pronoun ever has an apostrophe. A few examples of possessive pronouns in action:

> *your* completely unruly child — not your' completely unruly child (also wrong: that completely unruly child of yours')

> *our* extremely well-behaved youngster — not our' extremely well-behaved youngster (also wrong: the extremely well-behaved youngster of ours')

> *their* tendency to fight — not their' tendency to fight (also wrong: the tendency of theirs' not to fight)

> *his* call to the police — not his' call to the police

> *her* reading of the suspect's rights — not her' reading of the suspect's rights (also wrong: *her's*)

> *its* unreasonable verdict — not its' unreasonable verdict

Which sentence is correct?

A. Ratrug stole Cedric's mouthwash because of their' ancient feud.

B. Ratrug stole Cedric's mouthwash because of their ancient feud.

C. Ratrug stole Cedrics mouthwash because of their ancient feud.

Answer: Sentence B is correct. In sentence A, the apostrophe is needed in *Cedric's* because Cedric owns the mouthwash. However, *their* should not have an apostrophe because no possessive pronoun ever has an apostrophe. In sentence C, *their* is written correctly, but *Cedrics* lacks the apostrophe.

Just one more. Which sentence is correct?

A. Eggworthy claims that a weeks mouthwash is not worth fighting over and has pledged his support to Ratrug.

B. Eggworthy claims that a week's mouthwash is not worth fighting over and has pledged his' support to Ratrug.

C. Eggworthy claims that a week's mouthwash is not worth fighting over and has pledged his support to Ratrug.

Answer: Sentence C is correct. In sentence A, *a weeks* needs an apostrophe because the phrase means *a week of.* In sentence B, *his'* shouldn't have an apostrophe because (say it aloud — bellow it) no possessive pronoun ever has an apostrophe.

For more information on possessive pronouns, see Chapter 10.

Shortened Words for Busy People: Contractions

Are you in a hurry? Probably. So like just about everyone in our society, you probably use contractions when you speak. A *contraction* shortens a word by removing one letter or more and substituting an apostrophe in the same spot. For example, chop *wi* out of *I will,* throw in an apostrophe, and you have *I'll.* The resulting word is shorter and faster to say, with only one syllable (sound) instead of two.

Take a look at Table 12-1 for a list of common contractions. Notice that a couple of contractions are irregular. (*Won't,* for example, is short for *will not.*)

Table 12-1		Contractions	
Phrase	*Contraction*	*Phrase*	*Contraction*
are not	aren't	she is	she's
cannot	can't	that is	that's
could not	couldn't	they are	they're
do not	don't	they will	they'll
does not	doesn't	they would	they'd
did not	didn't	we are	we're
he will	he'll	we will	we'll

Phrase	Contraction	Phrase	Contraction
he would	he'd	we would	we'd
he is	he's	we have	we've
is not	isn't	what is	what's
it is	it's	who is	who's
I am	I'm	will not	won't
I will	I'll	would not	wouldn't
I would	I'd	you are	you're
I have	I've	you have	you've
she will	she'll	you will	you'll
she would	she'd	you would	you'd

If you'd like to make a contraction that isn't in Table 12-1, check your dictionary to make sure it's legal!

Common contraction mistakes

If you've gone to the mall — any mall — chances are you've seen a sign like this:

> Doughnuts 'N Coffee

or

> Skirts 'N Shirts

or

> Broken Grammar Rules

Okay, I doubt you've seen the last one, at least as a sign, but you've seen 'n as a contraction of *and*. And therefore, you've witnessed broken grammar rules at the mall. I know I'm fighting a losing battle here, and I know I should be worried about much more important issues, like the economy and the environment. Even so, I also care about the grammatical environment, and thus I make a plea to the store owners and sign painters of the English-speaking world. Please don't put 'n in anything. It's a grunt, not a word. Thank you.

Your right to use apostrophes

You're in trouble if *your* apostrophes are in the wrong place, especially when you're writing in the second person. (The second person is the form that uses *you, your, yours*, both singular and plural.) *You're* means *you are. Your* shows possession. These two words are not interchangeable. Some examples:

"*You're* not going to eat that rotten pumpkin," declared Ratrug. *(You are not going to eat.)*

"*Your* refusal to eat the pumpkin means that you will be given mystery meat instead," commented Cedric. (The refusal comes from *you* so you need a possessive word.)

"*You're* going to wear that pumpkin if you threaten me," said Lola. *(You are going to wear.)*

"I'm not afraid of *your* threats!" stated Legghorn. (The threats come from *you* so you need a possessive word.)

Woulda, coulda, shoulda. These three "verbs" are potholes on the road to better grammar. Why? Because they don't exist. Here's the recipe for a grammatical felony. Start with three real verb phrases:

would have

could have

should have

And turn them into contractions:

would've

could've

should've

Now turn them back into words. But don't turn them back into the words they actually represent. Instead, let your ears be your guide. (It helps if you have a lot of wax in your ears because the sounds don't quite match.) Now you say the following:

would of

could of

should of

These three phrases are never correct. Don't use them! Take a look at these examples:

WRONG: If Lochness had asked me to join the spy ring, I would of said, "No way."

RIGHT: If Lochness had asked me to join the spy ring, I would have said, "No way."

ALSO RIGHT: If Lochness had asked me to join the spy ring, I would've said, "No way."

Here's another set:

WRONG: In recruiting for the spy ring, Lochness could of been more polite.

RIGHT: In recruiting for the spy ring, Lochness could have been more polite.

ALSO RIGHT: In recruiting for the spy ring, Lochness could've been more polite.

Note one last group of examples:

WRONG: When I heard about the spy ring, I should of told the Central Intelligence Agency.

RIGHT: When I heard about the spy ring, I should have told the Central Intelligence Agency.

ALSO RIGHT: When I heard about the spy ring, I should've told the Central Intelligence Agency.

Which is correct?

A. Jane wouldnt go to the dentist even though she needed a new tooth.

B. Jane wouldn't go to the dentist, even though she needed a new tooth.

Answer: Sentence B is correct. *Wouldn't* is short for *would not.*

The questions never stop, do they? Try again. Which is correct?

A. The new tooth would of been fine, but she'll never learn.

B. The new tooth would've been fine, but she'll never learn.

C. The new tooth wouldve been fine, but she'll never learn.

Answer: Sentence B is correct. Sentence A contains an incorrect verb form, *would of.* The verb in sentence C lacks an apostrophe *(wouldve).*

Contractions you ne'er use except in poetry

Poets often create unusual contractions when they need a certain number of syllables in a line. In real life, no one ever says

o'er (over)	o' (of)	'gainst (against)
ne'er (never)	wi' (with)	ta'en (taken)
e'en (evening)	'twas (it was)	ow'st (owest)

and so forth. But in poems, these and other unusual contractions aren't uncommon. Poets writing in a strict format — the classic ten syllables a line, every other syllable stressed, sonnet form, for example — throw in an apostrophe when they need to drop one syllable from the line. (The reverse is also true. To add an extra syllable, poets place an accent mark above a normally silent letter — *markéd,* for example, is pronounced *mark-éd.*) They're cheating, but hey, poetry is tough to write.

Using Apostrophes with Symbols and Numbers

This rule is easy. To make the plural of a numeral or a symbol, you may add an apostrophe and then the letter *s.* Take a look at some examples:

Lulu's mother blushes whenever her daughter mentions the *1960's.* The computer that Lochness rewired prints only *#'s.*

When Eggworthy writes *0's,* they have a curious oval shape.

Cedric thinks that *&'s* are acceptable in formal writing! (They aren't.)

This rule may be on the way out. Recently, many publishers are simplifying their lives by adding only the letter *s.* Here are some examples:

Lola's mother turns pale when anyone mentions the 1950s.

Lochness writes #s on all his stolen microfilm.

Eggworthy's 0s seem fragile.

Cedric's teacher deducted points for all his &s.

So far, civilization hasn't crumbled from the shock. Stay tuned! For now, use both the apostrophe and the *s* when you really, really, really need to impress someone with your grammatical knowledge.

Chapter 13

Quotations: More Rules Than the Internal Revenue Service

*W*hen I correct the quotation marks in students' papers, I find that students are often puzzled. "Why did you move that period?" they ask. "Why did you change the single quotation marks to doubles? Do I really need a capital letter there?" They have a lot of questions for me (including that old favorite: "Why do we have to know this stuff?"). I always have one for them too (No, I don't ask, "Do you know the way to detention?" I'm much nicer than that.) I do ask them what rule they were following when they placed the quotation marks, the capital letters, the periods, and the commas. Surprisingly, they always have an answer. Then they quote a rule to me that justifies what they wrote. Unfortunately, the rules they quote don't exist; they're myths, not rules. Even more unfortunately, English grammar governs the use of quotation marks with a huge number of rules — more than our beloved governmental agency, the Internal Revenue Service.

In this chapter, I explain how to quote correctly and how to get the details right, including punctuation, capitalization, paragraphing, and all the other fun stuff. No myths here — just the facts.

And I Quote

A *quotation* is a written repetition of someone else's words — just one word or a whole statement or passage. You see quotations in almost all writing: newspapers, magazines, novels, essays, letters, and so on. To get an idea how to identify a quotation, take a look at the following story:

One day, while Felonia was on her way to a music lesson, she gazed through a shop window at a gleaming grand piano. Her heart beating wildly at the thought of playing such a marvel, she neglected to look up when everyone around her began to shout. Seconds later, another piano — an upright, not a grand — came whizzing through the air. One of the movers had taken a bite of his tuna fish sandwich, allowing the piano to break loose from the ropes hoisting it to the third floor. The piano landed a mere inch away from Felonia. What did Felonia say?

> She said that she was relieved.

This sentence tells you about Felonia and her feelings, but it doesn't give her exact words. It's a report of someone's ideas, but not a record of the words actually spoken or written. You can write exactly the same sentence if you heard Felonia say, "Thank God it missed me. My knees are shaking! I could have been killed."

You can also write the same sentence if you heard Felonia say, "Tomorrow's the big concert! What if it had hit me! I'm so glad it missed. Now I can play and become a star. Recording companies will come to me on bended knee, and my name will be all over the Internet. I'll even be a guest on Letterman."

And of course, you can write the same sentence if you heard Felonia say, "I am relieved."

As an observer, you can also record Felonia's reaction by writing:

> She said that she was "relieved."

This account of Felonia's reaction is a little more exact. Some of the sentence is general, but the reader knows that Felonia actually said the word "relieved" because it's in quotation marks. The quotation marks are signs for the reader; they mean that the material inside the marks is exactly what was said.

> Felonia said, "I am so relieved that I could cry."
>
> "I am so relieved that I could cry," Felonia said.

These two sentences quote Felonia. The words enclosed by quotation marks are exactly what Felonia said. The only thing added is a *speaker tag* — an identifying phrase that tells you who said the words (in this case, Felonia). You can place the speaker tag in the beginning of the sentence or at the end. (It can also land in the middle, but I talk about that later in this chapter.) The quotation marks enclose the words that were said or written.

Which sentences are quotations? Which sentences are general reports of what was said?

A. Blathersby doesn't get along with the conductor of the school orchestra, according to Lulu.

B. Besides placing exploding cushions on the conductor's chair, Blathersby has been heard talking about the conductor's "sentimental" choices of music for the next concert.

C. "I refuse to play anything that was composed before the twenty-first century," declared Blathersby.

Answer: Sentence A is a general report with none of Blathersby's exact words. Sentence B tells the reader that Blathersby said the word "sentimental." Sentence C is a quotation.

Punctuating Quotations

Here's a math problem for you:

Quotation + Punctuation = ?

Answer: A million dumb rules. Yes, I'm brave in calling the rules "dumb," even though I risk being expelled from the grammarians' union. In general, the rules for quotations are simply customs. Put a period inside, put a period outside — what difference does it make to your reader? Not much. But the illogical rules are just as important as the logical ones. You need to follow them, whether these rules make sense or not. So here goes: the earth-shattering topic of punctuating quotations.

Quotations with speaker tags

DUMB RULE 1: When the speaker tag comes first, put a comma after the speaker tag. The period at the end of the sentence goes *inside* the quotation marks.

The gang remarked, "Lola's candidate is a sure bet."

Ludwig added, "I am an absolute ruler and I like Lola's candidate."

Lola replied, "Don't get personal."

DUMB RULE 2: When the speaker tag comes last, put a comma *inside* the quotation marks and a period at the end of the sentence.

"Lola's candidate isn't a sure bet now," the gang continued.

"I declare war," screamed Lola.

"I have secret information about the election," said Lochness.

Now you know the first two (of far too many) quotation rules. Keep in mind that it doesn't matter where you put the speaker tag as long as you punctuate the sentence correctly.

Which sentence is correct?

A. Alonzo muttered, "I don't want to practice the piano".

B. Alonzo muttered, "I don't want to practice the piano."

Answer: Sentence B is correct, because the period is inside the quotation marks.

Here's another pair. Which sentence is correct?

A. "The equation that Agwamp wrote on the board is incorrect," trilled Analivia.

B. "The equation that Agwamp wrote on the board is incorrect", trilled Analivia.

Answer: Sentence A is correct, because the comma is inside the quotation marks.

How rude! Punctuating interrupted quotations with speaker tags

Sometimes a speaker tag lands in the middle of a sentence. To give you an example of this sort of placement, I revisit Felonia. Her saga continues with a visit to her lawyer.

"I think I'll sue," Felonia explained, "for emotional distress."

"You can't imagine," she added, "the feelings I felt."

"The brush of the piano against my nose," she sighed, "will be with me forever."

"The scent of tuna," she continued, "brings it all back."

"I can't go to the cafeteria," she concluded, "without suffering post-piano stress syndrome."

In each of these sample sentences, the speaker tag is in the middle of the quotation; it interrupts the quotation. Time for some more dumb rules for the punctuation of this sort of interrupted quotation.

DUMB RULE 3: In a sentence with an interrupted quotation, the comma is *inside* the quotation marks for the first half of a quotation.

DUMB RULE 4: In a sentence with an interrupted quotation, the speaker tag is followed by a comma *before* the quotation marks.

DUMB RULE 5: In a sentence with an interrupted quotation, the period at the end of the sentence is *inside* the quotation marks.

DUMB RULE 6: In a sentence with an interrupted quotation, the second half of a quotation does *not* begin with a capital letter.

Which sentence is correct?

A. "After the concert", said Lulu, "the piano goes to the third floor."

B. "After the concert," said Lulu, "The piano goes to the third floor."

Answer: Neither is correct. In sentence A, the comma after *concert* is in the wrong place. In sentence B, the second half of the quotation should not begin with a capital letter. Here is the correct sentence:

"After the concert," said Lulu, "the piano goes to the third floor."

Try another. Which sentence is correct?

A. "Although I am only a humble musician, said Felonia, "I have the right to a piano-free sidewalk."

B. "Although I am only a humble musician," said Felonia "I have the right to a piano-free sidewalk."

C. "Although I am only a humble musician," said Felonia, I have the right to a piano-free sidewalk."

D. "Although I am only a humble musician," said Felonia, "I have the right to a piano-free sidewalk."

Answer: Sentence D is correct. In sentence A, there should be a quotation mark after *musician*. In sentence B, a comma should be placed after *Felonia*. In sentence C, a quotation mark should be placed before *I*. (Annoying rules, aren't they? So many things can go wrong with this type of sentence.)

Notice that in all of the interrupted quotations I supply in this section, the quoted material adds up to only one sentence, even though it's written in two separate parts.

Avoiding run-on sentences with interrupted quotations

When you plop a speaker tag right in the middle of someone's conversation, make sure that you don't create a run-on sentence. A *run-on sentence* is actually two sentences that have been stuck together (that is, *run* together) with nothing to join them. (For more information on run-on sentences, see Chapter 7.) Just because you're quoting is no reason to ignore the rules about joining sentences. Check out this set of examples:

WRONG: "When you move a piano, you must be careful," squeaked Agwamp, "I could have been killed."

RIGHT: "When you move a piano, you must be careful," squeaked Agwamp. "I could have been killed."

The quoted material forms two complete sentences:

SENTENCE 1: When you move a piano, you must be careful.

SENTENCE 2: I could have been killed.

Because the quoted material forms two complete sentences, you must write two separate sentences. If you cram this quoted material into one sentence, you've got a run-on. Here's another set:

WRONG: "Felonia is my best friend," sobbed Agwamp, "on any other day I would have been walking with her and died instantly."

RIGHT: "Felonia is my best friend," sobbed Agwamp. "On any other day I would have been walking with her and died instantly."

WHY IT IS RIGHT: Your quotation is actually two complete sentences, so you can't run them together into one sentence. (Sentence 1 + *Felonia is my best friend.* Sentence 2 + *On any other day I would have been walking with her and died instantly.*)

Remove the speaker tag and check the quoted material. What is left? Enough for half a sentence? That's okay. Quoted material doesn't need to express a complete thought. Enough material for one sentence? Also okay. Enough material for two sentences? Not okay, unless you write two sentences.

Which is correct?

A. "A piano hits the ground with tremendous force," explained the physicist. "I would move to the side if I were you."

B. "A piano hits the ground with tremendous force," explained the physicist, "I would move to the side if I were you."

Answer: Sentence A is correct. The quoted material forms two complete sentences and you most quote it that way. Sentence 1 + *A piano hits the ground with tremendous force.* Sentence 2 + *I would move to the side if I were you.*

Here's another. Which is correct?

A. "I insist that you repeal the laws of physics, demanded Lola. "Pianos should not kill people."

B. "I insist that you repeal the laws of physics," demanded Lola, "Pianos should not kill people."

C. "I insist that you repeal the laws of physics," demanded Lola. "Pianos should not kill people."

Answer: C is correct. In A, a quotation mark is missing after the word *physics*. Choice B is a run-on. In C, the two complete thoughts are expressed in two sentences

Quotations without speaker tags

Not all sentences with quotations include speaker tags. The punctuation and capitalization rules for these sentences are a little different, though not more logical than other types of quotation mark rules. Check out these examples:

> According to the blurb on the book jacket, Analivia's history of geometry is said to be "thrilling and unbelievable" by all who read it.

> Unaccustomed to Analivia's monster ego, Plurabelle did not hesitate to say that "the book stinks."

> When Legghorn said that the book "wasn't as exciting as watching paint dry," Analivia threw a pie in his face.

> Analivia later told the press that the pie was "barely warm" and "quite delicious."

> Legghorn's lawyer is planning a lawsuit for "grievous injury to face and ego."

DUMB RULE 7: If the quotation doesn't have a speaker tag, the first word of the quotation is not capitalized.

DUMB RULE 8: No comma separates the quotation from the rest of the sentence if the quotation doesn't have a speaker tag.

Actually, rules 7 and 8 aren't completely dumb. Quotations without speaker tags aren't set off from the sentence; they're tucked into the sentence. You don't want to put a capital letter in the middle of the sentence, which is where nonspeaker-tag quotations usually end up. Also, omitting the comma preserves the flow of the sentence.

Notice that quotations without speaker tags tend to be short — a few words rather than an entire statement. If you're reporting a lengthy statement, you're probably better off with a speaker tag and the complete quotation. If you want to extract only a few, relevant words from someone's speech, you can probably do without a speaker tag.

Which is correct?

A. Eggworthy said that the latest nutritional research was "Suspect" because the laboratory was "Unfair."

B. Eggworthy said that the latest nutritional research was, "suspect" because the laboratory was, "unfair."

C. Eggworthy said that the latest nutritional research was "suspect" because the laboratory was "unfair."

Sentence C is correct. In sentence A, *suspect* and *unfair* should not be capitalized. In sentence B, no commas should be placed after *was*.

Quotations with question marks

Remember Felonia's piano from earlier in this chapter? When the piano nearly squashed Felonia, she said a few more things. (Not all of them are printable, but we'll ignore those remarks.) Here are additional remarks from our pianist:

> "Are you trying to kill me?" asked Felonia as she shook her fist at the piano mover.

> "Didn't you watch what you were doing?" she added, squinting into the sun.

> "How could you eat a tuna sandwich while hoisting a piano?" she continued as she eyed his lunch.

> "Could I have a bite?" she queried.

Let me put it another way:

> As she shook her first at the piano mover, Felonia asked, "Are you trying to kill me?"

> Squinting into the sun she added, "Didn't you watch what you were doing?"

> As she eyed his lunch she continued, "How could you eat a tuna sandwich while hoisting a piano?"

> She queried, "Could I have a bite?"

What do you notice about these two sets of quotations? That's right! The quoted words are questions. (Okay, I didn't actually hear your answer, but I'm assuming that because you were smart enough to buy this book, you're smart enough to notice these things.) And quotations that include questions follow the

NOT-SO-DUMB RULE 9: If you quote a question, put the question mark *inside* the quotation marks.

This rule makes good sense; it distinguishes a quoted question from a quotation embedded in a question. Time to look at one more part of Felonia's encounter with the falling piano. The piano mover answered Felonia, but no one could understand his words. (He had a mouthful of tuna fish.) I wonder what excuse he offered.

> Did he say, "I was just giving you a free piano"?
>
> Did he add, "I can't give you a bite of my sandwich because I ate it all"?
>
> Did he continue, "I hope you're not going to sue me"?
>
> Did he really declare, "It was just a piano"?

The quoted words in this set are not questions. However, each entire sentence is a question. Now it's time for more rules:

SLIGHTLY-LESS-DUMB RULE 10: If the quoted words aren't a question but the entire sentence is a question, the question mark goes *outside* the quotation marks. (This rule makes sense too, don't you think?)

To sum up the rules on question marks:

- ✔ If the quoted words are a question, put the question mark *inside* the quotation marks.
- ✔ If the entire sentence is a question, put the question mark *outside* the quotation marks.

I know that some of you detail-oriented (okay, picky) people have thought of one more possibility. What about the occasions when the quote and the sentence are both questions? English grammar has a response.

DUMB RULE 11: For those rare occasions when both the quoted words and the sentence are questions, put the question mark *inside* the quotation marks.

Here's an example of this rule:

> Did the mover really ask, "Is that lady for real?"

No matter what, don't use two question marks:

> WRONG: Did Felonia ask, "What's the number of a good lawyer?"?
>
> RIGHT: Did Felonia ask, "What's the number of a good lawyer?"

Which sentence is correct?

A. Did Lulu say, "I wish a piano would drop on me so that I could sue?"

B. Did Lulu say, "I wish a piano would drop on me so that I could sue"?

Answer: Sentence B is correct. Because the quoted words are not a question and the entire sentence is a question, the question mark goes outside the quotation marks.

Quotations with exclamation points

A word about exclamation points: These punctuation marks follow the same general rules as question marks. In other words,

NOT-SO-DUMB RULE 12: If the entire sentence is an exclamation, but the quoted words aren't, put the exclamation point *outside* the quotation marks.

NOT-SO-DUMB RULE 13: If the quoted words are an exclamation, put the exclamation point *inside* the quotation marks.

Here are some sample sentences with exclamation points:

> Ratrug said, "I can't believe it's not butter!" (The quoted words are an exclamation but the entire sentence is not.)

> I simply cannot believe that Ratrug actually said, "No, thank you"! (Now the entire sentence is an exclamation but the quoted words are not.)

For those of you who like to dot every i and cross every t:

DUMB RULE 14: If both the sentence and the quotation are exclamations, put the exclamation point *inside* the quotation marks.

Take a look at this example:

> I simply cannot believe that Ratrug actually said, "Not if it were my mother's dying wish would I run for president!"

No matter what, don't use two exclamation points:

> WRONG: I refuse to believe that Ratrug said, "In your dreams!"!

> RIGHT: I refuse to believe that Ratrug said, "In your dreams!"

Quotations with semicolons

Every hundred years or so you may write a sentence that has both a quotation and a semicolon. (In Chapter 15, I explain the semicolon rules in detail.) When you need to combine semicolons and quotations, here's the rule.

DUMB RULE 15: When writing a sentence that includes a quotation and a semicolon, put the semicolon *outside* the quotation marks.

Sneak a peek at this example:

> Cedric thinks that polyester is a food group; "I can't imagine eating anything else," he said.

and

> Cedric said, "I can't imagine eating anything but polyester"; he must have the IQ of a sea slug.

Okay, maybe that last sentence was a bit nasty. I apologize to sea slugs everywhere.

Quotations inside quotations

Now the topic of quotations becomes a little complicated. Sometimes you need to place a quotation inside a quotation. Consider this situation:

Agwamp, President of the Future Engineers of America, sees himself as a paragon of popularity. He doesn't want Archie to join the club because Archie wears a plastic pocket-protector filled with pens and pencils. Agwamp wants Archie to dump the pocket-protector, but Archie is outraged by the demand. You're writing a story about Archie and the Future Engineers of America. You're quoting Archie, who is quoting Agwamp. How do you punctuate this quotation?

> Archie says, "Agwamp had the nerve to tell me, 'Your pocket protector is nerd-city and dumpster-ready.'"

A sentence like this has to be sorted out. Without any punctuation, here's what Agwamp said:

> Your pocket protector is nerd-city and dumpster-ready.

Without any punctuation, here are all the words that Archie said:

> Agwamp had the nerve to tell me your pocket protector is nerd-city and dumpster-ready.

Agwamp's words are a quotation inside another quotation. So Agwamp's words are enclosed in single-quotation marks, and Archie's are enclosed (in the usual way) in double quotation marks. Which brings me to

DUMB RULE 16: A quotation inside another quotation gets single quotation marks.

British English Alert!

Just to make things even more difficult for writers of English everywhere, here's an important fact. Despite having settled their differences shortly after the Boston Tea Party, in some areas (grammar, for example) the British and the Americans are still fighting. Everything I've told you about quotation rules is true for American English grammar. The reverse is often true for British English grammar. The British frequently use single quotation marks when they're quoting, and double marks for a quotation inside another quotation. Thus a British book might punctuate Lulu's comment in the in this way:

> Lulu says, 'As a strong opponent of piercing, I am sorry to tell you that Lola told me, "I'm thinking of piercing my tongue."'

The name of the quotations marks is also different. In British English, the little squiggles are called "inverted commas." What's a puzzled grammarian to do? Follow the custom of the country he or she is in.

Another example: Lola says, "I'm thinking of piercing my tongue." Lulu tells Lola's mom about Lola's plan, adding a comment as she does so. Here's the complete statement:

> Lulu says, "As a strong opponent of piercing, I am sorry to tell you that Lola told me, 'I'm thinking of piercing my tongue.'"

Lola's words are inside single quotation marks and Lulu's complete statement is in double quotation marks.

Commas and periods follow the same rules in both double and single quotations.

Which sentence is correct?

A. Angel complained, "He said to me, 'You are a devil.'"

B. Angel complained, "He said to me, "You are a devil."

Answer: Sentence A is correct. You must enclose *You are a devil* in single quotation marks and the larger statement *He said to me you are a devil* in double quotation marks. The period at the end of the sentence goes inside both marks.

Quote or *quotation?* I've been using the term *quotation* because that's the correct word. In conversational English, *quote* and *quotation* are interchangeable. Strictly speaking, however, *quote* is what you do (in other words, a verb) and *quotation* is a thing (that is, a noun). See Chapter 1 for more information on when conversational English is acceptable.

Who Said That? Identifying Speaker Changes

In a conversation, people take turns speaking. Take a look at this extremely mature discussion:

"You sat on my tuna fish sandwich," Legghorn said.

"No, I didn't," Ludmilla said.

"Yes, you did," Legghorn said.

"Did not!" Ludmilla said.

"Did too!" Legghorn said.

Notice that every time the speaker changes, a new paragraph is formed. By starting a new paragraph every time the speaker changes, the conversation is easy to follow; the reader always knows who is talking.

Here's another version of the tuna fight:

"You sat on my tuna fish sandwich," Legghorn said.

"No, I didn't," Ludmilla said.

"Yes, you did."

"Did not!"

"Did too!"

Sounds better, doesn't it? The speaker tags are left out in this version, after the first exchange. Yet you can still figure out who is speaking because of the paragraph breaks.

DUMB RULE 17: Every change of speaker is signaled by a new paragraph.

This rule applies even if the argument deteriorates into single-word statements such as

"Yes!"

"No!"

or some other single-word statements (I won't specify, because this is a family-friendly book). A new paragraph signals each speaker change, no matter how short the quotation. (By the way, Ludmilla *did* sit on his tuna sandwich; I can tell by the mayonnaise stains on her skirt. However, Legghorn left the sandwich on her chair, so he is partly to blame.)

In novels, you may have a quotation from one speaker that is several paragraphs long. Budding novelists who are reading this book, please take note: The quotation begins with a quotation mark. Don't put a quotation mark at the end of any paragraph within the quotation. Whenever you begin a new paragraph, put a quotation mark. When the quotation is completely finished (at the end of the last paragraph), put a quotation mark.

Who said what? Label each statement, using the paragraph clues.

"Are you in favor of piano-tossing?" asked Lochness curiously.

"Not really," replied Cedric. "I like my pianos to have all four feet on the floor."

"But there's something about music in the air that appeals to me."

"There's something about no broken bones, no concussions, and no flattened bodies that appeals to me."

"You really have no artistic instinct!"

Answer: Here's the passage again, with the speakers' names inserted. (Note the punctuation.)

"Are you in favor of piano-tossing?" asked Lochness curiously.

"Not really," replied Cedric. "I like my pianos to have all four feet on the floor."

Lochness continued, "But there's something about music in the air that appeals to me."

Cedric countered, "There's something about no broken bones, no concussions, and no flattened bodies that appeals to me."

"You really have no artistic instinct!" shouted Lochness.

Using Sanitizing Quotation Marks

Possibly the most annoying grammatical habit (other than saying *'n* when you mean *and,* as in *Buns 'n Burgers*) is the *sanitizing quotation mark*. The sanitizing quotation mark tells the reader that you don't completely approve of the words inside the quotation marks. To get a better idea of what I'm describing, read this paragraph:

Quotation marks are a "necessary" part of writing. I don't like to look at little "squiggles" when I am concentrating on a story, but they show that I am a "hip" writer.

Now tell me, why are there three sets of quotation marks in that paragraph? I have no idea. I think people who write paragraphs like the one above are trying to be cute, while leaving themselves an out (an "out"?) in case the reader is not amused. These quotation marks put a little distance between the writer and what the writer says. They say, "I know this word is a little unusual or controversial. That's why I put it in quotation marks. If you don't like it, don't blame me. I'm only quoting." My advice? If you mean what you write, stand by it. Avoid using quotation marks to sanitize your writing.

Quoting Slang

Slang is highly informal speech that falls outside standard discourse. You hear slang every day — it becomes part of your culture — at home, work, school, and so on. (For more information on slang, see Chapter 1.) If you're quoting slang and you want to show that you know it's slang, quotation marks are helpful. Check out this example:

> Archie knew that the guys thought him "nerd-city," but he was determined not to abandon his beloved pocket protector just because it was considered "uncool."

The writer knows that "nerd-city" and "uncool" aren't correct, but those words show the ideas of Archie's co-workers. The quotation marks allow the writer to use slang without appearing ignorant. These sanitizing quotation marks are acceptable.

Don't overuse sanitizing quotation marks. Think of them as plutonium; a little goes a long way. Or, to sanitize that statement, a little goes a "long" way. See what I mean about annoying?

A useful little word is *sic*. *Sic* means that you're quoting exactly what was said or written, even though you know something is wrong. In other words, you put a little distance between yourself and the error by showing the reader that the person you're quoting made the mistake, not you. For example, if you're quoting from the works of Dan Quayle, former Vice President of the United States (and a *very* poor speller) you may write

> "I would like a potatoe [sic] for supper."

Punctuating Titles: When to Use Quotation Marks

In your writing, sometimes you may need to include the name of a magazine, the headline of a newspaper article, the title of a song or movie, and so on. When punctuating these names, headlines, and titles, keep in mind these two options:

1. **Put the title in quotation marks. Quotation marks enclose titles of smaller works or parts of a whole.**

or

2. **Set the title off from the rest of the writing with italics or underlining. By using italics or underlining, you set off titles of larger works or complete works.**

These options aren't interchangeable. Each option has a different use. To put it another way, quotation marks are for jockeys. Italics and underlining are for basketball players. One is for little, the other for big.

Use quotation marks for the titles of

- poems
- stories
- essays
- songs
- chapter titles
- magazine or newspaper articles
- individual episodes of a television series

Use italics or underlining for the titles of

- collections of poetry, stories, or essays
- titles of books
- titles of CD's or tapes or records (Do they still make records?)
- magazines or newspapers
- television shows
- plays

Here are some examples:

- ✔ "A Thousand Excuses for Missing the Tax Deadline" (a newspaper article) in *The Ticker Tape Journal* (a newspaper)
- ✔ "Ode to Taxes Uncalculated" (a poem) in *The Tax Poems* (a book of poetry)
- ✔ "I Got the W2 Blues" (a song title) on *Me and My Taxes* (a CD containing many songs)
- ✔ "On the Art of Deductions" (an essay) in *Getting Rich and Staying Rich* (a magazine)
- ✔ "Small Business Expenses" (an individual episode) on *The IRS Report* (a television series)
- ✔ *April 15th* (a play)

You may be wondering which letters you should capitalize in a title. For information on capitalization, see Chapter 16.

Add quotation marks and italics to the following paragraph.

Griselda slumped slowly into her chair as the teacher read The Homework Manifesto aloud in class. Griselda's essay, expressing her heartfelt dislike of any and all assignments, was never intended for her teacher's eyes. Griselda had hidden the essay inside the cover of her textbook, The Land and People of Continents You Never Heard Of. Sadly, the textbook company, which also publishes The Most Boring Mathematics Possible, had recently switched to thinner paper, and the essay was clearly visible. The teacher ripped the essay from Griselda's frightened hands. Griselda had not been so embarrassed since the publication of her poem I Hate Homework in the school magazine, Happy Thoughts.

Answer: Put "The Homework Manifesto" and "I Hate Homework" in quotation marks, because they're titles of an essay and a poem. Italicize *The Land and People of Continents You Never Heard Of* and *The Most Boring Mathematics Possible* and *Happy Thoughts,* because they're titles of books and a magazine.

Chapter 14

The Pause That Refreshes: Commas

. . . .

. . . .

Aloud, commas are the sounds of silence — short pauses that contrast with the longer pauses at the end of each sentence. Commas are really signals for your reader. Stop here, they say, but not for too long.

Commas also cut parts of your sentence away from the whole, separating something from everything around it in order to change the meaning of the sentence. When you're speaking, you do the same thing with your tone of voice and the timing of your breaths.

So why do so many commas land in the wrong place? Perhaps because some writers throw them in wherever the writer needs to stop and think. The key is to put the commas where the reader needs a break. The rules concerning commas aren't very hard. In fact, they actually have a logic to them. In this chapter, I guide you through the logic so you know where to put these punctuation marks in several common situations. For more information on comma use, see Chapters 13 and 25.

Distinguishing Items: Commas in Series

Let's say that you sent your friend Cedric to the store with a long grocery list. Because you have only a scrap of paper and because your electronic organizer is out of batteries, you write everything on one line.

flashlight batteries butter cookies ice cream cake

How many things does Cedric have to buy? Perhaps only three:

flashlight batteries

butter cookies

ice cream cake

Or five:

flashlight

batteries

butter cookies

ice cream

cake

How does Cedric know? He doesn't, unless you use commas. Here's what Cedric actually needs to buy — all four items:

flashlight batteries, butter cookies, ice cream, cake

To put it in a sentence:

Cedric has to buy flashlight batteries, butter cookies, ice cream, and cake.

The commas between these items are signals. When you read the list aloud, the commas emerge as breaths:

Cedric has to buy flashlight batteries [breath] butter cookies [breath] ice cream [breath] and cake.

You need commas between each item on the list, with one important exception. The comma in front of the word *and* is optional. Why? Because once you say *and,* you've already separated the last two items. But if you want to throw an extra comma there, you're welcome to do so. It's your choice.

Never put a comma in front of the first item on the list.

> WRONG: Cedric has to buy, flashlight batteries, butter cookies, ice cream and cake.

> RIGHT: Cedric has to buy flashlight batteries, butter cookies, ice cream and cake.

> ALSO RIGHT: Cedric has to buy flashlight batteries, butter cookies, ice cream, and cake.

> ALSO RIGHT, BUT NOT A GOOD IDEA: Cedric has to buy flashlight batteries and butter cookies and ice cream and cake.

You don't need commas at all in the last sentence because the word *and* does the job. Grammatically, that sentence is fine. In reality, if you write a sentence with three *ands,* your reader will think you sound like a little kid or a tape on continuous rewind.

Punctuate the following sentence.

> Jellibelle requested a jelly doughnut a silk dress four sports cars and a racehorse in exchange for the rights to the computer code she had written.

Answer: Jellibelle requested a jelly doughnut, a silk dress, four sports cars, and a racehorse in exchange for the rights to the computer code she had written. Note: You may omit the comma before the *and.*

Separating a List of Descriptions

Your writing relies on nouns and verbs to get your point across. But if you're like most people, you also enrich your sentences with descriptions. In grammar terminology, you add adjectives and adverbs. (For more information on adjectives and adverbs, see Chapter 8.) Notice the descriptions in the following sentences:

> "What do you think of me?" Jellibelle asked Jilly in an idle moment.

> Jilly took a deep breath, "I think you are a sniffling, smelly, pimple-tongued, frizzy-haired monster."

> "Thank you," said Jellibelle, who was trying out for the part of the wicked witch in the school play. "Do you think I should paint my teeth black too?"

Notice the commas in Jilly's answer. Four descriptions are listed: sniffling, smelly, pimple-tongued, frizzy-haired.

A comma separates each of the descriptions from the next, but there is no comma between the last description *(frizzy-haired)* and the word that it's describing *(monster).*

The four descriptions in the previous example are adjectives. All of these adjectives describe the noun *monster.*

Here's a little more of Jellibelle and Jilly's conversation:

"So do I get the part?" asked Jellibelle.

"Maybe," answered Jilly. "I have four sniffling, smelly, pimple-tongued, frizzy-haired monsters waiting to audition. I'll let you know."

Now look closely at Jilly's answer. This time there are five descriptions of the word *monster:* four, sniffling, smelly, pimple-tongued, frizzy-haired.

There are commas after *sniffling, smelly,* and *pimple-tongued.* As previously stated, no comma follows frizzy-haired because you shouldn't put a comma between the last description and the word that it describes. But why is there no comma after *four?* Here's why: sniffling, smelly, pimple-tongued, and frizzy-haired are more or less equal in importance in the sentence. They have different meanings, but they all do the same job — telling you how disgusting Jellibelle's costume is. *Four* is in a different category. It gives you different information. (It tells you how many monsters are waiting, not how they look), so it's not jumbled into the rest of the list.

Numbers aren't separated from other descriptions or from the word(s) that they describe. Don't put a comma after a number. Also, don't use commas to separate other descriptions from words that indicate number or amount — *many, more, few, less,* and so forth.

RIGHT: Sixteen smelly, bedraggled, stained hats were lined up on the shelf marked, "WITCH COSTUME."

WRONG: Sixteen, smelly, bedraggled, stained hats were lined up on the shelf marked, "WITCH COSTUME."

RIGHT: Additional stinky, mud-splattered, toeless shoes sat on the shelf marked, "GOBLIN SHOES."

WRONG: Additional, stinky, mud-splattered, toeless shoes sat on the shelf marked, "GOBLIN SHOES."

RIGHT: No drippy, disgusting, artificial wounds were in stock.

WRONG: No, drippy, disgusting, artificial wounds were in stock.

More descriptive words that you shouldn't separate from other descriptions or from the words that they describe include *other, another, this, that, these, those.*

> RIGHT: This green, glossy, licorice-flavored lipstick is needed for the witch's makeup kit.

> WRONG: This, green, glossy, licorice-flavored lipstick is needed for the witch's makeup kit.

> RIGHT: Those shiny, battery-powered, factory-sealed witches' wands are great.

> WRONG: Those, shiny, battery-powered, factory-sealed witches' wands are great.

Punctuate this sentence.

> Jilly was worried about the musical number in which one hundred scraggly fluorescent flowing beards come to life and dance around the stage.

Answer: Jilly was worried about the musical number in which one hundred scraggly, fluorescent, flowing beards come to life and dance around the stage.

Note: Don't put a comma after a number *(one hundred)* or after the last description *(flowing).*

In your writing, you may create other sentences in which the descriptions should not be separated by commas. For example, sometimes a few descriptive words seem to blend into each other to create one larger description in which one word is clearly more important than the rest. Technically the list of descriptions may provide two or three separate facts about the word that you're describing, but in practice, they don't deserve equal attention. Take a look at this example;

> Jilly just bought that funny little French hat.

You already know that you should not separate *that* from *funny* with a comma. But what about *funny, little,* and *French*? If you write

> Jilly just bought that funny, little, French hat.

you're giving equal weight to each of the three descriptions. Do you really want to emphasize all three qualities? Probably not. In fact, you're probably not making a big deal out of the fact that the hat is *funny* and *little*. Instead, you're emphasizing that the hat is *French*. So you don't need to put commas between the other descriptions.

Sentences like the example require judgment calls. Use this rule as a guide: If the items in a description are not of equal importance, don't separate them with commas.

You Talkin' to Me? Direct Address

When writing a message to someone, you need to separate the person's name from the rest of the sentence with a comma. Otherwise, your reader may misread the intention of the message. Take a look at the following note that Legghorn left on the door:

> Lochness wants to kill Wendy. I locked him in this room.

You think: Wendy is in danger. That's a shame. Oh well, I guess I'm safe. However, when you unlock the door and sit down for a pleasant chat, Lochness jumps up and starts chasing you around the room. You escape and run screaming to Legghorn. "Why didn't you tell me that Lochness was violent!" Legghorn pleads guilty to a grammatical crime. He forgot to put in the comma! Here's what he meant:

> Lochness wants to kill, Wendy. I locked him in his room.

It was your bad luck to read a note intended for Wendy. In grammarspeak, *Wendy* is in a direct-address sentence. Because you're speaking to Wendy, you separate out her name, cutting her off from the rest of the sentence with a comma. Direct address is also possible at the beginning or in the middle of a sentence:

> Wendy, Lochness wants to kill, so I locked him in his room.

> Lochness wants to kill, Wendy, so I locked him in his room.

Which sentence is correct?

A. The teacher called, Edwina, but I answered.

B. The teacher called Edwina, but I answered.

Answer: It depends. If you're talking to Edwina, telling her that Miss Sharkface phoned your house to report missing homework but you, not your mom, picked up the phone, then sentence A is correct. However, if you're explaining that the teacher screamed to Edwina, "Bring your homework up here *this minute!*" and instead you replied, "Miss Sharkface, Edwina asked me to tell you that a dog ate her homework," sentence B is correct.

Using Commas in Addresses and Dates

Commas are good, all-purpose separators. They won't keep you and your worst enemy apart, but they do a fine job on addresses and dates — especially when items that are usually placed on individual lines are put next to each other on the same line.

Addressing addresses

Where are you from? Jilly is from Mars, at least according to her friends. Jellibelle is from a small town called Bellyjelly. Here's her (fictional) address:

> Ms. Jellibelle Tumtum
>
> 223 Center Street
>
> Bellyjelly, New York 10001

If you put Jellibelle's address into a sentence, you have to separate each item of the address, as you see here:

> Jellibelle Tumtum lives at 223 Center Street, Bellyjelly, New York 10001.

Here's the address (envelope style) for her best friend Jilly:

> Jilly Willy
>
> 53 Asimov Court
>
> Mars Colonial Hills Estate
>
> Mars 50001

And now the sentence version:

> Jilly Willy lives at 53 Asimov Court, Mars Colonial Hills Estate, Mars 50001.

Notice that the house number and street are not separated by a comma, nor are the state (or planet) and the zip code.

If the sentence continues, you must separate the last item in the address from the rest of the sentence with another comma:

> Jellibelle Tumtum lives at 223 Center Street, Bellyjelly, New York 10001, but she is thinking of moving to Mars in order to be closer to her friend Jilly.

Jilly Willy lives at 53 Asimov Court, Mars Colonial Hills Estate, Mars 50001, but she is thinking of moving to Venus in order to be closer to her friend Alex.

If there is no street address — just a city and a state — put a comma between the city and the state. If the sentence continues after the state name, place a comma after the state.

Jellibelle Tumtum lives in Bellyjelly, New York, but she is thinking of moving to a Martian colony.

Jilly Willy used to live in Bellyjelly, New York, near the launch pad.

Commas also separate countries from the city/state/province:

Lochness lives in Edinburgh, Scotland, near a large body of water. His brother Legghorn just built a house in Zilda, Wisconsin.

Punctuate the following sentence.

Police believe that the missing salamander ran away from his home at 77 Main Street Zilda Wisconsin because of a dispute over the number of insects he would receive for each meal.

Answer: Police believe that the missing salamander ran away from his home at 77 Main Street, Zilda, Wisconsin, because of a dispute over the number of insects he would receive for each meal.

Here's another sentence that needs additional punctuation:

Responding to a 553 (salamander in the garden) call on the radio, police cruisers proceeded to 99-09 Center Street Wilda Illinois where they discovered the missing animal.

Answer: Responding to a 553 (salamander in the garden) call on the radio, police cruisers proceeded to 99-09 Center Street, Wilda, Illinois, where they discovered the missing animal.

Punctuating dates

If I click on the toolbar of my word-processing program to insert the date and time, I see several options, including:

September 28, 2000

9/28/2000

Sept. 28, 2000

If you aren't sure how to abbreviate a particular month (or any other word), check your dictionary.

Any of the three dates above are fine for the top of a letter. When the date is alone on a line, the only comma you have to worry about is the one after the day of the month.

In many countries, the custom is to place the day before the month:

28 September, 2000

In this case, place the comma between the month and the year, but not between the day and the month.

To insert a date into a sentence, I need one more comma:

On September 28, 2000, Lulu ate several thousand gummy candies.

or

Lulu was especially hungry on September 28, 2000, when she ate several thousand gummy candies.

Always use commas to separate the year from the rest of the sentence.

Punctuate this sentence.

Lola testified under oath that on December 18 1999 she saw Lulu place a carton of gummy bears under the counter without paying for them.

Answer: Lola testified under oath that on December 18, 1999, she saw Lulu place a carton of gummy bears under the counter without paying for them.

Try another.

Lulu's testimony was that on January 8 2001 Lola herself stole a carton of gummy bears.

Answer: Lulu's testimony was that on January 8, 2001, Lola herself stole a carton of gummy bears.

Flying Solo: Introductory Words

Yes, this section introduces a comma rule. No, it's not optional. Well, you probably know it already. Oh, I'll explain it anyway. Okay, the rule is that you must separate words that aren't part of the sentence but instead comment on the meaning of the sentence. I'll put it another way:

yes

no

well

oh

okay

These words are known as *introductory words*. They frequently appear at the beginning of a sentence and are set off from what follows by commas. If you omit these words, the sentence still means the same thing. Read these examples twice, once with the introductory words and once without. See how the meaning stays the same?

Yes, you are allowed to chew gum balls during class, but don't complain to me if you break a tooth.

No, you are not allowed to write the exam in blood as a protest against the amount of studying you need to do in order to pass this course.

Well, you may consider moving on to another topic if you have exhausted the creative possibilities of "My Favorite Lightbulb."

Oh, I didn't know that you needed your intestine today.

Okay, I'll try to hit the ball, not the catcher this time.

To sum up the rule on introductory words: Use commas to separate them from the rest of the sentence, or omit them entirely.

Which sentence is correct?

A. Well Ludmilla plays the piano well when she is in the mood.

B. Well, Ludmilla plays the piano, well, when she is in the mood.

C. Well, Ludmilla plays the piano well when she is in the mood.

Answer: Sentence C is correct. If you omit the first word, the sentence means exactly the same thing. *Well* is an introductory word that a comma should separate from the rest of the sentence. In sentence A, there is no comma after *well*. In sentence B, the first comma is correct, but the second *well* shouldn't be separated from the rest of the sentence because it's not an introductory word.

Chapter 15

Adding Information: Semicolons, Dashes, and Colons

- -

In This Chapter

▶ Joining two sentences with semicolons

▶ Using semicolons with fake joiners and in lists

▶ Knowing where to place a colon in a business letter, list, and quotation

▶ Separating two parts of a sentence with a colon

▶ Using dashes effectively

- -

In a classic episode of an old detective show, *The Rockford Files,* the hero's sidekick writes a book. He hands a thick pile of typing paper to Rockford and waits for his reader's reaction. Jim Rockford studies the manuscript for a moment and points out that the entire thing is written as one sentence. There is no punctuation whatsoever. The author explains that he's going to put "all that stuff" in later.

Many writers sympathize with the hero's sidekick. "All that stuff" is a real pain. Who has time to worry about punctuation when the fire of creativity burns? But the truth is that without punctuation, you may not get your point across. In this chapter, I explain three useful little items — semicolons, colons, and dashes.

Gluing Complete Thoughts Together: Semicolons

Semicolons (a dot on top of a comma — ;) can glue one complete sentence to another. An example:

Sentence 1: Arthur had only one shoelace left.

Sentence 2: He went to the store.

You can glue these two sentences together with a semicolon:

Arthur had only one shoelace left; he went to the store.

You can also join sentences together with words such as *and, but, or, nor, since, because, so,* and so forth. In general, semicolons attach sentences to each other without joining words. The sentences that semicolons attach should have a logical relation to each other. For more information on joining sentences and a complete discussion of how to do so with semicolons, see Chapter 7.

Joining words are called conjunctions. *And, or, but, yet, nor, so,* and *for* are co-ordinate conjunctions. *Because, since, after, although, where, when,* and so forth are subordinate conjunctions. For more information on conjunctions, see Chapter 7.

Using semicolons with false joiners

It's almost time for the marathon. As you stretch your muscles and focus your mind, you notice that the sole of your sneaker is loose. A gaping hole gives you a fine view of your sweat socks. What to do? You run into a nearby store and grab a stapler. Five quick clicks and you're on your way to glory.

I don't think so! The stapler looks like a solution to your problem, but in reality, it was never intended to attach soles to sneakers. (What really happens? Your sneaker falls apart on the far turn, a staple sticks you, and you drop out about 26 miles too soon. Then you get arrested for shoplifting the stapler.)

Some words are like a stapler at a marathon. Think of them as *false joiners*. At first glance they look like conjunctions. Analyze the meaning of each, and you see that they relate one idea to another. But grammatically they aren't conjunctions, and they were never intended to attach one sentence to another. These false joiners don't do the job. If you use them improperly, your sentence loses the race. Here's an example:

Maxwell ran into the house to get his silver hammer, however, the butler could not find it.

Why is the sentence incorrect? You've got two complete sentences:

SENTENCE 1: Maxwell ran into the house to get his silver hammer.

SENTENCE 2: The butler could not find it.

However is not a joining word, even though it looks like one. So the two complete sentences are jammed into one long sentence, with nothing holding them together. In grammarspeak, they've become a *run-on sentence*. (For more information on run-on sentences, see Chapter 7.) If you want to keep the *however,* add a semicolon. Here's a legal combination:

> Maxwell ran into the house to get his silver hammer; however, the butler could not find it.

Or, you may decide to make two sentences:

> Maxwell ran into the house to get his silver hammer. However, the butler could not find it.

The most common false joiners are *however, consequently, also, moreover, therefore, nevertheless, besides, thus, indeed,* and *then.* Don't put these words on your no-no list, because they add lots of meaning to a sentence. Just make sure that you use them with semicolons or with a single idea. Never use them to combine sentences.

The false joiners listed in the preceding tip are adverbs. (For more information on adverbs, see Chapter 8.)

A few phrases — *for example* and *for instance* — also look like joiners, but they aren't. They are prepositional phrases, not conjunctions. Here's another example of a run-on and its correction:

> RUN-ON: Agwamp is noted for his temper tantrums, for example, he threw a lemon at Lulu when she refused to make him a glass of lemonade.

The sample sentence is a run-on because it contains two complete sentences:

> SENTENCE 1: Agwamp is noted for his temper tantrums.

> SENTENCE 2: He threw a lemon at Lulu when she refused to make him a glass of lemonade.

The phrase *for example* is not strong enough to join these ideas. Use a semicolon or make two sentences:

> Agwamp is noted for his temper tantrums; for example, he threw a lemon at Lulu when she refused to make him a glass of lemonade.

or

> Agwamp is noted for his temper tantrums. For example, he threw a lemon at Lulu when she refused to make him a glass of lemonade.

A comma sets apart most of these false joiners from the second half of the sentence. If you've made two separate sentences, a comma probably sets off the false joiner from the rest of the sentence.

Correct or incorrect?

A. Aretha sang with all her heart; therefore, the glass in the recording booth shattered.

B. Aretha sang with all her heart, therefore, the glass in the recording booth shattered.

C. Aretha sang with all her heart. Therefore, the glass in the recording booth shattered.

Answer: Sentences A and C are correct, but sentence B is incorrect. *Therefore* is a false joiner. If you want to use it, add a semicolon or a true joining word (a conjunction). You may also make two sentences.

Here's the bottom line: in combining two complete sentences, be sure to use a semicolon or a conjunction. Don't use a comma, an adverb, or a prepositional phrase.

Separating items in a list with semicolons

Salamander is writing his guest list for the annual Reptile-Amphibian Ball. He plans to invite quite a few important people. Here, without punctuation, are some of the lucky guests:

> Oscar Diamondback the nation's leading reptile historian Annamaria Komodo the dragon expert a keeper from the local zoo the movie villain known as "The Snake" and of course Newt a former congressman

Confusing, isn't it? Perhaps commas will help:

> Oscar Diamondback, the nation's leading reptile historian, Annamaria Komodo, the dragon expert, a keeper from the local zoo, the movie villain known as "The Snake," and of course, Newt, a former congressman

The caterer wants to know how many orders of reptile chow are required, but the list has some names and some titles. A few of the names and titles are paired, indicating one person. A few are not paired, indicating two people. How can you tell the difference?

If the list isn't punctuated or is punctuated only with commas, you can't tell the difference. All those names and titles are jumbled together. You need something stronger than a comma to separate the elements of the list. You need — super comma! Well, actually you need semicolons. Here's the correct version:

Salamander is making out his guest list for the annual Reptile-Amphibian Ball. He plans to invite Oscar Diamondback; the nation's leading reptile historian; Annamaria Komodo, the dragon expert; a keeper from the local zoo; the movie villain known as "The Snake"; and of course, Newt, a former congressman.

The rule for semicolons in lists is very simple:

- When any items in a list include commas, separate all the items with semicolons.
- Don't put a semicolon before the first item on the list.
- Put a semicolon between the last two items on the list (before the conjunction).

Which is correct?

A. During the race Festus the Frog vowed that he would invite all the lizards, who are notoriously picky eaters, to a barbecue, make speeches about the effect of swamp pollution on the wildlife habitat, and begin a petition to remove the word "amphibious" from all motor vehicles.

B. During the race Festus the Frog vowed that he would invite all the lizards, who are notoriously picky eaters, to a barbecue; make speeches about the effect of swamp pollution on the wildlife habitat; and begin a petition to remove the word "amphibious" from all motor vehicles.

Answer: The punctuation of sentence B is correct. One of the items in the list has commas in it:

that he would invite all the lizards, who are notoriously picky eaters, to a barbecue

so you must separate the items on the list by semicolons. Notice that you need a semicolon before the word _and_.

Creating a Stopping Point: Colons

A colon is one dot on top of another — :. It shows up when a simple comma isn't strong enough. The colon shows more intensity. (It also shows up in those smiley faces — the so-called _emoticons_ — that people write in their e-mails.) In this section, I look at the colon in a few of its natural habitats: business letters, lists, and quotations.

Addressing a business letter

Colons appear in business letters, as you see in the following examples.

Dear Mr. Ganglia:

You are getting on my nerves. You're fired.

                Sincerely,

I.M. Incharj

To Whom It May Concern:

Everyone in the division is fired also.

Sincerely,

I.M. Incharj

The colon makes a business letter more formal. The opposite of a business letter is what English teachers call a *friendly letter,* even if it says something like "I hate you." When you write a friendly letter, put a comma after the name of the person who will receive the letter.

Introducing lists

When you insert a short list of items into a sentence, you don't need a colon. (For more information on how to use commas in lists, see Chapter 14.) When you're inserting a long list into a sentence, however, you may sometimes use a colon to introduce the list. Think of the colon as a good-sized gulp of air that readies the reader for a good-sized list. The colon precedes the first item. Here are some sentences that use colons at the beginning of long lists:

Ethelred needed quite a few things: a horse, an army, a suit of armor, a few million arrows, a map, and a battle plan.

Lulu's trail plan was quite ambitious and included the following tasks: reach the summit of Mount Everest, create a storm shelter using only twigs, rebalance the ecology of the natural habitat, and chant "om" until world peace occurred.

Lochness sent each spy away with several items: an excerpt from the encyclopedia entry on espionage, a collection of the essays of Mata Hari, a photocopy of the nation's policy on treason, and a poison pill.

If you put a colon in front of a list, check the beginning of the sentence — the part before the colon. Does it make sense? Can it stand alone? If so, no problem. The words before the colon must form a complete thought. If not, don't use a colon. Here are some examples:

> WRONG: The problems with Ethelred's battle plan are: no understanding of enemy troop movements, a lack of shelter and food for the troops, and a faulty trigger for the retreat signal.

> WHY IT'S WRONG: The words before the colon *(The problems with Ethelred's battle plan are)* can't stand alone. They form an incomplete thought.

> RIGHT: The problems with Ethelred's battle plan are numerous: no understanding of enemy troop movements, a lack of shelter and food for the troops, and a faulty trigger for the retreat signal.

> WHY IT'S RIGHT: The words before the colon *(The problems with Ethelred's battle plan are numerous)* can stand alone. They form a complete thought.

Here's another set:

> WRONG: You should: build a fire, arrest Lochness, sedate Lulu, and return to your grammar studies.

> WHY IT'S WRONG: The words before the colon *(you should)* do not form a complete thought.

> RIGHT: You should accomplish the following: build a fire, arrest Lochness, sedate Lulu, and return to your grammar studies.

> WHY IT'S RIGHT: The words before the colon are a complete sentence. (I know. When you say *the following* you're waiting for more information. However, grammatically they form a complete sentence. For more information on complete sentences, see Chapter 5.)

Introducing long quotations

The rule concerning colons with quotations is fairly easy. If the quotation is short, introduce it with a comma. If the quotation is long, introduce it with a colon. (In other words, you can precede pretty much everything a politician says with a colon, assuming you quote every precious, patriotic phrase and don't go for the sound bite. However, you can precede everything your friend says, when she's in one of her moods and you're trying to pry information about of her tight little mouth, with a comma.) Take a look at the following two examples for comparison.

What did Lola say at the meeting? Not much.

Lola stated, "I have no comment on the bedbug incident."

Lola made a short statement, which a speaker tag *(Lola stated)* and a comma introduce.

What did Ethelred say at the press conference? Too much.

> Ethelred explained: "The media has been entirely too critical of my preparations for war. Despite the fact that I have spent the last ten years and two million gold coins perfecting new and improved armor, I have been told that I am unready to fight."

Ethelred made a long statement, which a speaker tag *(Ethelred explained)* and a colon precede.

When you write a term paper or an essay, you may put some short quotations (up to three lines) into the text. However, you shouldn't place quotations that are longer than three lines in the text. Instead, you should double-indent and single-space the quoted material so that it looks like a separate block of print. Such quotations are called *block quotations*. Introduce the blocked quotation with a colon, and don't use quotation marks. (The blocking shows that you're quoting, so you don't need the marks.) Here's an example:

Flugle, in his essay entitled, "Why Homework is Useless," makes the following point:

> Studies show that students who have no time to rest are not as efficient as those who do. When a thousand teens were surveyed, they all indicated that sleeping, listening to music, talking on the phone, and watching television were more valuable than schoolwork.

If you're writing about poetry, you may use the same block format:

> The post-modern imagery of this stanza is in stark contrast to the imagery of the Romantic period:
>
> Roses are red,
> Violets are blue,
> Eggworthy is sweet,
> And stupid, too.

Joining explanations

Colons sometimes show up inside sentences, joining one complete sentence to another. Usually joining words such as *and, but,* and so on glue one sentence to another, or a semicolon does the job. (See "Gluing Complete Thoughts: Semicolons," earlier in this chapter.) But in one special circumstance, a colon may take over.

When the second sentence explains the meaning of the first sentence, you may join them with a colon.

> Smellyhead has only one problem: His new wig fell in a vat of perfume.

Notice that I've capitalized the first word after the colon. Some writers prefer lower case for that spot. This decision is a matter of style, not grammar. Check with the authority figure in charge of your writing (teacher, boss, warden, and so on) for the officially approved style.

Notice that the first sentence tells you that Smellyhead has a problem. The second sentence tells you the problem. Here's one more example:

> Lola has refused to take the job: She believes the media will investigate every aspect of her life.

The second half of the sentence explains why Lola doesn't want to run for president. Actually, it explains why almost no Americans want to run for president.

Which sentence is correct?

A. Lochness's portrayal of the monster was panned by the critics, they called his disappearance into the murky water "melodramatic."

B. Lochness's portrayal of the monster was panned by the critics; they called his disappearance into the murky water "melodramatic."

C. Lochness's portrayal of the monster was panned by the critics: They called his disappearance into the murky water "melodramatic."

Answer: Both B and C are correct. Sentence A is a run-on sentence, with two complete thoughts joined only by a comma. Not allowed! Sentence B has a semicolon, and sentence C has a colon. Both are acceptable.

Giving Additional Information — Dashes

Dashes have two jobs. First job: They tell the reader that you've jumped tracks onto a new subject, just for a moment. Here are some examples:

> After we buy toenail clippers — the dinosaur in that exhibit could use a trim, you know — we'll stop at the doughnut shop.

Standing on one manicured claw, the dinosaur — I forgot to tell you that the Creature Company finally delivered him to the museum — is the star of the exhibit.

Oggle the Caveperson slinks in the background — painted in fluorescent orange by a curator who "wanted to liven the place up" — although everyone knows that dinosaurs and human beings never co-existed.

The information inside the dashes is off-topic. Take it out, and the sentence makes sense. The material inside the dashes relates to the information in the rest of the sentence, but it acts as an interruption to the main point that you're making.

Second job: The dash turns something general into something specific, or it introduces a definition. Check out the following examples:

I think I have everything I need for the first day of camp — bug spray, hair spray, sun block, and DVD player.

Everything I need is general; *bug spray, hair spray, sun block, and DVD player* is specific.

Goggle said that he would perform the *ugu-ug-ba* — the ritual unwrapping of the season's first piece of chewing gum.

The definition of *ugu-ug-ba* is *the ritual unwrapping of the season's first piece of chewing gum*.

Grammatically, you may use dashes for the two reasons I just explained. There are many more reasons *not* to use a dash:

- ✔ Don't use a dash to replace a period at the end of a sentence.
- ✔ Don't use a dash to indicate that someone is speaking.
- ✔ Don't use a dash to separate items in a list.
- ✔ Don't use a dash inside a word. (To divide a word, use a hyphen, which is a shorter line.)

Here are some examples:

WRONG: With infinite slowness he raised his hand — he lifted an arm and tore off the bandage — he stood up.

RIGHT: With infinite slowness he raised his hand. He lifted an arm and tore off the bandage. He stood up.

WHY IT'S RIGHT: The three complete thoughts are now expressed as three complete sentences.

WRONG: — I'm alive. I'm alive!

RIGHT: "I'm alive. I'm alive!"

WHY IT'S RIGHT: Quoted material should be placed inside quotation marks.

WRONG: When I grow up I'm going to become president — climb Mt. Everest — travel to Mars.

RIGHT: When I grow up I'm going to become president, climb Mt. Everest, and travel to Mars.

WHY IT'S RIGHT: Commas separate the items in the list, not dashes.

Try reading the paragraph about Zangfroid aloud.

> Zangfroid went to Ye Olde Doughnut Shoppe — he likes coconut twists — and plunked down five dollars — the cost of a dozen. The clerk — not a fan of doughnuts himself but working his way through journalism school — frowned. "Are you sure you want to eat those greasy globs — not that there's anything wrong with that — and raise your cholesterol level? Are you aware of the ingredients — oil, fat, a little more oil, and sugar?

Do you notice how choppy it sounds? Every time you hit a dash, your voice probably changes. It's almost as though you were interrupting yourself. (I don't know your friends, but if they're like mine, they do enough interrupting to take care of all of us. I don't have to add any interruptions of my own.)

Dashes are tempting because they flow easily out of your mind and onto the paper. They seem to be the ideal punctuation mark. Got a new idea? Dash it in. Need to explain something that's vague? Dash into a definition. Tired of those old, boring punctuation marks? Try the new, improved dash!

Dashes may be fun to write, but they're not fun to read. Used legally (according to the laws of grammar), dashes are fine. For a little change of pace dash a new idea into your sentence. Just don't dash in too often!

Is the following sentence legal or grounds for arrest by the grammar police?

> Smiling broadly and brushing his long ears with one paw, the rabbit — yes, there really is a rabbit — hurried down the rabbit hole.

Answer: Legal. This sentence makes sense without the information inside the dashes. The information inside the dashes is a change of topic, but not a completely unrelated idea.

Here's another. Is this sentence legal or grounds for arrest by the grammar police?

> The sweet sounds of a thousand tubas wafted through the air — she fell asleep.

Answer: If you said legal, you get five to ten in the punctuation penitentiary. You need a period after *air* because *The sweet sounds of a thousand tubas wafted through the air* is a complete sentence. *She fell asleep* is also a complete sentence. You may not connect two complete sentences with a dash. The correct sentence reads

> The sweet sounds of a thousand tubas wafted through the air. She fell asleep.

Chapter 16

CAPITAL LETTERS

● ●

In This Chapter

▶ Referring to titles of people, family members, and the Deity

▶ Giving directions and naming areas of the country, seasons of the year, and other times

▶ Capitalizing school courses and subjects and the titles of creative works

▶ Writing eras, events, and abbreviations

▶ Capitalizing lines of poetry

● ●

*F*ortunately, the rules for capital letters are easy. Here are the basics:

✔ Begin every sentence with a capital letter. (See Chapter 5.)

✔ Capitalize *I*. (See Chapter 10.)

✔ Begin quotations with a capital letter, unless you're jumping to the middle of a quotation. (See Chapter 13.)

The rest of this chapter covers a few of the stickier points about capitalization.

Capitalizing (or Not) References to People

If human beings were content to be called only by their names, life would be much simpler, at least in terms of capital letters. Unfortunately, most people pick up a few titles as they journey through life. Even more unfortunately, along with the titles come rules for capitalization. In this section I tell you what's up (*up* as in *upper case,* or capital letters) when you refer to people.

Addressing Chief Dogcatcher and other officials

Allow me to introduce myself. I'm *Ms.* Woods, *Chief Grammarian* Woods, and *Apostrophe-Hater-in-Chief* Woods (see Chapter 12). Notice the capitals? All these titles start with what kindergarten kids call "the big letters" because they're attached to the front of my name. In a sense, they've become part of my name.

Allow me to introduce my friend Eggworthy. He's *Mr.* Eggworthy Henhuff, *director of poultry* at a nearby farm. Next year *Director of Poultry* Henhuff plans to run for *state senator,* unless the vegetarian-voting block opposes his candidacy. Eggworthy may then settle for a nomination to the office of *sheriff.*

Now what's going on with the capitals? The title *Mr.* is capitalized because it's attached to Eggworthy's last name. Other titles — *state senator* and *sheriff* — are not. In general, write titles that aren't connected to a name in *lower case,* or what the kindergarten kids call "small letters."

Notice that *Director of Poultry* is capitalized when it precedes Eggworthy's last name but not capitalized when it follows Eggworthy's name. *Director of Poultry Henhuff* functions as a unit. If you were talking to Eggworthy, you might address him as *Director of Poultry Henhuff.* So the first *Director of Poultry* in the paragraph above functions as part of the name. When the title follows the name, it gives the reader more information about Eggworthy, but it no longer acts as part of Eggworthy's name. Hence, the second *director of poultry* in the paragraph above is in lower case.

No self-respecting rule allows itself be taken for granted, so this capitalization rule has an exception or two, just to make sure that you're paying attention. You must capitalize very important titles even when they appear without the name of the person who holds them. What's very important? Definitely these:

- ✔ President of the United States
- ✔ Secretary-General of the United Nations
- ✔ Chief Justice of the Supreme Court
- ✔ Vice President of the United States
- ✔ Prime Minister of Great Britain

Here's an example of one of these titles, President of the United States, in action:

> The President of the United States addressed the nation tonight. In her address, the President called for the repeal of all illogical grammar rules.

Of course, there's some leeway with the rule on titles, with the boss or editor or teacher making the final decision. (When in doubt, check with the authority in question.) The following titles are often but not always lower case when they appear without a name:

- ✔ senator
- ✔ representative
- ✔ ambassador
- ✔ consul
- ✔ justice
- ✔ cabinet secretary
- ✔ judge
- ✔ sheriff

Nameless titles that are even lower on the importance ladder are strictly lower case:

- ✔ assistant secretary
- ✔ dogcatcher-in-chief
- ✔ officer
- ✔ ensign

When capitalizing a hyphenated title, capitalize both words (*Chief* Justice) or neither (*assistant secretary*). One exception (sigh) to the rule is for *exes* and *elects:*

- ✔ ex-President
- ✔ President-elect

Writing about family relationships

It's not true that Legghorn's *grandma* was imprisoned for felonious vocabulary. I know for a fact that *Uncle Bart* took the rap, although Legghorn's *brother* Alfred tried desperately to convince *Grandma* to make a full confession. "My *son* deserves to do the time," said *Grandma*, "because he split an infinitive when he was little and got away with it."

What do you notice about the family titles in the preceding paragraph? Some of them are capitalized, and some are not. The rules for capitalizing the titles of family members are simple. If you're labeling a relative, don't capitalize.

(I'm talking about kinship — aunt, sister, son, and so on — not appearance or personality flaws — tubby, sweet-face, dishonest, and so on.) If the titles take the place of names (as in *Uncle Bart*), capitalize them. For example:

> Lulu's *stepsister* Sarah took care to pour exactly one cup of ink into every load of wash that Lulu did. (*stepsister* = label, not a name in this sentence)

> Sarah's motivation was clear when she told *Mother* about the gallon of paint thinner that Lulu had tipped over Sarah's favorite rose bush. (*Mother* = name, not a label in this sentence)

> I was surprised when my *father* took no action; fortunately *Aunt Aggie* stepped in with a pail of bleach for Lulu. (*father* — label; *Aunt Aggie* — name in this sentence)

If you can substitute a real name — Mabel or Jonas, for example — in the sentence, you probably need a capital letter:

> I told *Father* that he needed to shave off his handlebar moustache and put it on his bicycle. (original sentence)

> I told *Jonas* that he needed to shave off his handlebar moustache and put it on his bicycle. (The substitution sounds fine, so capitalize *Father*.)

If the substitution sounds strange, you probably need lower case:

> I told my *grandmother* that she should definitely not shave off her moustache for any reason. (original sentence)

> I told my *Mabel* that she should definitely not shave off her moustache for any reason. (The substitution doesn't work because you don't say *my Mabel*. Use lower case for *grandmother*.)

The word *my* and other possessive pronouns *(your, his, her, our, their)* often indicate that you should lowercase the title. (For more information on possessive pronouns, see Chapter 17.)

Which sentence is correct?

A. Ever since he heard that housework causes acute inflammation of elbow grease, Archie helps mother around the house as little as possible.

B. Ever since he heard that housework causes acute inflammation of elbow grease, Archie helps Mother around the house as little as possible.

Answer: Sentence B is correct. *Mother* is used as a name, not a label, so you must capitalize it. (Try the *Mabel* test; it works!)

Capitalizing the Deity

Okay, technically a divine being isn't a *person* per se, but words referring to God still require a special capitalization rule. Traditionally, believers capitalize all words that refer to the being they worship, including pronouns. Look at this line from a famous hymn:

> *God* works in mysterious ways *His* wonders to perform.

On the other hand, you capitalize mythological gods only when giving their names:

> The Greeks offered tributes of wine to their *gods,* but the most lasting tribute is the collection of stories immortalizing their names. Who is not familiar with the stories of *Zeus, Hermes, Hera,* and other deities?

Capitalizing Geography: Directions, Places, and Languages

If you are a world traveler, you deal with capitalization and geography every day. But even if nothing more than your imagination leaves the living room, you still need to know the rules for capitalizing the names of places, languages, geographical features, regions, and directions. Here's a complete guide to capitalizing geography.

Directions and areas of a country

Alice and Archie, my parakeets, don't migrate for the winter. (Instead, they sit on the window frame and squawk at their friends, the pigeons of New York.) If they did fly away, though, where would they go — south or South? It depends. The *direction* of flight is south (lower case). The *area of the country* where they work on a tan, grow a few new feathers, and generally enjoy themselves is the South (upper case). Got it? From New York City you drive west to visit the West (or the Midwest).

The names of other, smaller areas are often capitalized too. Plopped in the center of New York City is Central Park, which the West Side and the East Side flank. Chicago has a South Side and London has Bloomsbury. Note the capital letters for areas of the city.

Capitalizing geographic features

Capitalize locations within a country when the proper name is given (the name of a city or region, for example). Be sure to capitalize the entire name. Here are some examples:

- ✔ Mississippi River
- ✔ the Pyrenees
- ✔ Los Angeles
- ✔ the Congo

Is *the* part of the name? Usually not, even when it's hard to imagine the name without it. In general, don't capitalize *the*.

When the name doesn't appear, lowercase geographical features:

- ✔ mountain
- ✔ valley
- ✔ gorge
- ✔ beach

An exception to the rule on country names

In general, you should capitalize the names of countries and languages. One exception to this rule: A few countries have kindly lent their names to common objects: *french fries, scotch whiskey, venetian blinds,* and so forth. By attaching itself to a common object, the language or country name takes on a new meaning. The name no longer makes the reader think of the country or language. Instead, the reader simply thinks of an everyday object. In situations such as this, the country or language name loses its capital letter. For example:

> The people of France speak French, but they eat *french fries.* (The expression *french fries* refers to common objects, associated more with fast food outlets than with the country of France.)

> I love *French* food. (Now *French* refers to the country, not to a common object.)

> The people of China have probably never heard of *chinese checkers.* (The expression *chinese checkers* refers to a game, not to the country of China.)

> I love *Chinese* food. (Now *Chinese* refers to the country.)

> Do Turks dry themselves with *turkish towels?* (The expression *turkish towels* refers to household items, not to the country of Turkey.)

If you're not sure whether or not to capitalize the geographical part of a common item, use a capital letter.

Correct the capitalization in this paragraph.

> When Alex sent his little brother Abner to Italy, Abner vowed to visit mount Vesuvius. Alex asked Abner to bring back some venetian blinds, but Abner returned empty-handed. "Let's go out for chinese food," said Abner when he returned. "Some sesame noodles will cheer me up."

Here is the answer, with explanations in parentheses:

> When Alex sent his little brother Abner to Italy (correct — country name), Abner vowed to visit Mount Vesuvius (capitalize the entire name of the mountain). Alex asked Abner to bring back some venetian blinds (correct — lower case for the name of a common object), but Abner returned empty-handed. "Let's go out for Chinese food (because this isn't the name of one specific item, such as french fries, capitals are better)," said Abner when he returned. "Some sesame noodles will cheer me up."

Tackling race and ethnicity

If you come from Tasmania, you're Tasmanian. If you come from New York, you're a New Yorker. (Don't ask me about Connecticut; I've never been able to get an answer, though I've asked everyone I know from that state.)

Those examples of capitalization are easy. But what about race and ethnicity? As the names change, so do the grammar books. But grammar authorities are always a little behind on this topic. Like everyone else, grammarians struggle to overcome the legacy of a racist society and its language. Here are some guidelines concerning capitalization and race:

- ✔ White and Black (or white and black) are acceptable, but be consistent. Don't capitalize one and not the other. Always capitalize *Asian* because the term is derived from the name of a continent.

- ✔ European American, Asian American, African American (and the less popular Afro-American) are all in capitals.

- ✔ Mexican American, Polish American, and other descriptions of national origin are written with capital letters because the terms are derived from country names.

- ✔ To hyphenate or not to hyphenate, that is the question. *Afro-American* is generally written with a hyphen. As for terms such as Asian American, Mexican American, African American, and the like, the answer depends on your politics. Without the hyphen, *American* is the primary word, described by the word that precedes it. So without the hyphen, you emphasize the identity of *American*. With the hyphen, both words are equal, so both parts of the identity have equal importance.

Marking Seasons and Other Times

Lochness hates the *summer* because of all the tourists who try to snap pictures of what he calls "an imaginary monster." He's been known to roar something about *"winter's* peaceful *mornings,"* even though he never wakes up before *3 p.m.*

After reading the preceding example, you can probably figure out this rule without me. Write the seasons of the year in lower case, as well as the times of day. The only exception is in poetry, but everyone knows that poets make up their own rules, so those exceptions don't count.

I have good news and bad news about the abbreviations for morning and afternoon — a.m. and p.m. Some books tell you to capitalize them (A.M. and P.M.) and some specify lower case. So no matter what you do, half your readers will think you're right (the good news) and half will think you're wrong (the bad news). By the way, a.m. stands for *ante meridian* (when the sun hasn't yet reached its highest point). The other term — p.m. — stands for *post meridian,* when the sun has passed its highest point in the sky.

The abbreviations for a.m. and p.m. come from Latin, in which *ante* and *post* mean *before* and *after.*

Schooling: Courses, Years, and Subjects

As every student knows, school is complicated. So is the rule concerning the capitalization of school-related terms. Don't capitalize subjects and subject areas unless the names refer to a language. Check out these examples:

- history
- science
- physics
- mathematics
- English
- Spanish
- physical education
- economics

On the other hand, capitalize the titles of courses. Here are some examples:

- ✔ Economics 101
- ✔ Math for Poets
- ✔ Intermediate Chemistry
- ✔ Physics for Nuclear Terrorists
- ✔ Spanish Translation and You!
- ✔ The Meaning of the Paper Clip in American History

The years in school, while interminable and incredibly important, are not capitalized.

- ✔ seventh grader
- ✔ eighth grader
- ✔ freshman
- ✔ sophomore
- ✔ junior
- ✔ senior

Correct the capitalization in this paragraph.

> Hurrying to his Chemistry class, Kneejerk slipped on the ice on the very first day of his Senior year. He was carrying a small jar of purple crystals, which, when added to water, were guaranteed to produce dense, purple smoke. Kneejerk wanted to impress the love of his life, Freshman Lilac Jones, who had enrolled in history of the ancient world with Professor Krater. Lilac's class, deep in the study of history, never knew the peril they had escaped.

Answer: Here's the correct version, with the reasons in parentheses:

> Hurrying to his chemistry (don't capitalize subjects) class, Kneejerk slipped on the ice on the very first day of his senior year (never capitalize years in school). He was carrying a small jar of purple crystals, which, when added to water, were guaranteed to produce dense, purple smoke. Kneejerk wanted to impress the love of his life, freshman (never capitalize years in school) Lilac Jones, who had enrolled in History of the Ancient World (capitalize course titles) with Professor Krater. Lilac's class, deep in the study of history (this one is correct — lower case for subject areas), never knew the peril they had escaped.

Writing Capitals in Book and Other Titles

Lochness is hosting a book party to celebrate the publication of his new book, *I AM NOT A MONSTER*. He has postponed the party three times because he can't decide how to capitalize the title. What should he do?

Actually, he should scrap the book, which consists of 540 pages of unbelievably boring detail about his humdrum life. Apart from that issue, here's what Lochness should do:

- ✔ Capitalize *I* and *Monster*. *I* is always upper case and *Monster* is an important word. Also, *I* is the first word of the title, and the first word of the title is always capitalized.

- ✔ Capitalize *Am* because it's a verb, and verbs are at the heart of the title's meaning. (See Chapter 2.)

- ✔ Capitalize *Not* because it changes the meaning of the verb and thus has an important job to do in the sentence.

- ✔ Lowercase the only word left — a. Never capitalize articles (a, an, and the) unless they're the first words in the title.

Do you see the general principles that I've applied? Here is a summary of the rules for all sorts of titles:

- ✔ Capitalize the first word in the title.

- ✔ Capitalize verbs and other important words.

- ✔ Lowercase unimportant words.

The problem, of course, is deciding what is important and what is unimportant. Authorities vary. (See the sidebar on manuals of style at the end of this chapter.) In the following list, I summarize the general principles for deciding what's important and unimportant (for words that aren't at the beginning of the title):

- ✔ Lowercase articles *(a, an, the)*.

- ✔ Lowercase conjunctions, the connecting words *(and, or, but, nor, for)*.

- ✔ In general, lowercase prepositions. Some style manuals say that you should capitalize long prepositions — those with more than four letters. Others tell you to lowercase all prepositions, even the huge ones *(concerning, according to,* and so on). See Chapter 9 for a list of common prepositions.

Bottom line: Check with your immediate authority (editor, boss, teacher, and so on) to make sure that you write in the style to which he or she is accustomed.

When writing the title of a magazine or newspaper, should you capitalize the word *the?* Yes, if *the* is part of the official name, as in *The New York Times.* No, if the publication doesn't include *the* in its official name, as in the *Daily News.*

Which words should you capitalize in these titles?

the importance of being lochness

romeo and lulu

slouching towards homework

Answers:

The Importance of Being Lochness (*The* is the first word of the title. *Importance, Being,* and *Lochness* are important words. Lowercase *of* because it's not an important word.)

Romeo and Lulu (*Romeo* is the first word of the title and is also a name. Similarly, *Lulu* is a name. Lowercase *and* because it's not an important word.)

Slouching Towards Homework (*Slouching* is the first word of the title. *Homework* is important. *Towards* can go either way. It's a preposition — a relationship word — and thus may be lower case, at least according to some grammarians. It's also a long word, which makes it suitable for capitalization in the opinion of other grammarians.)

Concerning Historic Capitals: Events and Eras

Bobo entered her time machine and set the dial for the *Middle Ages.* Because of a tiny glitch in the power supply, Bobo instead ended up right in the middle of the *Industrial Revolution.* Fortunately for Bobo, the *Industrial Revolution* did not involve a real *war.* Bobo still shudders when she remembers her brief stint in the *Civil War.* She is simply not cut out to be a fighter, especially not a fighter in the *nineteenth century.* On the next *Fourth of July,* Bobo plans to fly the bullet-ridden flag she brought back from the *Battle of Gettysburg.*

The story of Bobo's adventures should make the rules concerning the capitalization of historic events and eras easy. Capitalize the names of specific time periods and events but not general words. Hence

✔ Capitalized: Middle Ages, Industrial Revolution, Civil War, Fourth of July, Battle of Gettysburg

✔ Lowercase: war, nineteenth century

Some grammarians capitalize *Nineteenth Century* because they see it as a specific time period. Others say that you should lowercase numbered centuries. I prefer to lowercase the century.

Correct the capitalization in this paragraph.

> Bobo has never met Marie Antoinette, but Bobo is quite interested in the French revolution. With her trusty time-travel machine, Bobo tried to arrive in the Eighteenth Century, just in time for Bastille Day. However, once again she missed her target and landed in the middle of the first crusade.

Answer, with explanations in parentheses:

> Bobo has never met Marie Antoinette, but Bobo is quite interested in the French Revolution. (Capitalize the name of a war.) With her trusty time-travel machine, Bobo tried to arrive in the eighteenth century, (Optional, but most grammarians write numbered centuries in lower case.) just in time for Bastille Day. (Correct. Capitalize the names of important days.) However, once again she missed her target and landed in the middle of the First Crusade. (Capitalize the name of the war.)

If U Cn Rd Ths, U Cn Abbreviate

Faster! Faster! You're falling behind! Does that message sound familiar? Or am I the only one who sees life as an out-of-control train? I suspect that everyone occasionally feels the need to speed things up — when listening to a lecture on the joys of grammar, for example.

I can't cite a historical source, but I suspect that abbreviations stem from the need to get-it-over-with-quickly. Why spend eleven letters when two will do the job? Why write *New York City* when you can write *N.Y.C.?*

Why? Well, for several reasons. First of all, you want people to understand you. The first time you saw *e.g.,* did you know that it meant *for example?* If so, fine. If not, you probably didn't understand what the author was trying to say. Second, abbreviations clash with formal writing. Formal writing implies thought and care, not haste.

Now that you know why you shouldn't abbreviate, here's how to do so correctly:

✔ Capitalize abbreviations for titles and end the abbreviation with a period. For example, *Mrs.* Snodgrass, *Rev.* Tawkalot, *Sen.* Veto, Jeremiah Jones, *Jr.,* and *St.* Lucy.

✔ In Britain, omitting the period after *Mr, Mrs,* and *Ms* is acceptable.

✔ Capitalize geographic abbreviations when they're part of a name but not when they're alone. Put a period at the end of the abbreviation: Appalachian Mts. or Amazon R., for example. On a map you may write mt. (mountain).

✔ The United States Postal Service has devised a list of two-letter state abbreviations. Don't put periods in these abbreviations. Examples: *AZ* (Arizona), *CO* (Colorado), *WY* (Wyoming), and so on.

✔ Write measurements in lower case and end the abbreviation with a period. (Metric abbreviations are sometimes written without periods.) For example:

- yds. (yards)
- ft. (foot or feet)
- lbs. (pounds)
- km (kilometer)
- cm (centimeter)
- g (gram)

Don't confuse abbreviations with acronyms. Abbreviations generally chop some letters out of a single word. Acronyms are new words made from the first letters of each word in a multi-word title. Some common acronyms include the following:

NATO: North Atlantic Treaty Organization

OPEC: Organization of Petroleum Exporting Countries

AIDS: Acquired Immune Deficiency Syndrome

You generally write abbreviations with periods, but acronyms without periods.

Want to drive your teacher crazy? Write a formal essay with &, w/, w/o, or b/c. (For the abbreviation-deprived, & means *and,* w/ means *with,* w/o means *without,* b/c means *because.*) These symbols are fine for your notes but not for your finished product.

Correct Legghorn's homework.

Yesterday (Tues.) I went in the a.m. to CO. I saw Mr. Pimple, who told me that the EPA had outlawed his favorite pesticide. I have three gal. in the basement, & I'll have to discard it.

Answer:

(Tuesday) I went in the morning to Colorado. I saw Mr. Pimple, who told me that the EPA had outlawed his favorite pesticide. I have three gallons in the basement, and I'll have to discard it.

Explanation: Don't abbreviate in homework assignments except for titles (Mr. Pimple) and easily understood acronyms (EPA, or Environmental Protection Agency). If this had been a note to a friend, however, the abbreviations would have been perfectly acceptable.

Giving the Last Word to the Poet

One summer's morn

Upon the lawn

Did Legghorn cry,

"Forlorn! Forlorn

Am I and so shall sigh

Until I die. Goodbye."

One of the advantages of poetry is that you can usually convince people that your grammar mistakes are artistic choices. (Try it on your teacher, but no guarantees.) But poetry does have a system of rules for capital letters:

✔ In formal poems you usually capitalize the first word of each line.

✔ Regardless of where you are in the line, begin a new sentence with a capital letter.

✔ In quoting poetry, capitalize everything the poet capitalized. Put a slash to show where a line ends.

What this year's comma is wearing: Manuals of style

Not quite as exciting as a designer's collection are fashions in grammar. Yes, fashions. A comma here, a comma there. A period on one side of the Atlantic but not on the other. Capital letters for the abbreviation of a few centuries and then lowercase.

In this whirl of changing grammar rules, how can conscientious writers be sure that they're in style? Easy. Just check a manual. Many institutions publish manuals of style; each manual lists the institution's preferences for punctuation, capitalization, citation, and a whole other list of -*ations* that you've never heard of. All you have to do is check the index to find the answer to your grammatical dilemma. (You'd have to be institutionalized if you sat down and read the whole thing. *Boring* doesn't even begin to describe them, but they are good for reference.)

Your teacher/boss/editor (whoever's judging your writing) will be able to tell you which manual of style he or she prefers. Then you know that your work will be in fashion, or at least in the fashion that your particular authority figure likes.

A few popular manuals of style are the Modern Language Association (MLA) Handbook for Writers of Research Papers (Modern Language Association of America), The Chicago Manual of Style (The University of Chicago Press), and The New York Times Manual of Style and Usage (Crown).

Part IV

Polishing Without Wax — The Finer Points of Grammar

The 5th Wave   By Rich Tennant

"Okay people, remember — when writing your extortion letters, place the pronoun close enough to its antecedent to ensure clarity."

In this part . . .

Think of this part of the book as sandpaper — a set of scratchy, annoying rules that rub the rough edges off of your writing. After you polish a paragraph according to the information in this part, the finished product will have the correct pronouns (Chapter 17), the appropriate verb tense (Chapter 18), and no misplaced descriptions (Chapter 19). All of your comparisons will be logical and complete (Chapter 20), and none of your sentences will be unbalanced (Chapter 21). For the finer points of grammar, read on.

Chapter 17

Pronouns and Their Cases

Edgar Rice Burroughs' famous character Tarzan is a smart fellow. Not only can he survive in the natural world, but he also teaches himself a fair-sized English vocabulary, saves his beloved Jane from quicksand, and — when he travels to England — learns how to tie his shoelaces. Despite all these accomplishments, one task trips him up. He never seems to grasp pronoun-verb pairs. "Me Tarzan, you Jane," he says over and over. "I am Tarzan" is apparently beyond him.

Millions of suffering grammar students know exactly how Tarzan feels. Choosing the correct pronoun is enough to give even a thirteen-year-old a few gray hairs. (I have a whole section on my head from the *who/whom* issue.) But there's actually a logic to pronouns, and a few tips go a long way toward making your choices more obvious. In this chapter I cover the three sets, or cases, of pronouns — subject, object, and possessive. So grab a vine and swing into the jungle of pronouns.

Me Like Tarzan: Choosing Subject Pronouns

The subject is the person or thing that is talked about in the sentence. (For more on locating the subject, see Chapter 4.) You can't do much wrong when you have the actual name of a person, place, or thing as the subject — in other words, a noun — but pronouns are another story.

A subject pronoun is said to be in the *nominative case.*

Legal subject pronouns include *I, you, he, she, it, we, they, who,* and *whoever.* If you want to avoid a grammatical felony, stay away from *me, him, her, us, them, whom,* and *whomever* when you're selecting a subject.

Here are some examples of pronouns as the subject of a sentence:

> *I* certainly did tell Lulu not to remove her nose ring in public! (*I* is the subject of the verb *did tell.*)

> Agwamp and *she* will bring the killer bees to the next Unusual Pets meeting. (*She* is the subject of the verb *will bring.*)

> *Whoever* marries Ludwig next should negotiate a good prenuptial agreement. (*Whoever* is the subject of the verb *marries.*)

Compounding interest: Pairs of subjects

Most people do okay with one subject, but sentences with two subjects are a different story. For example, I often hear my otherwise grammatically correct students say such things as

> *Him* and *me* are going to the supermarket for some chips.

> Although *her* and *I* haven't met, we plan to have dinner soon.

See the problem? In the first sample sentence, the verb *are going* expresses the action. To find the subject, ask *who* or *what are going.* The answer right now is *him and me are going,* but *him* and *me* aren't subject pronouns. Here's the correct version:

> *He* and *I* are going to the supermarket for some carrots and celery. (I couldn't resist correcting the nutritional content too.)

In the second sample sentence, the action — the verb — is *have met.* (*Not* isn't part of the verb.) *Who* or *what have met?* The answer, as it is now, is *her* and *I. I* is a legal subject pronoun, but *her* is not. The correct version is as follows:

> Although *she* and *I* haven't met, we plan to have dinner soon.

Pairs or even larger groups of subjects are called *compound subjects.* Each of the preceding sample sentences includes a compound subject.

One good way to check your pronouns is to look at each one separately. If you've developed a fairly good ear for proper English, isolating the pronoun helps you decide whether you've chosen correctly. You may have to adjust the verb a bit when you're speaking about one subject instead of two, but the principle is the same. If the pronoun doesn't sound right as a solo subject, it isn't right as part of a pair either. Here is an example:

> ORIGINAL SENTENCE: *Ludmilla* and *her* went to the spitball-shooting contest yesterday.

> CHECK 1: *Ludmilla* went to the spitball-shooting contest yesterday. Verdict: sounds okay.

> CHECK 2: *Her* went to the spitball-shooting contest yesterday. Verdict: sounds terrible. Substitute *she.*

> CHECK 3: *She* went to the spitball-shooting contest yesterday. Verdict: much better.

> RECOMBINED, CORRECTED SENTENCE: *Ludmilla* and *she* went to the spitball-throwing contest yesterday.

Which sentence is correct?

A. Mudbud, you, and me appointed the judges for the spitball-shooting contest, so we have to live with their decisions, however wrong.

B. Mudbud, you, and I appointed the judges for the spitball-shooting contest, so we have to live with their decisions, however wrong.

Answer: Sentence B is correct. *I* is a subject pronoun, and *me* is not. If you take the parts of the subject separately, you can hear the correct answer.

Attracting appositives

Do you want to say the same thing twice? Use an appositive. An *appositive* is a noun or a pronoun that is exactly the same as the noun or pronoun that precedes it in the sentence. Check out these examples:

> Raven, the girl whose hair matches her name, is thinking of changing her name to Goldie.

> Tee Rex, holder of the coveted Dinosaur of the Year trophy, has signed an endorsement deal with a company that makes extra-large sneakers.

> Lochness, the Spy of the Month, will hold a press conference tomorrow at 10 a.m.

> Lola, a fan of motorcycles, acknowledges that life in the fast lane is sometimes hard on the complexion.

Do you see the pair of matching ideas in each sentence? In the first, *Raven* and *the girl whose hair matches her name* are the same. In the next sentence, *Tee Rex* and *holder of the coveted Dinosaur of the Year trophy* make a pair. In the third, *the Spy of the Month* is the same as *Lochness*. In the last sentence, *Lola* and *a fan of motorcycles* are the same. The second half of each pair *(the girl whose hair matches her name, holder of the coveted Dinosaur of the Year trophy, the Spy of the Month,* and *a fan of motorcycles)* is an appositive.

Appositives fall naturally into most people's speech and writing, perhaps because human beings feel a great need to explain themselves. You probably won't make a mistake with an appositive unless a pronoun or a comma is involved. (See Chapter 25 for more information on appositives and commas.)

Pronouns can serve as appositives, and they show up mostly when you have two or more people or things to talk about. Here are some sentences with appositives and pronouns:

> The winners of the raffle — Ali and he — will appear on the *Tonight Show* tomorrow. (Appositive = *Ali* and *he*)

> The judges for the spitball contest, Saliviata and she, wear plastic rain-coats. (Appositive — *Saliviata* and *she*)

> The dancers who broke their toenails, Lulu and I, will not appear in the closing number. (Appositive = *Lulu* and *I*)

Why are *he, she* and *I* correct? In these sample sentences, the appositives are paired with the subjects of the sentence *(winners, judges, dancers).* In a sense, the appositives are potential substitutes for the subject. Therefore, you must use a subject pronoun.

The appositive pronoun must always match its partner; if you pair it with a subject, the appositive must be a subject pronoun. If you pair it with an object, it must be an object pronoun.

You can confirm pronoun choice with the same method that I describe in the previous section. Take each part of the pair (or group) separately. Adjust the verb if necessary, and then listen to the sentence. Here's the check for one of the sentences that I used earlier:

> CHECK 1: The judges for the spitball contest wear plastic raincoats. Verdict: sounds okay.

> CHECK 2: Saliviata wears plastic raincoats. (You have to adjust the verb because *Saliviata* is singular, not plural, but the pronoun sounds okay.)

> CHECK 3: She wears plastic raincoats. (Again, you have to adjust the verb, but the pronoun sounds okay.)

Bottom line: Isolate the pronoun and listen. If it sounds fine, it probably is.

Picking pronouns for comparisons

Lazy people that we are, we all tend to take shortcuts, chopping words out of our sentences and racing to the finish. This practice is evident in comparisons. Read the following sample sentences:

Lulu denied that she had more facial hair than he.

That sentence really means

Lulu denied that she had more facial hair than he had.

If you say the entire comparison, as in the preceding example, the pronoun choice is a cinch. However, when you drop the verb *(had),* you may be tempted to use the wrong pronoun, as in this sentence:

Lulu denied that she had more facial hair than him.

Sounds right, doesn't it? But the sentence is wrong. The words you say must fit with the words you don't say. Obviously you aren't going to accept

Lulu denied that she had more facial hair than him had.

Him had is just too gross. The technical reason? *Him* is an object pronoun, but you're using it as the subject of *had.*

Whenever you have an implied comparison — a comparison that the sentence suggests but doesn't state completely — finish the sentence in your head. The correct pronoun becomes obvious.

Implied comparisons often contain the word *than* (as in the preceding sample sentences). The words *so* and *as* are also frequently part of an implied comparison:

The sponges that Legghorn grew do not sop up so much moisture as they.

Eggworthy gave Ludwig as much trouble as her.

Ratrug, live in concert on Broadway, is as entertaining as she.

The complete comparisons are as follows:

The sponges that Legghorn grew do not sop up so much moisture as they do.

Eggworthy gave Ludwig as much trouble as Eggworthy gave her.

Ratrug, live in concert on Broadway, is as entertaining as she is.

In some incomplete comparisons more than one word is missing. For example:

> Grandmother gives my sister more souvenirs than me.

means

> Grandmother gives my sister more souvenirs than Grandmother gives to me, because my sister is a spoiled brat and is always flattering the old bat.

and

> Grandmother gives my sister more souvenirs than I.

means

> Grandmother gives my sister more souvenirs than I do because I have better things to do with my allowance.

Think before you make a decision, because the pronoun choice determines the meaning of the sentence.

Which sentence is correct?

   A. Tee Rex broke more claws than I during the fight with Godzilla.

   B. Tee Rex broke more claws than me during the fight with Godzilla.

Answer: Sentence A is correct. Read the sentence this way: Tee Rex broke more claws than *I did* during the fight with Godzilla. You can't say *me did*.

Last one! Which is correct?

   A. Lochness told me more atomic secrets than she.

   B. Lochness told me more atomic secrets than her.

Answer: Both are correct, depending on the situation. Sentence A means that Lochness told me more atomic secrets than *she told me*. Sentence B means that Lochness told me more atomic secrets than *he told her*.

Connecting pronouns to linking verbs

Think of linking verbs as giant equal signs, equating two halves of the sentence. All forms of the verb *to be* are linking verbs, as well as verbs such as *seem, appear, smell, sound,* and *taste.* The type of pronoun that begins the equation (the subject) must also be the type of pronoun that finishes the equation. (For more information on finding linking verbs and the pronouns that go with them, see Chapter 2.) In this section, I talk about pairs of subject pronouns with linking verbs. Looking at pairs of words is helpful because choosing pronouns for compound subjects is always hard. Check out this sentence:

> The new champions, who spelled "sassafras" correctly for the first and only time, are him and me.

Correct or incorrect? Here's how to check. Think of the equal sign (the linking verb). If the pronouns are correct, you should be able to reverse the sentence. After all, $2 + 2 = 4$ and $4 = 2 + 2$.

If I reverse the preceding sample sentence, I get

> Him and me are the new champions who spelled "sassafras" correctly for the first and only time.

Uh oh. *Him and me are*. Not a good idea. What would you really say? *He and I are*. So go back to the original sentence. Change the pronouns. Now the sentence reads

> The new champions, who spelled "sassafras" correctly for the first and only time, are he and I.

In conversation, many people ignore the *reversibility rule* and choose an object pronoun. In conversation you can get away with such a choice, but in formal writing the rules are tighter. If you have a linking verb followed by a pronoun, choose from the subject set.

Which sentence is correct?

A. The students voted "Most Likely to Go to Jail Before Graduation" are Lizzy and I.

B. The students voted "Most Likely to Go to Jail Before Graduation" are Lizzy and me.

Answer: In formal English, sentence A is correct. Reverse the sentence: *Lizzy and I are* the students voted "Most Likely to Go to Jail Before Graduation." Verdict: Fine. If you reverse sentence B, you get *Lizzy and me are*. This phrasing is not a good idea, though it is acceptable in conversational English. (See Chapter 1 for more information on formal and conversational English.)

Using Pronouns as Direct and Indirect Objects

Previously in this chapter, I've concentrated on subject pronouns, but now it's time to turn to the receiver of the sentence's action — the object. Specifically, it's time to turn to *object pronouns*. (For more information on finding the object, see Chapter 6.) Pronouns that may legally function as objects include *me, you, him, her, it, us, them, whom,* and *whomever.* Here are some examples of direct and indirect object pronouns, all in italics:

> Ticktock smashed *him* right on the nose for suggesting that "the mouse ran down the clock." (*smashed* is the verb; *Ticktock* is the subject; *him* is the object)

> Archie married *us,* despite our parents' objections, in a quadruple ring ceremony. (*married* is the verb; *Archie* is the subject; *us* is the object)

> Olivier, president and chief operating officer of Actors Inc., sent *me* a horrifying *letter.* (*sent* is the verb; *Olivier* is the subject; *letter* and *me* are objects)

A *direct object* receives the action directly from the verb, answering the questions *whom* or *what* after the verb. An *indirect object* receives the action indirectly (clever, those grammar terms), answering the questions *to whom* or *to what* after the verb. In the previous sample sentence, *letter* is the direct object and *me* is the indirect object. For more information on direct and indirect objects, see Chapter 6.

Which sentence is correct?

A. After a great deal of discussion, the principal punished we, the innocent, for the small nuclear device that disrupted the cafeteria yesterday.

B. After a great deal of discussion, the principal punished us, the innocent, for the small nuclear device that disrupted the cafeteria yesterday.

Answer: Sentence B is correct. *Us* is the object of the verb *punished.*

Choosing objects for prepositions

Prepositions — words that express relationships such as *about, after, among, by, for, behind, since,* and others — may also have objects. (For a more complete list of prepositions, see Chapter 9.) Here are some examples:

Pinkworm, fearful for his pet tarantula, gave his dog *to us* yesterday.

Jellibelle's dance solo is a problem *for her* because she can't find a suitable costume.

Legghorn's latest play received a critical review *from them*.

Archibald didn't like the window so he simply plastered *over it*.

Notice that the object word answers the usual object questions *(whom? what?)*:

Pinkworm, fearful for his pet tarantula, gave his dog to whom? Answer: to *us*.

Jellibelle's dance solo is a problem for whom? Answer: for *her*.

Legghorn's latest play received a critical review from whom? Answer: from *them*.

Archibald didn't like the window, so he simply plastered over what? Answer: over *it*.

Also notice that all the pronouns — *us, him, her, them, it* — come from the set of object pronouns.

Which sentence is correct?

A. The conversation between Agwamp and I always revolves around piano-throwing.

B. The conversation between Agwamp and me always revolves around piano-throwing.

Answer: Sentence B is correct. *Between* is a preposition. *Between* whom? *Between Agwamp and me*. *Me* is one of the objects of the preposition *between*.

For some reason, the phrase *between you and I* has caught on. However, it's time to unhook it! *Between* is a preposition, so object pronouns follow it. The pronoun *I* is for subjects, and *me* is for objects. So between you and me, *me* is the word you want.

Seeing double causes problems

You'll probably choose the correct object pronoun when there's only one in the sentence, but compounds (pairs or larger groups), cause problems. The solution is fairly easy: Check each part of the compound separately. Your ear helps you find the right choice. Here are some examples:

ORIGINAL SENTENCE: Paris, pleading poverty, presented Perry and me with a check for fifteen cents.

CHECK 1: Paris, pleading poverty, presented Perry with a check for fifteen cents. Verdict: The sentence sounds fine.

CHECK 2: Paris, pleading poverty, presented me with a check for fifteen cents. Verdict: The sentence sounds fine. When you isolate the pronoun, *me* is obviously the correct choice. You're unlikely to accept *Paris, pleading poverty, presented I with a check for fifteen cents.*

Try another one.

ORIGINAL SENTENCE: Perry, claiming to be far richer than Ted Turner, presented the government and he with a billion dollars.

CHECK 1: Perry, claiming to be far richer than Ted Turner, presented the government with a check for a billion dollars. Verdict: The sentence is fine.

CHECK 2: Perry, claiming to be far richer than Ted Turner, presented he with a check for a billion dollars. Verdict: *presented he?* Nope. The sentence doesn't work.

CHECK 3: Perry, claiming to be far richer than Ted Turner, presented him with a check for a billion dollars. Verdict: Now the sentence sounds right.

RECOMBINED SENTENCE: Perry, claiming to be far richer than Ted Turner, presented the government and him with a check for a billion dollars.

Pronouns of Possession: No Exorcist Needed

Possessive pronouns show (pause for a drum roll) possession. Not the movie head-twisting-backwards kind, but the kind where you own something. Possessive pronouns include *my, your, his, her, its, our, their, mine, yours, hers, ours, theirs,* and *whose.* Check out the following sample sentences:

Legghorn took *his* apple out of the refrigerator marked "Open Only in Case of Emergency."

Sure that the computer had beeped *its* last beep, Lola shopped for a new model.

To *our* dismay, Lochness and Lulu opened *their* birthday presents two days early.

Vengeance is *mine.*

Lester slapped the dancer *whose* stiletto heels had wounded Lola's big toe.

The possessive pronouns in these examples show that the apple belongs to Legghorn, the beep belongs to the computer, the dismay belongs to us, and the presents belong to Lochness and Lulu. Vengeance belongs to *me*. (*Mine* is the possessive pronoun that refers to something *I* own, something that belongs to *me*.) The last sentence is a little more complicated. The word *whose* refers to the *dancer*. The stiletto heels belong to the dancer. The big toe belongs to Lola, but possession is shown in this example with a possessive noun (*Lola's*) not a possessive pronoun (*her*).

Notice that none of the possessive pronouns have apostrophes. They never do! Ever! Never ever! Putting apostrophes into possessive pronouns is one of the most common errors. (*It's* doesn't mean *belongs to it. It's* means *it is*.)

Why don't possessive pronouns have apostrophes? I have no idea. Logically, you expect possessive pronouns to have apostrophes, because apostrophes show possession for nouns (*Angie's mug*, for example). But logic and grammar aren't always friends or even acquaintances, and (as you may have noticed) possessive pronouns don't have apostrophes. Ever.

Which sentence is correct?

A. Smashing the pumpkin on his mother's clean floor, Rocky commented, "I believe this gourd is yours."

B. Smashing the pumpkin on his mother's clean floor, Rocky commented, "I believe this gourd is your's."

Answer: Sentence A is correct. No possessive pronoun has an apostrophe, and *yours* is a possessive pronoun.

Dealing with Pronouns and "-Ing" Nouns

The rule concerning possessive pronouns and "-ing" nouns is broken so often that it may be a losing battle. However, the rule isn't completely useless, like many of the other rules that people break. Moreover, this rule is actually logical. Some nouns that end in *-ing* are created from verbs. (In grammarspeak, they're called gerunds. See Chapter 24 for more information.) When you put a pronoun in front of one of these nouns, you must be sure that the pronoun is possessive. Here are some examples:

> Just because I once got a speeding ticket, my parents object to *my taking* the car for even short drives. (not *me taking*)

> Lola knows that *their* creating a dress code has nothing to do with the fact that she recently pierced her toes. (not *them* creating)

Eggworthy likes *his* singing in the shower. (not *him* singing)

The goldfish accept *our* placing food in the tank so long as we don't try to shake their fins. (not *us placing*)

Why possessive? Here's the reasoning. If you put a possessive pronoun in front of the noun, the noun is the main idea, Therefore:

My parents object to the *taking* of the car. They don't object to *me*.

Lola knows something about the *creating* of a dress code. She may not know anything about *them*.

Eggworthy likes the *singing*. Eggworthy may not like *him*.

The goldfish accept *placing* food. They don't accept *us*.

Some *-ing* words weren't created from verbs, and some *-ing* words aren't nouns. Don't worry about distinguishing between one and the other. Just apply this simple test: You need a possessive if the meaning of the sentence changes radically when you drop the *-ing* word. Check out this example:

Lochness loves me singing and always invites me to perform at his concerts.

If I drop the *-ing* word, the sentence says

Lochness loves me.

Now there's a radical change of meaning. Clearly the sentence is incorrect. The correct version is

Lochness loves my singing.

Now the focus is on *singing,* not on *me*.

Which sentence is correct?

A. Stunned by my low batting average, the coach forbade my swinging at every pitch.

B. Stunned by my low batting average, the coach forbade me swinging at every pitch.

Answer: Sentence A is correct. The coach went on and on about *my swinging at every pitch* and never mentioned anything about my personal life. (In sentence B, he's forbidding *me,* all of me.)

Chapter 18

Fine-tuning Verbs

● ●

● ●

*H*ave you ever written a letter and then, after reading it, gone back and crossed out half the words? Do the verbs tie your tongue (well, actually, your pen) in knots. Are you constantly editing yourself to avoid verb problems. If so, this chapter is for you.

Giving Voice to Verbs

Verbs can have two voices. No, not soprano and tenor. Verbs can be either active or passive. Take a look at these two examples:

> "The window *was broken* yesterday," reported Eggworthy, carefully tucking his baseball bat under the sofa.

> "I *broke* the window yesterday," reported Eggworthy, carefully tucking his baseball bat under the sofa.

How do the two versions differ? Grammatically, Eggworthy's statement in version one focuses on the receiver of the action, the *window*, which received the action of *breaking*. The verb is *passive* because the subject is not the person or thing doing the action but instead the person or thing receiving the action. In version two the verb is in active voice because the subject *(I)* performed the action *(broke)*. When the subject is acting or being, the verb is *active*.

To find the subject of a sentence, locate the verb and ask who or what before the verb. For more information on subjects, see Chapter 4. For more information on the basics of verbs, see Chapter 2.

Here are some active and passive verbs:

> Lulu *gives* a free-tattoo coupon to Lola. (active)
>
> Lola *is convinced* by Lulu to get a tattoo. (passive)
>
> Lochness *slaps* Lulu. (active)
>
> Lulu *is tattooed* by Lola. (passive)

Making the Better Choice: Active Voice

Unless you're trying to hide something or unless you truly don't know the facts, you should make your writing as specific as possible. Specifics reside in active voice. Compare these pairs of sentences:

> The president of the Egg-Lovers' Club *was murdered* yesterday. (The cops are still looking for the villain who wielded the hammer and crushed the president's skull like a . . . well, like an eggshell.)
>
> Murgatroyd murdered the president of the Egg-Lovers' Club yesterday. (Murgatroyd is on the lam.)

> It *is recommended* that the furnace not be cleaned until next year. (Someone wants to save money, but no one is taking responsibility for this action. If the furnace breaks when the thermometer hits twenty below because too much glop is inside, no one's name comes up for blame.)
>
> The superintendent *recommends* that the furnace not be cleaned until next year. (Now the building's residents may storm the superintendent's office after they chip icicles off their noses.)

Do you notice how the active-verb sentences provide extra information? In the first pair of sample sentences, we know the name of the murderer. In the second pair, we know who recommends deferring maintenance of the furnace. Knowing (in life as well as in grammar) is usually better than not knowing, and active voice is usually better than passive voice.

Active voice is also better than passive because active voice uses fewer words to say the same thing. Compare the following sentences:

> Murdlock was failed by the teacher because the grammar book was torn up by Murdlock before it was ever opened. (20 words)
>
> The teacher failed Murdlock because Murdlock tore up the grammar book before opening it. (14 words)

Okay, six words don't make the difference between a 900-page novel and a three-page story, but those words do add up. If you're writing a letter or an essay, switching from passive to active voice may save you one-third of your words — and therefore one-third of the reader's energy and patience. Right about now you may be remembering a past homework assignment: the teacher asked for 500 words on Hamlet and you had only one teeny idea about the play. You may have thought that padding was a good idea! Wrong. Your teacher (or boss) can see that you've buried only one teeny idea in those piles of paragraphs. Besides losing points for knowing too little, you're likely to lose points for wasting the reader's time. The solution? Write in active voice and don't pad your writing.

Label the verbs in these sentences as active or passive.

A. The omelet was made with egg whites, but the yolks were discarded.

B. Eggworthy slobbers when he eats eggs.

Answer: Sentence A is passive *(was made, were discarded),* and sentence B is active *(slobbers, eats).*

Try one more. Which is active and which is passive?

A. The nail was hammered into that sign by Lochness.

B. Lochness is building a tank for his pet piranhas.

Answer: Sentence A is passive *(was hammered),* and sentence B is active *(is building).*

Putting It in Order: Sequence of Tenses

All verbs express information about three time periods: the present, the past, and the future. Unfortunately, human beings have a tendency to want more specific information about timing. Enter about a million shades of meaning, closely followed by about a million rules.

For information on the basic tenses of verbs, see Chapter 3. In this chapter I focus on some special cases — which verbs to use when more than one thing is happening.

To clarify what's happening when, timelines accompany some of the examples in this section. Match the events on the timeline to the verbs in the sentence to see where in time each tense places an action.

Case 1: Simultaneous events — main verbs

Look at the italicized verbs in each of these sample sentences:

Trueheart *swiped* a handkerchief and daintily *blew* her noise. (*swiped* and *blew* = two events happening at almost the same moment; both verbs are in past tense)

Trueheart *will be* in court tomorrow, and the judge *will rule* on her case. (*will be* and *will rule* = two events happening at the same time; both verbs are in future tense)

Trueheart *is* extremely sad about the possibility of a criminal record, but she *remains* hopeful. (*is* and *remains* = states of being existing at the same time; both verbs are in present tense)

If two actions take place at the same time (or nearly the same time), use the same tense for each verb.

Case 2: Simultaneous events — verbals

The verb doesn't express all the action in a sentence. Some verb forms don't act as the official verb in the sentence; in fact, they don't act as verbs at all, even though they give you some information about an event. These verb forms are called *verbals.* In the following sentences, check out the italicized words. The first is a verbal and the second is the main verb. Notice that the same verbal matches with present, past, and future verbs and places the two actions at the same time or close enough in time to make the difference irrelevant. Also notice that none of the verbals are formed with the words *have* or *had.* (*Have* and *had* help express actions taking place at different times. See Case #6 later in this section.)

Swiping a handkerchief, Trueheart daintily *blows* her nose. (The *swiping* and the *blowing* take place at nearly the same time — in the present.)

Swiping a handkerchief, Trueheart daintily *blew* her nose. (The *swiping* and the *blowing* took place at nearly the same time — in the past.)

Swiping a handkerchief, Trueheart *will* daintily *blow* her nose. (The *swiping* and the *blowing* will take place at nearly the same time — in the future.)

Another variation:

To blow her nose daintily, Trueheart swipes a handkerchief. (The *blowing* and the *swiping* take place at nearly the same time — in the present.)

To blow her nose daintily, Trueheart swiped a handkerchief. (The *blowing* and the *swiping* took place at nearly the same time — in the past.)

To blow her nose daintily, Trueheart will swipe a handkerchief. (The *blowing* and the *swiping* will take place at nearly the same time — in the future.)

Participles are verb forms that may act as adjectives. In the preceding sample sentences, *swiping* is a present participle, and *swiping a handkerchief* is a participial phrase describing *Trueheart.* The action expressed by the present participle takes place at the same time (or nearly the same time) as the action expressed by the main verb. For more information on participles, see Chapter 24. *To blow* is an infinitive, the basic form of a verb. Infinitives never function as verbs in the sentence. In the previous sample sentences, *to blow her noise daintily* is an infinitive phrase describing *Trueheart.* For more information on infinitives, see Chapter 2. For tips on using infinitives creatively, see Chapter 24.

Case 3: Events at two different times in the past

Everything in the past happened at exactly the same moment, right? Oh, if only this statement were true. History tests would be much easier, and so would grammar. Sadly, you often need to talk about events that took place at different times in the past. The verb tenses you use create an order of events — a timeline — for your reader. Check the italicized verbs in this sentence:

Trueheart *had* already *swiped* the handkerchief when she *discovered* the joys of honesty.

There are two events to think about, one taking place before the other. (Unfortunately for Trueheart, the joy of honesty came after the theft, for which she's doing ten to twenty in the penitentiary.) Note the timeline:

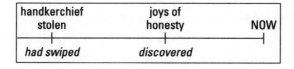

For two events in the past, write the earlier event with *had* and the more recent event in simple past tense (without *had*). For grammar-lovers only: Verbs written with *had* are in the past perfect tense. (See Chapter 3 for definitions of tenses.)

Check out these examples:

Because of Lulu's skill with a needle, where a hole in the sock *had gaped*, a perfect heel now *enclosed* her tender foot. (Event 1: the hole in the sock gapes; event 2: the mended sock covers the foot.)

When Lochness *had inserted* the microfilm, he *sewed* the hole in the now illegal teddy bear. (Event 1: Lochness inserts the microfilm; event 2: Lochness sews the bear.)

Though she *had lost* her wallet, Ludmilla *kept* a tight grip on her sanity. (Event 1: Ludmilla loses her wallet; Event 2: Ludmilla does not lose her mind.)

After the song *had* been *played* at least twelve times, Legghorn *shouted*, "Enough!" (Event 1: The song is played twelve times; event 2: Legghorn loses it.)

A common error is using *had* for everything. Wrong! Don't use *had* unless you're consciously putting events in order:

WRONG: Trueheart had dried her eyes, and then she had gone to see the judge.

RIGHT: After Trueheart had dried her eyes, she went to see the judge.

Also, sometimes you may want to talk about events in the past without worrying about specific times. You *went* on vacation, *had* a great time, *sent* some postcards, *ate* a lot of junk food, and *came* home. No need for *had* in this description because the order isn't the point. You're just making a general list. Use *had* when the timing matters. Don't overuse it.

Note: You may encounter one other use of *had*, the subjunctive. See Chapter 22 if you have to know absolutely everything about *had* — and believe me, you don't.

Which sentence tells you about events that happened at different times?

A. Slipping the judge a fifty-dollar bill, Trueheart hoped for mercy.

B. Although she had slipped the judge only one fifty-dollar bill, Trueheart hoped for mercy.

Answer: Sentence B reports events at different times. Trueheart tried the bribe at 10 a.m. and spent the rest of the day planning a trip to Rio (cancelled when her ten-to-twenty-year jail term was announced). In sentence A, Trueheart bribes and hopes at the same time.

One more question. Which sentence reports events happening at two different times?

A. To prepare for her trial, Trueheart bought a copy of *Be Your Own Lawyer!*

B. Trueheart had bought a copy of *Be Your Own Lawyer!* when the trial began.

Answer: Sentence B has two events, one earlier than the other. The purchase of the book *(had bought)* happened before the trial *(began)*. In sentence A, the two events *(to prepare, bought)* happen at the same time.

Case 4: More than two past events, all at different times

This rule is similar to the one described in Case 3. Apply this rule when you talk about more than two events in the past:

Trueheart *had baked* a cake and *had inserted* a sharp file under the icing before she *began* her stay in jail.

Now the timeline is as follows:

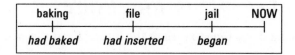

baking	file	jail	NOW
had baked	had inserted	began	

What do you notice? The most recent event *(began her stay in jail)* is written without *had*. In other words, the most recent event is in simple past tense. Everything that happened earlier is written with *had* — that is, in past perfect tense. For more information on tenses, see Chapter 3.

Here are some examples:

Murgatroyd *had bent* his knees and *had bowed* his head before he *shot* the spitball. (Events 1 and 2: Murgatroyd tries to look respectful. Event 3: Murgatroyd shoots the spitball, proving once and for all that he can't act respectfully.)

Legghorn *had planned* the shower, and Lola *had* even *planned* the wedding by the time Ludmilla *agreed* to marry Ludwig. (Events 1 and 2: Legghorn and Lola visit the wedding coordinator. Event 3: Ludmilla makes the biggest mistake of her life.)

Felonia *had composed* a sonata, *played* it for royalty, and *signed* a recording contract before she *reached* her tenth birthday. (Events 1, 2, and 3: Felonia writes the music, performs it, and makes big bucks. Event 4: Felonia's mom puts ten candles on the cake.)

In the last example three verbs — *composed, played,* and *signed* — form a list of the actions that Felonia performed before her tenth birthday. They all have the same subject *(Felonia)*. The word *had* precedes only *composed,* the first verb of the three. You may omit the word *had* in front of *played* and *signed* because they are part of the same list and they all have the same subject. The reader knows that the word *had* applies to all three of the verbs. In other words, the reader understands that *Felonia had composed, had played,* and *had signed.*

Identify the events in this sentence and put them in order.

Where patriots had fought and wise founders had written a constitution, a fast-food catfish restaurant stood.

Answer: Events 1 and 2: People with a better idea fight the old government and write a plan for a new government. Event 3: In the free and successful society that results, someone builds a restaurant after suing the landmarks preservation commission for the right to tear down a historic building.

Case 5: Two events in the future

Leaving the past behind, it's time to turn to the future. Read this sentence:

Ratrug *will have completed* all 433 college applications before they are due.

Ratrug's applications will be error-filled — he spelled his name *Ratrig* on at least three — but they will be done before the deadline. *Deadline* is the important word here, at least regarding verb tense. The *have* form of the future, also called *future perfect tense,* involves a deadline. You don't necessarily have two verbs in the sentence, but you do have two events:

Past		Future	applications
	NOW	Ratrug works on applications	due
		will have completed	*are*

Use the future perfect tense to talk about the earlier of the two events.

Here are a few examples:

Ms. Trueheart *will have served* all of her sentence before the parole board meets. (The deadline in the sentence is the parole board meeting.)

By nine tonight, Eggworthy *will have* successfully *scrambled* the secret message. (The deadline in the sentence is nine o'clock.)

Analivia *will have left* for Lulu's trip up Mount Everest by the time the mountaineering supply company sends her gear. (The deadline in the sentence is the delivery of mountain-climbing supplies.)

Which sentence is correct?

A. Shakey will have tossed the salad tonight.

B. Shakey will have tossed the salad out the window before anyone has a chance to taste it.

Answer: Sentence B is correct. Future perfect tense involves a deadline, which in this sentence is *before anyone has a chance to taste it.*

Case 6: Different times, different verb forms

Remember those weird verb forms from Case 2, earlier in the chapter? The verbals? When they express different times, a helping verb *(having* or *have)* is involved. Check out this sentence:

Having sealed the letter containing his job application, Nobrain *remembered* his name.

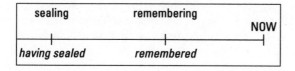

In other words, Nobrain's job application — unless he rips open the envelope — is anonymous because the *sealing* of the letter took place before the *remembering* of his name.

Here are additional examples:

Having finished her homework, Felonia *turned* on the television to watch the oatmeal-wrestling tournament. (Event 1: Felonia finishes her homework at 2 a.m. Event 2: The tournament begins at 3 a.m. For some reason, the networks are reluctant to broadcast the match during prime time.)

Having won all the votes, Lola named herself "Empress-in-Chief." (Event 1: Lola gets 100 percent of the votes. Event 2: Lola loses her head.)

Having exhibited the painting in Mudbud's new gallery, Felonia considered herself an all-around artistic genius. (Event 1: Felonia convinces Mudbud to hang her *Homework Blues* still life. Event 2: Felonia adds an art link to her Web page.)

The present participle (*finishing,* for example) combines with present, past, and future verbs to show two events happening at the same time or at nearly the same time. The present perfect form of the participle (*having finished*) combines with present, past, and future verbs to show two events happening at different times.

She done him wrong

The word *done* is never a verb all by itself. A true party animal, this verb form insists on being accompanied by helping verbs. In grammar-speak, *done* is a past participle of the verb *to do.* Naked, shivering, totally-alone participles never function as verbs. Here are some examples:

WRONG: He done all he could, but the sky fell anyway.

RIGHT: He had done all he could, but the sky fell anyway.

WRONG: She done him wrong.

RIGHT, BUT A BAD SENTENCE: She has done him wrong.

BETTER SENTENCE: What she has done to him is wrong.

You may blame the fact that so many people create sentences like the first example *(He done all he could)* on one of the many joys of English grammar. Some past participles — those of regular verbs — look exactly the same as the plain past tense. Consider the verb *to walk:*

PLAIN PAST TENSE: I *walked* twenty miles.

PRESENT PERFECT TENSE: I *have walked* twenty miles.

WHAT THESE TWO SENTENCES HAVE IN COMMON: The word *walked,* which is a verb in the first example and a past participle — part of a verb — in the second example.

WHY ENGLISH DOES THIS: I have no idea.

BOTTOM LINE: You may use *walked* alone or with a helper because the same word may be both a past tense verb and a participle. You may not use *done* by itself as a verb, however, because it's not the past tense of *to do.* The past tense of *to do* is *did.*

Another one of the verb-forms-that-aren't-verbs, the infinitive, may also show events happening at two different times. The present perfect infinitive (*to have finished,* for example) is the one that does this job. Don't worry about the name; just look for the *have.* Here's an example:

> It was helpful *to have bought the cookbook* before the dinner party.
> (Event 1: Pre-party, panicked trip to the bookstore. Event 2: Guests arrive, unaware that they're about to eat Alfalfa Stringbean Surprise.)

The *have* form (the present perfect form) of the infinitive always places an event *before* another in the past. Don't use the *have* form unless you're putting events in order:

> WRONG: I was sorry to have attended the party.

> RIGHT: I was sorry to attend the party. The music was terrible and there was nothing to eat but vegetables.

> ALSO RIGHT: I was sorry to have attended the party before I got a chance to investigate the menu. Shakey's salad was terrible.

Which sentence shows two events happening at the same time, and which shows two events happening at different times?

A. Running up the clock, the mouse spoke with his friends.

B. Having run up the clock, the mouse spoke with his friends.

Answer: Sentence A shows two events happening at the same time. The mouse is running and speaking with his friends. Sentence B shows two events happening at different times. The mouse has arrived at the top of the clock and is now speaking with his friends (notice that the word *having* is involved, indicating that different events are occurring at different times).

Reporting Information: The Verb Tells the Story

Flipping his hair over each of his three shoulders, the alien *told* us about the explosion on his planet. The gas of three rocket tanks *caught* fire and *destroyed* the spaceport terminal, he *said.* He *went* on to explain that almost everyone on the planet *was affected,* including the volleyball team, which *sustained* significant losses. All their courts, he *said, were covered* with rubble, and they *forfeited* the intergalactic tournament.

The alien's story is summarized speech. I'm not quoting him directly. If I were, I'd insert some of his exact words:

"Oh, the humanity!" he cried.

In the previous summarized speech, the verbs are all in past tense. Although rare, it's possible to summarize speech in present tense also. Present tense adds an extra dose of drama:

Flipping his hair over each of his three shoulders, the alien *tells* us about the explosion on his planet. The gas of three rocket tanks *catches* fire and *destroys* the spaceport terminal, he *says*. He *goes* on to explain that almost everyone on the planet *is affected,* including the volleyball team, which *sustains* significant losses. All their courts, he *says, are covered* with rubble, and they *forfeit* the intergalactic tournament.

When reporting information, either present or past tense is acceptable. However, mixing tenses is *not* acceptable. Don't move from one to the other, except for one special case, which I describe in the next section, "Recognizing Eternal Truths: Statements That Are Always in Present Tense."

WRONG: Shakey *said* that he *had tossed* the salad out the window. It *hits* a pedestrian, who *sues* for lettuce-related damages. (The first two verbs are in past tense, and the next two are in present tense.)

RIGHT: Shakey *said* that he *had tossed* the salad out the window. It *hit* a pedestrian, who *sued* for lettuce-related damages. (All verbs are in a form of the past tense.)

Correct the verb tense in this paragraph. The verbs are in italics.

Lola *testified* that she *excavated* at the town dump every Tuesday afternoon before she *attends* choir practice. She often *found* arrow heads, broken pottery, discarded automobile tires, and other items of interest. One day she *discovers* a metal coil about two feet long. On one end of the coil *was* a piece of gum. As she thoughtfully *removes* the gum and *starts* to chew, a whistle *blew*. Lochness *sprinted* into the dump at top speed. "Get your hands off my gum," he *exclaims*. Lochness *smiles*. His anti-gum-theft-alarm *had worked* perfectly.

Answer: The story is in two different tenses, past and present. To correct it, choose one of the two. Here is the past tense version, with the changed verbs underlined:

Lola *testified* that she *excavated* at the town dump every Tuesday afternoon before she <u>*attended*</u> choir practice. She often *found* arrow heads, broken pottery, discarded automobile tires, and other items of interest. One day she <u>*discovered*</u> a metal coil about two feet long. On one end of the coil *was* a piece of gum. As she thoughtfully <u>*removed*</u> the gum and *started* to chew, a whistle *blew*. Lochness *sprinted* into the dump at top speed. "Get your hands off my gum," he *exclaimed*. Lochness *smiled*. His anti-gum-theft-alarm *had worked* perfectly.

Here is the present tense version, with the changed verbs underlined:

Lola *testifies* that she *excavates* at the town dump every Tuesday afternoon before she *attends* choir practice. She often *finds* arrow heads, broken pottery, discarded automobile tires, and other items of interest. One day she *discovers* a metal coil about two feet long. On one end of the coil *is* a piece of gum. As she thoughtfully *removes* the gum and *starts* to chew, a whistle *blows*. Lochness *sprints* into the dump at top speed. "Get your hands off my gum," he *exclaims*. Lochness *smiles*. His anti-gum-theft-alarm *has worked* perfectly.

One special note: When you're not reporting what someone says, you can make a general statement about something that always happens (someone's custom or habit) using present tense. You can easily combine such a statement with a story that focuses on one particular incident in the past tense. Therefore, the preceding story may begin in present tense and move to past tense in this way:

Lola *excavates* at the town dump every Tuesday afternoon before she *attends* choir practice. She often *finds* arrow heads, broken pottery, discarded automobile tires, and other items of interest.

Up to here in the story, all the verbs are in present tense because the story tells of Lola's habits. The story isn't reporting what someone said. In the next sentence, the story switches to past tense because it examines one particular day in the past.

One day she *discovered* a metal coil about two feet long. On one end of the coil *was* a piece of gum. As she thoughtfully *removed* the gum and *started* to chew, a whistle *blew*. Lochness *sprinted* into the dump at top speed. "Get your hands off my gum," he *exclaimed*. Lochness *smiled*. His anti-gum-theft-alarm *had worked* perfectly.

Recognizing Eternal Truths: Statements That Are Always in Present Tense

What's wrong with these sentences?

Analivia explained that one plus one *equaled* two.

Ms. Belli said that the earth *was* round.

She added that diamonds *were made* of carbon.

Well, you may be thinking,

> *Equaled* two? What does it equal now? Three?

> *Was* round? And now it's a cube?

> *Were* made of carbon? Now they make diamonds from pastrami?

In others words, the verb tense is wrong. All of these statements represent eternal truths — statements that will never change. When you write such statements, you must always write in present tense, even if the statement was made in the past:

> Analivia explained that one plus one *equals* two.

> Ms. Belli told us that the earth *is* round.

> She went on to say that diamonds *are made* of carbon.

Which sentence is correct?

A. Legghorn said that Lulu had a cold.

B. Leggorn said that Lulu has a cold.

Answer: Sentence A is correct. Lulu's cold is not an eternal truth, though it has lasted three weeks and shows no signs of letting up. Be consistent in verb tense.

Chapter 19

Saying What You Want to Say: Descriptive Words and Phrases

● ●

In This Chapter

▶ Placing descriptions so that the sentence says what you mean

▶ Beginning a sentence with a description

▶ Using infinitives as descriptions

▶ Avoiding double meanings for descriptive words

▶ Omitting words without losing meaning

● ●

*O*nce upon a time, ye olde ancestor of our Modern English, Old English, was the language of the land. Most words had many forms: one to show that the word received an action and one to show that it performed an action. Because the words themselves carried so many aspects of meaning, you could arrange them in many ways and still say the same thing. Word order was less important in Old English than it is in Modern English.

The good news is that speakers of Modern English don't have to learn dozens of forms of words. The bad news is that Modern English speakers have to be careful about word order. Most people do all right with nouns and verbs, but descriptive words are another matter. In this chapter, I show you some common mistakes of placement. Specifically, I show you how placing a description in the wrong spot can completely wreck your sentence.

Ruining a Perfectly Good Sentence: Misplaced Descriptions

Can you spot what's wrong with this sentence?

Lulu put a ring into her pierced nose that she had bought last week.

The describing words *that she had bought last week* follow the word *nose*. The way the sentence is now, *that she had bought last week* describes *nose*. The Internet sells plenty of unusual items, but not noses (yet), though I imagine a Web address for plastic surgeons offering discount nose jobs is out there somewhere.

Here's the correction:

> Into her pierced nose Lulu put a ring that she had bought last week.

Now *that she had bought last week* follows ring, which Lulu really did buy last week.

The description *that she bought last week* is an adjective clause. It modifies the noun *ring*. For more information on adjective clauses, see Chapter 24.

Here's another description that wandered too far from home:

> Lulu also bought a genuine, 1950-model, fluorescent pink hula-hoop with a credit card.

According to news reports, toddlers and dogs have received credit card applications, but not plastic toys — at least as far as I know. Yet the sentence says that the hula-hoop comes with a credit card. How to fix it? Move the description:

> With a credit card Lulu also bought a genuine, 1950-model, fluorescent pink hula-hoop.

Granted, most people can figure out the meaning of the sentence, even when the description is in the wrong place. Logic is a powerful force. But chances are your reader or listener will pause a moment to unravel what you've said. The next couple of sentences may be a washout because your audience is distracted.

The rule concerning description placement is simple: Place the description as close as possible to the word that it describes.

Which sentence is correct?

A. Lochness put the paper into his pocket with atomic secrets written on it.

B. Lochness put the paper with atomic secrets written on it into his pocket.

Answer: Sentence B is correct because the paper has atomic secrets written on it, not the pocket.

With atomic secrets is a prepositional phrase, specifically, an adjectival prepositional phrase (those grammatical terms really roll off the tongue, don't they?) describing *paper*. *Written on it* is a participle, a verb form that isn't used as a verb. Participles describe nouns and pronouns. In this sentence, *written on it* describes the noun *secrets*. For more information on prepositional phrases, see Chapter 9. For more information on participles, see Chapter 24.

Try another. Which sentence is correct?

A. Analivia peddled to the Mathematics Olympics on her ten-speed bicycle with a complete set of differential equations.

B. Analivia peddled on her ten-speed bicycle to the Mathematics Olympics with a complete set of differential equations.

C. With a complete set of differential equations, Analivia peddled on her ten-speed bicycle to the Mathematics Olympics.

Answer: Sentence C is correct. In sentence A, the bicycle has ten speeds, two tires, and a set of equations — not very useful in climbing hills and swerving to avoid taxis! In sentence B, the Mathematics Olympics has a complete set of differential equations. Perhaps so, but the sentence revolves around Analivia, so the more likely meaning is that Analivia has the equations. Only in sentence C does Analivia have the equations. By the way, she won a silver medal in speed-solving.

Keeping Your Audience Hanging: Danglers

How can you describe something that isn't there? Descriptions must have something to describe. Read this sentence:

Munching a buttered sausage, the cholesterol really builds up.

Who is munching? You? Eggworthy? Everyone in the local diet club? In the sentence above, no one is munching. Descriptive verb forms that have nothing appropriate to describe are called *danglers* or *dangling modifiers*. To correct the sentence, add a muncher:

Munching a buttered sausage, Eggworthy smiled and waved to his cardiologist.

Some sentences start with a verb form — a participle or an infinitive, for those of you who like grammatical terms — that doesn't act as a verb but instead describes a noun or a pronoun. (For more information on participles and infinitives, see Chapter 24.) In sentences beginning with a descriptive verb form, the subject of the sentence must perform the action mentioned in the descriptive verb form. In the sample sentence, Eggworthy is the subject of the sentence. The sentence begins with a descriptive verb form, *munching a buttered sausage*. Thus, Eggworthy is the one who is munching. (For more information on identifying the subject of a sentence, see Chapter 4.) If you want the cardiologist to munch, say

> Munching a buttered sausage, the cardiologist returned Eggworthy's wave.

Munching a buttered sausage is an *introductory participle*. It modifies the subject *cardiologist* in the preceding example. The introductory participle always describes the subject of the sentence.

Here's another example:

> Sitting on the park bench, the speeding space shuttle briefly delighted the little boy.

Oh really? The space shuttle is sitting on a bench and speeding at the same time? Defies the laws of physics, don't you think? Try again:

> Sitting on the park bench, the little boy was briefly delighted by the speeding space shuttle.

Now *little boy* is the subject of the sentence, so the introductory description applies to him, not to the space shuttle. Another correction may be

> The speeding space shuttle briefly delighted the little boy who was sitting on the park bench.

Now the descriptive words *sitting on the park bench* are placed next to little boy, who in fact is the one sitting, being delighted by the speeding space shuttle.

Which one is correct?

- A. Sailing swiftly across the sea, Samantha's boat was surely a beautiful sight.
- B. Sailing swiftly across the sea, the sight of the beautiful boat made Samantha sob.

Answer: Sentence A is correct. *Sailing swiftly across the sea* describes Samantha's boat. Samantha's boat is performing that action. Sentence B is wrong because in sentence B *sight,* the subject, is sailing. (And of course, a *sight* can't sail.)

A common dangler is an infinitive (to + verb) that begins a sentence.

> To sew well, strong light is necessary.

This sentence may sound correct to you. After all, sewing in the dark is hard. But think about the meaning for a moment. Who is sewing? No one, at least the way the sentence is now written. Moving the infinitive may make the sentence sound better to your ears, but the move doesn't solve the problem:

> A strong light is necessary to sew well.

There's still no one sewing, so the sentence is still incorrect. To fix the problem, you must add a person:

> To sew well, you need a strong light. (*You* are sewing.)

> To sew well, sit near a strong light. (*You* is understood in this command sentence.)

> To sew well, everyone needs a strong light. (*Everyone* is sewing.)

> To sew well, Felonia insists on at least a 75-watt bulb. (*Felonia* is sewing.)

Which sentence is correct?

A. To enjoy a good cup of coffee, a clean coffee pot is essential.

B. A clean coffeepot is essential to enjoy a good cup of coffee.

Answer. Neither A nor B is correct. (I threw in one of those annoying teacher tricks just to keep you alert.) Neither sentence has a coffee drinker in it. So who's enjoying the coffee? No one. A true correction must add a person:

> To enjoy a good cup of coffee, *you* start with a clean coffeepot.

> To enjoy a good cup of coffee, caffeine *addicts* start with a clean coffeepot.

> To enjoy a good cup of coffee, *Analivia* starts with a clean coffeepot.

> To enjoy a good cup of coffee, start with a clean coffeepot. (Now *you* [understood in this command sentence] are the coffee drinker.)

Avoiding Confusing Descriptions

Take a look at the following example:

> The teacher that Lochness annoyed often assigned detention to him.

What does the sentence mean? Did Lochness *often annoy* the teacher? Perhaps the teacher *often assigned* detention to Lochness.

The problem with the sample sentence is that *often* is between *annoying* and *assigning* and may be linked to either of those two actions. The sentence violates a basic rule of description: All descriptions must be clear. You shouldn't put a description where it may have two possible meanings.

How do you fix the sentence? You move *often* so that it is closer to one of the verbs, thus showing the reader which of two words *only* describes. Here are two correct versions, each with a different meaning:

> The teacher that Lochness often annoyed assigned detention to him.

In this sentence *often* is closer to *annoyed*. Thus, *often* describes *annoyed*. The sentence communicates to the reader that after 514 spitballs, the teacher finally flipped and assigned detention to Lochness.

Here's a second possibility:

> The teacher that Lochness annoyed assigned detention to him often.

Now *often* is closer to *assigned*. The reader understands that *often* describes *assigned*. The sentence tells the reader that the teacher vowed "not to take anything from that little brat" and assigned detention to Lochness every day of the school year, including winter break and Presidents' Day.

Correct or incorrect? You decide.

> The pig chewing on pig chow happily burped and made us all run for gas masks.

Answer: Incorrect. You don't know if the pig is *chewing happily* or *burping happily*. Here's how to correct the sentence:

> The pig chewing happily on pig chow burped and made us all run for gas masks.

or

> The pig chewing on pig chow burped happily and made us all run for gas masks.

You may be tempted to fix a description by tucking it inside an infinitive:

> Felonia's song is strange enough to *intensely* captivate creative musicians.

Technically, you shouldn't split an infinitive (to + verb — *to captivate* in this sentence).

> Right: to captivate intensely

> Wrong: to intensely captivate

This rule is often ignored and probably on the way out of the grammar rule books. But if you're writing for a super-strict reader, be careful of split infinitives.

The most commonly misplaced descriptions are single words: *only, just, almost,* and *even.* See Chapter 8 for a complete explanation of how to place these descriptive words correctly.

Finding the Subject When Words Are Missing from the Sentence

In the never-ending human quest to save time, words are often chopped out of sentences. The assumption is that the sentence is still understandable because the listener or reader supplies the missing piece. Not a bad assumption, as long as you understand what you can chop and what you need to leave alone. Check out these examples:

> After sleeping for exactly 33 minutes, Johann yawned and woke up.

> Although screaming in rage, Lola managed to keep an eye on the clock.

> If caught, Lochness will probably deny everything.

> Calla Lily snored when dreaming of little sheep.

Do you understand what these sentences mean? With all the words present, the sentences read as follows:

> After *he had been* sleeping for exactly 33 minutes, Johann yawned and woke up.

> Although Lola was screaming in rage, *she* managed to keep an eye on the clock.

> If *Lochness is* caught, he will probably deny everything.

> Calla Lily snored when *she was* dreaming of little sheep.

In the sample sentences, the missing part of the sentence is the subject. Sometimes part of the verb is missing also. You need to remember only one rule for these sentences: The missing subject must be the same as the subject that is present. In other words, if your sentence lacks more information, the reader or listener will assume that you're talking about the same person or thing in both parts of the sentence. Here are some examples:

> WRONG: While missing a shovel, the hole in Lulu's backyard was dug by a backhoe.

> UNINTENDED MEANING: While the hole was missing a shovel, the hole in Lulu's backyard was dug by a backhoe.

> CORRECTION: While missing a shovel, Lulu rented a backhoe to dig a hole in her backyard.

> MEANING OF CORRECTED SENTENCE: While she was missing a shovel, Lulu rented a backhoe to dig a hole in her backyard.

> ADDITIONAL UNINTENDED EFFECT: Lulu, not knowing how to drive a backhoe, hit a power line and brought down the entire electrical system of the Northeast. The Internet has still not recovered.

Which sentence is correct?

A. Since conducting the leak test, Dripless's pipe has been watertight.

B. Since conducting the leak test, Dripless reported that the pipe was watertight.

C. Since he conducted the leak test, Dripless's pipe has been watertight.

Answer: Sentences B and C are both correct. The missing subject in sentences A and B is *Dripless*. In sentence A *Dripless's pipe* is the subject of the second part of the sentence, so there is a mismatch between the two parts of the sentence. In sentence B *Dripless* is the subject of the second part of the sentence. The two halves of the sentence match. In sentence C a subject *(he)* is supplied, so the two halves of the sentences don't have to have the same subject.

Chapter 20

Good, Better, Best: Comparisons

Is your knowledge of comparisons *more better* or *less worse*? If you chose one of those two alternatives, this chapter is for you, because *more better* and *less worse* are both incorrect. English has two ways of creating comparisons, but you can't use them together and they're not interchangeable. In this chapter, I show you how to tell the difference between the two types of comparisons, how to use each correctly, and how to avoid some of the common errors of comparisons. I don't, however, tell you which comparisons to avoid altogether, such as *Which dress makes me look fat?* and *Am I a better dancer than your last date?* You have to figure out those dilemmas yourself.

Ending It with -Er or Giving It More

Lochness's smile is *more evil* than Legghorn's, but Legghorn's giggle sounds *cuter*.

Eggworthy searched for the *least efficient* sports utility vehicle, believing that global warming is *less important* than having the *raciest* image in the parking lot.

Felonia's *most recent* symphony was *less successful* than her *earlier* composition.

Analivia's *older* sister is an even *greater* mathematician than Analivia herself, though Analivia has the edge in geometry.

Lulu's *latest* tattoo is *grosser* than her first, but Lulu, not the *shyest* girl in the class, is looking for the *most extreme* design for her next effort.

What did you notice about the comparisons in the preceding sample sentences? Here's the stripped-down list: *more evil, cuter, least efficient, less important, raciest, most recent, less successful, earlier, older, greater, grosser, latest, shyest, most extreme.*

Some of the comparisons were expressed by adding *-er* or *-est,* and some were expressed by adding *more, most, less,* or *least* to the quality that's being compared. How do you know which is appropriate? (Or, to use a comparison, how do you know which is *better?*) The dictionary is the final authority, and you should consult one if you're in doubt about a particular word. However, there are some general guidelines:

- ✔ Add *-er* and *-est* to most single-syllable words.

- ✔ If the word already ends in the letter *e,* don't double the *e* by adding *-er* or *-est.* Just add *-r* or *-st.*

- ✔ *-Er* and *-est* endings are not usually appropriate for words ending in *-ly.*

The dictionary is your friend

You can learn a lot from the dictionary, with only a little boredom. The following is a list of what the average dictionary entry tells you about each word:

- ✔ the part of speech

- ✔ the pronunciation

- ✔ the definitions of the word, listed in order of importance

- ✔ some common expressions using the word

- ✔ other forms of the word

- ✔ something about the history of the word — its earlier forms or its linguistic ancestors

- ✔ a ruling on whether the word is acceptable in formal English

All that information is packed into only an inch or two of writing! But to fit in everything, the publishers rely on abbreviations. Therefore, reading a dictionary entry may resemble a trip to a foreign country — one where everyone else seems to know the language and customs and is happy to leave you out of the picture.

Let me put you in the picture. Here's a very special dictionary entry, with the parts decoded for the average reader. (By the way, don't look for this word in a real dictionary; I made it up.) Just match the letters in the dictionary entry with the explanations below.

A. chukblok B. (chuck–blahk) **C.** n. **D.** *pl.* chukbloks. **E.** 1. The state currency of Ludwig's country. 2. The national bank of Ludwig's country. 3. In economics, a very high protective tariff: a *chukblok* against imported bananas. **F.** 4. *Informal* extremely rich person: he's a walking *chukblok.* **G.** 5. *obs.* A coin made of chewing gum. **H.** – *adj.* 1. rich: She put a *chukblok* icing on that cake. 2. illegal: The *chukblok* plan was bound to backfire. **I.** [<O.L. *chublah*<ML. chubare a coin.] **J. Syn.** n. coins, money, moolah, spending green. *adj.* well-heeled, well-off, illicit. **K.** – **to see chukbloks in the trees** *Slang.* To assume that one is about to get rich. –

to flip one's chukblok *Informal.* To bet all of one's money on the throw of the dice.

Here are the letter identifications:

A. The word

B. The pronunciation. The symbols here are a little confusing, but most dictionaries provide a key in the front of the book. The key explains the pronunciation symbols by showing you the same sound in some easily recognizable words.

C. The part of speech.

D. The abbreviation *pl.* means *plural,* and this part of the entry tells you how to form the plural of this word.

E. The definitions. The most commonly used definitions are first.

F. *Informal* tells you that you shouldn't use that particular meaning in formal writing. If the word isn't labeled, it's acceptable in formal writing.

G. *Obs.* means *obsolete* and tells you that a meaning is no longer used.

H. Another part of speech. The *adj.* abbreviation tells you that you can also use *chukblok* as an adjective, in addition to using it as a noun. The meanings listed after *adj.* explain what the word means when it is used as an adjective. Again, the definitions are in order from the most common meaning to the rarest.

I. These symbols tell you the family tree of the word *chukblok.* The abbreviation *O.L.* refers to *Old Ludwig,* a language that I made up. *ML.* is an abbreviation; it refers to *Middle Lolean,* another language that I made up. In the brackets, you learn that you can trace the history of *chukblok* to the Old Ludwig word *chublah,* which in turn may be traced to a Middle Lolean word *chubare,* meaning *coin.*

J. Another abbreviation. *Syn.* means *synonym.* Following this symbol are words that mean the same as the noun and adjective versions of *chukblok.*

K. The meaning of common expressions with the word *chukblok.* One is slang and the other informal; neither is acceptable in formal writing.

Table 20-1 is a chart of some common descriptions of Lola, with both the *-er* and *-est* forms. Note: To understand Lola's personality, you need to know to what (or to whom) she's being compared, so I include a few clues.

Table 20-1	Common Descriptions	
Description of Lola	*-ER form*	*-EST form*
able	abler than Lulu	ablest of all the budding scientists in her atom-splitting class
bald	balder than an eagle	baldest of the models
cute	cuter than an elf	cutest of all the assassins

(continued)

Table 20-1 *(continued)*

Description of Lola	-ER form	-EST form
dumb	dumber than a sea slug	dumbest of the presidential candidates
edgy	edgier than caffeine	edgiest of the atom splitters
friendly	friendlier than a grizzly bear	friendliest person on the block
glad	gladder than the loser	gladdest of all the lottery winners
heavy	heavier than a before ad for a diet book	heaviest of all the sumo wrestlers
itchy	itchier than she was before she sat in poison ivy	itchiest of all the patients in the skin clinic

Notice that when the last letter is *y*, you must often change the *y* to *i* before you tack on the ending.

Table 20-2 contains even more descriptions of Lola, this time with *more, less, most,* and *least* added:

Table 20-2	Two-word Descriptions	
Description of Lola	More/Less form	Most/Least form
(Lola runs) jerkily	more jerkily than the old horse	most jerkily of all the racers
knock-kneed	less knock-kneed than an old sailor	least knock-kneed of all the beauty pageant contestants
lily-livered	less lily-livered than the saloon owner in an old movie	least lily-livered of all the florists
magnificent	more magnificent than a work of art	most magnificent of all the ninjas
notorious	more notorious than a princess	most notorious of the florists
oafish	less oafish than the young prince	least oafish of all the cab drivers

Description of Lola	More/Less form	Most/Least form
prune-faced	less prune-faced than her teacher	least prune-faced of the grammar students
queenly	more queenly than Queen Elizabeth	most queenly of all the models
rigid	less rigid than a grammarian	least rigid of the traffic cops

These two tables give you a clue about another important comparison characteristic. Did you notice that the second column is always a comparison between Lola and *one other* person or thing? The addition of *-er* or *more* or *less* compares two things. In the last column of each chart, Lola is compared to a group with more than two members. When the group is larger than two, *-est* or *most* or *least* creates the comparison and identifies the extreme.

To sum up the rules:

   ✔ Use *-er* or *more/less* when comparing only two things.

   ✔ Use *-est* or *most/least* when singling out the extreme in a group that is larger than two.

   ✔ Never combine two comparison methods, such as *-er* and *more*.

The *-er* or *less/more* form of comparison is called *comparative* and the *-est* or *least/most* form of comparison is called *superlative*.

Which sentence is correct?

   A. Lola, fresh from drinking a cup of cream, was the more cheerful of all her friends in the dairy bar.

   B. Lola, fresh from drinking a cup of cream, was the most cheerful of all her friends in the dairy bar.

Answer: Sentence B is correct. The sentence singles out Lola as the extreme in a group, so you need *most* here, not *more*.

Try another:

Which sentence is correct?

   A. Eggworthy's design for a new egg carton is simpler than the one his competitor hatched.

   B. Eggworthy's design for a new egg carton is more simpler than the one his competitor hatched.

Answer: Sentence A is correct. Never combine two forms of comparison. Sentence B combines the *-er* form with the word *more*.

Last one. Which sentence is correct?

A. Of all the cars in the parking lot, Eggworthy's is the newer.

B. Of all the cars in the parking lot, Eggworthy's is the newest.

Answer: Sentence B is correct. Eggworthy's car is compared to more than one other car.

Breaking the Rules: Irregular Comparisons

Whenever English grammar gives you a set of rules that make sense, you know it's time for the irregulars to show up. Not surprisingly, then, you have to create a few common comparisons without *-er, -est, more/less,* or *most/least.* Look at the following examples:

Legghorn's trumpet solo is *good,* but Lochness's is *better,* and according to Lulu, her trumpet solo is the *best* of all.

Lulu's habit of picking at her tattoo is *bad,* but Ratrug's constant sneezing is *worse.* Eggworthy's tendency to crack jokes is the *worst* habit of all.

Mudbud has a *good* earthquake prevention kit. The kit made by Mudbud's major competitor is *better* than Mudbud's. The kit sold by a little-known Parisian company is the *best* of all the brands now on the market.

Got the idea? Here is a list of the irregular comparisons:

✔ good, better, best

✔ bad, worse, worst

✔ well, better, best

Similarly, here are two more that I've also used:

✔ little, less, least

✔ many (or much), more, most

These irregulars break the rules, but they are easy to remember. Three of the irregulars judge quality (good, bad, well) and two judge quantity (little, many). The comparative form compares one thing to another, and the superlative form identifies the extreme in the group.

Answer this question in correct English (and then correct the question itself).

Who's the baddest kid in the playground?

Answer: The *worst* (not *baddest*) kid in the playground is Lochness, unless Lola is in one of her moods. The correct question is *Who's the worst kid in the playground?*

Here's another:

Who plays more better blues?

Answer: No one. Use *more* or *better,* but not both, to make the comparison. Other ways to word the question include:

Who plays better blues — Legghorn or Lulu?

Who plays the best blues?

Who plays the blues best?

Of the two saxophonists, who plays better blues?

Last one. Which sentence is correct?

  A. Legghorn says that he is feeling worse today than yesterday, but his statement must be considered in light of the fact that today is the algebra final.

  B. Legghorn says that he is feeling more bad today than yesterday, but his statement must be considered in light of the fact that today is the algebra final.

Answer: Sentence A is correct. *More bad* is incorrect; use *worse.*

Never More Perfect: Using Words That You Can't Compare

Is this chapter more unique than the previous chapter? No, definitely not. Why? Because nothing is *more unique.* The word *unique* means "one of a kind." Either something is one of a kind, or it's not. Yes or no, true or false, one or zero (when you're speaking in computer code). No halfway point, no degrees of uniqueness, no . . . well, you get the idea. You can't compare something that's unique to anything but itself. Check out the following examples:

WRONG: The vase that Eggworthy cracked was more unique than the Grecian urn.

ALSO WRONG: The vase that Eggworthy cracked was fairly unique.

ALSO WRONG: The vase that Eggworthy cracked was almost unique.

WRONG AGAIN: The vase that Eggworthy cracked was very unique.

RIGHT: The vase that Eggworthy cracked was unique.

ALSO RIGHT: The vase that Eggworthy cracked was unique, as was the Grecian urn.

RIGHT AGAIN: The vase that Eggworthy cracked was more unusual than the Grecian urn.

WHY IT'S RIGHT: *Unusual* is not an absolute term, so you can use it in comparisons.

The word *unique* is not unique. Several other words share its absolute quality. One is *perfect*. Something is perfect or not perfect; nothing is *very perfect* or *unbelievably perfect* or *quite perfect*. (I am bound, as a patriotic American, to point out one exception: The United States Constitution contains a statement of purpose citing the need to create "a more perfect union.") Another absolute word is *round*. Your shape is *round* or *not round*. Your shape isn't *a bit round, rounder,* or *roundest*. Here are some examples:

WRONG: "Lola is *extremely perfect* when it comes to grammar, as I am," said Lulu.

WHY IT'S WRONG: *Perfect* is absolute. There are no degrees of perfection.

RIGHT: "Lola is *nearly perfect* when it comes to grammar, as I am," said Lulu.

WHY IT'S RIGHT: You can approach an absolute quality, comparing how close someone or something comes to the quality. Lola approaches perfection (as does Lulu), but neither achieves it.

ALSO RIGHT: "Lola is *perfect* when it comes to grammar, as I am," said Lulu.

WHY THEY'RE RIGHT: You may approach *perfect,* as in *nearly perfect*. You may also be *perfect,* without any qualifiers.

WRONG: Of the two circles drawn on the chalkboard, mine is rounder.

WHY IT'S WRONG: The shape is round or it's not round. It can't be *rounder*. Also, by definition circles are *round*.

RIGHT: Of the two *shapes* drawn on the chalkboard, mine is *more nearly round*.

RIGHT AGAIN: Neither of the two shapes drawn on the chalkboard is *round,* but mine approaches *roundness*.

As some of the "RIGHT" sentences in the preceding examples illustrate, you can't compare absolute qualities, but you can compare how close people or things come to having those qualities. Look at these examples:

> Lola thinks that her latest nose ring is an *almost perfect* accessory.

> Ratrug's new hooked rug is *more nearly circular* than his previous effort.

> Lulu's style of relaxation *approaches uniqueness.*

One more word causes all sorts of trouble in comparisons: *equally.* You hear the expression *equally as* quite frequently. You don't need the *as,* because the word *equally* contains the idea of comparison. For example:

> WRONG: Lochness got a lighter sentence than Lulu, but he is *equally as* guilty because of the nature of his doughnut-based terrorism.

> RIGHT: Lochness got a lighter sentence than Lulu, but he is *equally* guilty because of the nature of his doughnut-based terrorism.

> ALSO RIGHT: Lochness got a lighter sentence than Lulu, but he is as guilty as she is because of the nature of his doughnut-based terrorism.

Which sentence is correct?

A. Legghorn's recent drama is even more unique than his last play.

B. Legghorn's recent drama is even more unusual than his last play.

C. Legghorn's recent drama is unique, as was his last play.

Answer: Sentences B and C are correct. Sentence A incorrectly compares an absolute *(unique).* In sentence B *more unusual* expresses a correct comparison. Sentence C tells you that Legghorn's recent drama is unique and that his last play was also unique. The absolute is not being compared but simply applied to two different things.

Which is correct?

A. Analivia's last chess move, when compared to the grandmaster's, is equally mistaken.

B. Analivia's last chess move, when compared to the grandmaster's, is equally as mistaken.

Answer: Sentence A is correct. Do not say *equally as* because the word *equally* expresses the concept of comparison.

Leaving Your Audience in Suspense: Incomplete Comparisons

What's wrong with this sentence?

> Octavia screamed more chillingly.

Maybe these hints will help:

> Octavia screamed more chillingly. Uh oh, thought Olivier, yesterday I thought she would burst my eardrum. If she screamed more chillingly today, I'd better get my earplugs out before it's time for tomorrow's lungfest.

or

> Octavia screamed more chillingly. Olivier, rushing to aid Hypatia, whose scream of terror had turned his blood to ice, stopped dead. Octavia sounds even worse, he thought. I'd better go to her first.

or

> Octavia screamed more chillingly. "Please," said the director, "I know that you have just completed take 99 of this extremely taxing verbal exercise, but if you are going to star in my horror movie, you'll have to put a little more into it. Try again!"

Now the problem is clear. The comparison in the examples is incomplete. Octavia screamed more chillingly than . . . than what? Until you finish the sentence, your readers are left with as many possibilities as they can imagine. Bottom line: Don't stop explaining your comparison until you get your point across. Look at the following example:

WRONG: Octavia screamed more chillingly.

RIGHT: Octavia screamed more chillingly than the cat did the day Lulu drove a truck over its tail.

ALSO RIGHT: Octavia screamed more chillingly than she ever had before, and Olivier resolved to come to her aid as soon as he had finished all five courses of his lunch.

RIGHT AGAIN: Octavia screamed more chillingly than she had in the previous takes, but the director still decided to go with the mute actress who had brought so many fans into the theater for the previous twelve installments of the horror series.

Here's another comparison with a fatal error. Can you spot the problem?

> Lulu loved sky-diving more than Lola.

Need another hint? Read on:

> Lulu loved sky-diving more than Lola. Lola sobbed uncontrollably as she realized that Lulu, whom she had always considered her best friend, was on the way to the airport instead of on the way to Lola's house. What a disappointment!

or

> Lulu loved sky-diving more than Lola. Lola was fine for the first 409 jumps, but then her enthusiasm began to flag. Lulu, on the other hand, was climbing into the airplane eagerly, as if it were her first jump of the day and as if the rattler had not crawled into her parachute on the last landing.

See the problem? *Lulu loved sky-diving more than Lola* is incomplete. Your reader can understand the comparison in two different ways, as the two stories illustrate. The rule here is simple: Don't omit words that are necessary to the meaning of the comparison.

> WRONG: Lulu loved sky-diving more than Lola.

> RIGHT: Lulu loved sky-diving more than she loved Lola.

> ALSO RIGHT: Lulu loved sky-diving more than Lola did.

One more time. What's the problem now?

> "My life is the best," explained Ratrug.

This one is so easy that you don't need stories. *Best* how? In money, fame, love, health, lack of body odor, winning lottery tickets, access to boy-band concerts? Ratrug's friends may understand his statement, but no one else will.

Remember: In making a comparison, be clear and complete.

Which sentence is correct?

A. My cat Agatha slapped her tail more quickly.

B. My cat Agatha slapped her tail more quickly than Dorothy.

Answer: Both are wrong. (Sorry! Trick question.) The meaning is unclear in both A and B. In sentence A, the reader is left asking *more quickly than what?* In sentence B, the sentence may mean *my cat Agatha slapped her tail more quickly than she slapped Dorothy* or *my cat Agatha slapped her tail more quickly than Dorothy slapped the cat's tail.* Neither comparison is complete.

Try another. Which sentence is correct?

A. Felonia played that piano concerto as emotionally as Legghorn did, but with fewer mistakes.

B. Felonia played that piano concerto just as emotionally, despite the fact that she has no real feeling for "The Homework Blues #3."

Answer: Sentence A is correct. In sentence B, the reader wonders about the basis of comparison for the emotions of Felonia's playing. Did she play the concerto *as emotionally as the other works on her program, such as "The Falling Piano Concerto"?* Or did she play the concerto *as emotionally as Lochness, who has less technical skill but a deep-seated hatred of homework.* Sentence A expresses the basis of comparison.

Joe DiMaggio Played Better Than Any Baseball Player: Illogical Comparisons

Before I start, here's an explanation of the heading for those of you who (gasp of pity here) don't like baseball. Joe DiMaggio was a baseball player. Actually, a great baseball player — one of the best, and a New York Yankee. So what's wrong with the title sentence? It takes (gasp of astonishment) Joltin' Joe out of the group of baseball players. It makes him (swoon of sorrow) a *non*-baseball player. To keep Joltin' Joe in the sport, add *other:*

WRONG: Joe DiMaggio played better than any baseball player.

RIGHT: Joe DiMaggio played better than any other baseball player.

ALSO RIGHT: The Yankees rule! (Sorry, can't help myself. I'm a fan.)

The rule for comparisons here is very simple: Use the word *other* or *else* when comparing someone or something to other members of the same group. Check out the following examples:

WRONG: The star soprano of the Santa Lola Opera, Sarah Screema, sings louder than anyone in the cast.

WHY IT'S WRONG: The sentence makes it clear that Sarah is in the cast, but the comparison implies that she's not in the cast. Illogical!

RIGHT: The star soprano of the Santa Lola Opera, Sarah Screema, sings louder than anyone *else* in the cast.

WRONG: That robot short-circuits more frequently than any mechanical device.

WHY IT'SWRONG: A robot is, by definition, a mechanical device, but the comparison takes the robot out of the group of mechanical devices.

RIGHT: That robot short-circuits more frequently than any *other* mechanical device.

Here's another problem. Can you find it?

Mudbud's nose is longer than Legghorn.

Okay, before you say anything, I should mention that Legghorn is tall — not skyscraper tall, but at least six-two. Now do you see what's wrong with the sentence? Mudbud's nose, a real tourist attraction for its length *and* width (not including the pimple at the end) is about four inches long. It is *not* longer than Legghorn. It is longer than Legghorn's *nose*.

WRONG: Mudbud's nose is longer than Legghorn.

RIGHT: Mudbud's nose is longer than Legghorn's nose.

ALSO RIGHT: Mudbud's nose is longer than Legghorn's.

One more example:

Ahab's toe ring is as wide as Dmitri.

I don't think so. Dmitri is a fairly trim fellow, but even so his waist measures 33 inches. If Ahab wore a toe ring that wide, no shoes would fit and walking would be a real adventure. Thus

WRONG: Ahab's toe ring is as wide as Dmitri.

RIGHT: Ahab's toe ring is as wide as Dmitri's toe ring.

ALSO RIGHT: Ahab's toe ring is as wide as Dmitri's.

Here's the bottom line:

- Make sure your comparisons are logical.
- Check to see that you have compared what you want to compare — two things that are at least remotely related.
- If the first part of the comparison involves a possessive noun or pronoun (showing ownership), the second part of the comparison probably needs a possessive also. For more information on possessive nouns, see Chapter 12. For more information on possessive pronouns, see Chapter 17.

Getting Two for the Price of One: Double Comparisons

No one will misunderstand you if you break this rule, but grammarians everywhere will hunt you down and tsk-tsk you into outer space: When you're making two comparisons at the same time, finish the first one before you begin the second. In other words, don't say,

> Dubdub is as dumb, if not dumber than Elvin.

In the previous sentence, you're really trying to say two different things:

1. Dubdub is as dumb as Elvin.
2. Dubdub may be dumber than Elvin.

First of all, and completely apart from grammar, you ought to make a decision. As dumb as? Dumber than? Don't leave your reader in suspense. Take the plunge and express your real opinion. Grammatically, you may sit on the fence, but only if you finish the first comparison before going on to number two. Here's how you finish:

> Dubdub is as dumb as Elvin, if not dumber.

What a difference an *as* makes! Now the sentence is complete after the word *Elvin,* so the *if* statement is an add-on, as it should be. In the incorrect version, you're missing an *as*. (I did warn you that only grammarians would care, remember?)

Chapter 21

Parallels Without the Lines

• •

In This Chapter

▶ Constructing parallel sentences

▶ Being consistent in form, tense, and voice

▶ Using pairs of conjunctions correctly

▶ Keeping comparisons parallel

• •

*I*n art class you draw parallels. In math class you plot them on a graph. In grammar, you create parallel constructions. When I say parallel constructions, I'm not talking about lines that look like train tracks. I'm talking about the need for balance in speech and writing, the need to create sentences that aren't lopsided. I'm talking about the reason Hamlet says, "To be or not to be" instead of "Being or not to be." In this chapter, I show you how to avoid several everyday errors of parallelism, or what the hard-hatted grammarian calls *faulty construction*.

Constructing Balanced Sentences

Ludwig wanted with all his heart to find a bride who was smart, beautiful, and had millions of chukbloks, the currency of his native land.

Not counting Ludwig's matrimonial ideas, the sentence has another problem: It's not parallel. Concentrate on the part of the sentence following the word *was*. Ludwig's dream bride was supposed to have these characteristics:

✔ smart

✔ beautiful

✔ had millions of chukbloks

Do you see that these three descriptions don't match? The first two are adjectives. The third consists of a verb *(had)* and an object *(millions of chukbloks)*. (For more information on adjectives, see Chapter 8. For more information on verbs and objects, see Chapters 2 and 6.) But all three descriptions are doing the same job in the sentence — describing Ludwig's dream bride. Because they're doing the same job, they should match, at least in the grammatical sense. Here's one revised list:

- ✔ smart
- ✔ beautiful
- ✔ rich in chukbloks
- ✔ nearsighted (I added this one because I've actually seen Ludwig.)

And here's another:

- ✔ intelligence
- ✔ beauty
- ✔ millions of chukbloks
- ✔ bad eyesight

Both lists are fine. In the first set, all the characteristics of Ludwig's bride are adjectives. In the second set, all the characteristics are nouns. You can use either list. Just don't take some elements from one and some from another. Here are the revised sentences:

> Ludwig wanted with all his heart to find a bride who was smart, beautiful, nearsighted, and rich in chukbloks, the currency of his native land.

> Ludwig wanted with all his heart to find a bride with intelligence, beauty, bad eyesight, and millions of chukbloks, the currency of his native land.

Now for another lopsided sentence. Can you spot the problem?

> To visit the stately dome, swimming the sacred river Alph, and becoming CEO of Kubla Khan, Inc. were Ludwig's goals.

Perhaps a list will help you. Ludwig's goals are as follows:

- ✔ to visit the stately dome
- ✔ swimming the sacred river Alph
- ✔ becoming CEO of Kubla Khan, Inc.

Which one doesn't match? *To visit the stately dome.*

To visit is an infinitive, but the next two items in the list are not. *Swimming* and *becoming* are gerunds. Gerunds and infinitives are all *verbals* — forms of a verb that don't function as verbs in the sentence. For more information on verbals, see Chapter 24.

All three of Ludwig's goals are subjects of the sentence. Because they're doing the same job in the sentence, they should be the same grammatically. Here are two possible corrections:

- ✔ visiting the stately dome
- ✔ swimming the sacred river Alph
- ✔ becoming CEO of Kubla Khan, Inc.

or

- ✔ to visit the stately dome
- ✔ to swim the sacred river Alph
- ✔ to become CEO of Kubla Khan, Inc.

Here are the two corrected sentences:

> To visit the stately dome, to swim the sacred river Alph, and to become CEO of Kubla Khan, Inc. were Ludwig's goals.

> Visiting the stately dome, swimming the sacred river Alph, and becoming the CEO of Kubla Khan, Inc. were Ludwig's goals.

Items in a sentence with the same job (function) should have the same grammatical identity. Whenever you have more than one subject, object, verb, or other element of the sentence, make a list and check it twice, whether or not you believe in Santa Claus.

Here are some additional examples:

> NOT PARALLEL: Analivia said that whenever anything went wrong, whenever someone let us down, or in case of disaster, she would "feel our pain."

> WHAT'S WRONG: The three things that Analivia said are not parallel. Two have subject–verb combinations *(anything went, someone let),* and one *(in case of disaster)* does not.

> PARALLEL: Analivia said that whenever anything went wrong, whenever someone let us down, or whenever disaster struck, she would "feel our pain."

> WHY IT'S PARALLEL: Now the three things that Analivia said are all subject–verb combinations.

> ALSO PARALLEL: Analivia said that in the event of mistakes, disloyalty, or disaster, she would "feel our pain."

> WHY IT'S PARALLEL: Now the things that Analivia said are all expressed as nouns: *mistakes, disloyalty, disaster.*

Try another set:

> NOT PARALLEL: Eggworthy, a gourmet cook and renowned for his delicious no-cholesterol omelets, thinks that French cooking is "overrated."

> WHAT'S WRONG: The *and* joins two descriptions of Eggworthy. One is a noun *(cook)* and one is a verb form *(renowned for his delicious no cholesterol omelets)*.

> PARALLEL: Eggworthy, a gourmet cook renowned for his delicious no-cholesterol omelets, thinks that French cooking is "overrated."

> WHY IT'S PARALLEL: Once you remove the *and,* the problem is solved. Now the descriptive verb form *(renowned)* describes the noun *(cook)*.

Which is correct?

A. Ludwig found the honeymoon suite restful, exotic, tasteful, and in the less-populated section of his kingdom.

B. Ludwig found the honeymoon suite restful, exotic, and tasteful. It was located in the less-populated section of his kingdom.

C. Ludwig found the honeymoon suite restful, exotic, tasteful, and remote.

Answer: Sentences B and C are correct. If you list the qualities of Ludwig's honeymoon suite as expressed in sentence A, you have

✔ restful

✔ exotic

✔ tasteful

✔ in the less-populated section of his kingdom

The first three are adjectives, but the last is a prepositional phrase. (For more information about prepositional phrases, see Chapter 9.) Because they don't match, the sentence is not parallel. In sentence B, the three adjectives are alone in one sentence. The prepositional phrase is in its very own sentence. Sentence C expresses all the characteristics of Ludwig's honeymoon suite as adjectives.

To avoid parallelism errors, you don't have to know the correct grammatical terms. Even without the fancy grammatical names, the list shows you the odd man out. Just use your common sense and listen. A parallel sentence has balance. A non-parallel sentence doesn't.

Shifting Grammar into Gear: Avoiding Stalled Sentences

If you've ever ridden in a car with a stick shift, you know that smooth transitions are rare (at least when I'm driving). If something is just a little off, the car bucks like a mule. The same thing is true in sentences. You can, at times, shift in tense, voice, or person, but even the slightest mistake stalls your sentence. In this section, I explain how to avoid unnecessary shifts and how to check your sentence for consistency.

Steering clear of a tense situation

Check out this sentence with multiple verbs:

> Ludwig begs Ludmilla to marry him, offers her a crown and a private room, and finally won her hand.

Now make a list of the verbs in the sentence:

- begs
- offers
- won

The first two verbs are in present tense, but the third shifts into past for no valid reason. Stall! If the verbs in this sentence were gears in a stick shift, your car would conk out. All three verbs should be in present tense or all three should be in past tense. Here are the corrected versions of the sentence:

> Ludwig begs Ludmilla to marry him, offers her a crown and a private room, and finally wins her hand. (All three verbs are in present tense.)

or

> Ludwig begged Ludmilla to marry him, offered her a crown and a private room, and finally won her hand. (All three verbs are in past tense.)

Sometimes in telling a story, you must shift tense because the action of the story requires a change in time. For example:

> Felonia always *practices* for at least ten hours a day, unless she *is giving* a concert. Last week she *flew* to Antarctica for a recital. When she *arrived,* the piano *was frozen.* Nevertheless, the show *went* on. Next week Felonia *will practice* twelve hours a day to make up for the time she *lost* last week.

Felonia's story has present *(practices)*, present progressive *(is giving)*, past *(flew, arrived, was frozen, went, lost)*, and future tenses *(will practice)*. Each change of tense is justified by the information in the story. (For more information on verb tense, see Chapters 3 and 18.) Here are some additional examples of justified and unjustified shifts in verb tense:

> WRONG: Ratrug *slips* on the ice, and after obsessively checking every inch of his skull in the mirror, *decided* that *had hurt* his head.

> WHY IT'S WRONG: The first verb is in present tense. The sentence shifts to past tense for no reason.

> RIGHT: Ratrug *slipped* on the ice, and after obsessively checking every inch of his skull in the mirror, *decided* that he *had hurt* his head.

> SENTENCE THAT LOOKS WRONG BUT ISN'T: Murgatroyd *needs* a loan because he *bet* his entire paycheck on a horse that *came* in first in the eighth race. (Unfortunately, the horse was running in the seventh race.)

> WHY IT LOOKS WRONG: The first verb is in present tense, and the next two are in past tense.

> WHY IT'S RIGHT: Both tenses are justified. The first part talks about Murgatroyd now, explaining his present condition with a reference to the past. The shift is acceptable because the meaning of the sentence makes the shift necessary.

Which sentence is correct?

A. Eggworthy scrambled to the finish line a nano-second before the next fastest racer and then raised his arms in victory.

B. Eggworthy scrambles to the finish line a nano-second before the next fastest racer and then raises his arms in victory.

Answer: Both sentences are correct. (Don't you hate trick questions?) In sentence A, both *scrambled* and *raised* are in past tense. No shift, no problem. In sentence B, both *scrambles* and *raises* are in present tense. Again, no shift, again no problem.

Keeping your voice steady

The voice of a verb — not baritones and tenors — is either *active* or *passive*. (For more information on voice, see Chapter 18.) Like tense, the voice of the verbs in a sentence should be consistent unless there's a good reason for a shift. I should point out that a shift in voice is not a grammar felony; think misdemeanor or maybe even parking ticket. Nevertheless, avoid unnecessary shifts if you can do so without writing yourself into a corner. Here's a sentence with an unjustified shift in voice:

Ludwig *polished* the diamond engagement ring, *rechecked* the certificate of authenticity, and *was* completely *demolished* when his intended bride *said* no.

Do you see the problem? A checklist makes it obvious:

- ✔ polished
- ✔ rechecked
- ✔ was demolished
- ✔ said

The first two verbs and the last one are in active voice, but the third is in passive voice.

A number of changes can take care of the problem:

Ludwig *polished* the diamond engagement ring, *rechecked* the certificate of authenticity, and *cried* like a baby when his intended bride *said* no.

or

Ludwig *polished* the diamond engagement ring and *rechecked* the certificate of authenticity. His intended bride completely demolished him with her refusal.

Notice that the list of verbs in the corrected sentences are all in active voice: *polished, rechecked, cried* and *polished, rechecked, demolished.*

Which is correct?

   A. Lulu popped the cork from the champagne, reached for the chilled glasses, and was shocked to learn that the caviar had been confiscated by customs officials.

   B. Lulu popped the cork from the champagne, reached for the chilled glasses, and was shocked to learn that customs officials had confiscated the caviar.

   C. Lulu popped the cork from the champagne, reached for the chilled glasses, and staggered in shock when she heard that customs officials had confiscated the caviar.

Answer: Sentence C is best because all of the verbs *(popped, reached, staggered, heard,* and *had confiscated)* are in active voice.

Knowing the right person

Ah, loyalty. One of the most celebrated virtues, in life as well as in grammar! Loyalty in grammar relates to consistency of person. You shouldn't start out talking about one person and then switch to another in a sentence, unless you have a valid reason for doing so. Here's an example of an unnecessary shift in person:

> To celebrate his marriage, Ludwig promised amnesty to all the bigamists currently in his jails because you need to do something spectacular on such occasions.

The first part of the sentence talks about *Ludwig.* The second part of the sentence, which begins with the word *because,* shifts to *you.* Making the correction is simple:

> To celebrate his marriage, *Ludwig* promised amnesty to all the bigamists currently in his jails because *he* needs to do something spectacular on such occasions.

or

> To celebrate his marriage, *Ludwig* promised amnesty to all the bigamists currently in his jails because *everyone* needs to do something spectacular on such occasions.

or

> To celebrate his marriage, *Ludwig* promised amnesty to all the bigamists currently in his jails because *rulers* need to do something spectacular on such occasions.

All three of the preceding sentences are correct. Why? In the first, *Ludwig* is the subject of the first part of the sentence, and *he* is the subject of the second part. No problem. The second and third corrections are a bit more complicated. Grammarians refer to three *persons.* In *first person,* the subject narrates the story: In other words, *I* or *we* acts as the subject of the sentence. In *second person,* the subject is being spoken to, and *you* (either singular or plural) is the subject. In *third person,* the subject is being spoken about, using *he, she, it, they,* or any other word that talks *about* someone or something. In the second correction, Ludwig (third person) is matched with *everyone* (a third person pronoun). In the third correction example, Ludwig is matched with *rulers,* a noun.

Here is another example:

> WRONG: *I* am planning to pick up some of those coins; *you* can't pass up a chance for free money!

WHY IT IS WRONG: The first part of the sentence is in first person (*I*) and the second part of the sentence shifts to *you,* the second person form. Why shift?

RIGHT: *I* am planning to pick up some of those coins; *I* can't pass up a chance for free money!

Make sure your sentences are consistent in person. Unless there's a logical reason to shift, follow these guidelines:

- ✔ If you begin with first person (*I* or *me*), stay in first person.
- ✔ If you begin with second person (*you*), stay in second person.
- ✔ If you begin with third person, talking *about* someone or something, make sure that you continue to talk *about* someone or something.

Which sentence is correct?

A. Whenever a person breaks a grammar rule, you get into trouble.

B. Whenever a person breaks a grammar rule, he or she gets into trouble.

C. Whenever a person breaks a grammar rule, they get into trouble.

Answer: Sentence B is correct. *A person* matches *he or she* because both talk about someone. In sentence A, *a person* does not match *you.* Sentence A shifts from third to second person for no logical reason. Sentence C stays in third person, talking about someone, but *a person* is singular and *they* is plural — a mismatch. (For more information on singular and plural pronouns, see Chapter 10.)

Try one more. Which is correct?

A. Everybody loves somebody sometime because all you need is love.

B. Everybody loves somebody sometime because all anybody needs is love.

Answer: Sentence B is correct. Sentence A shifts from third person (*everybody*) to second (*you*) with no reason other than a pathetic attempt to quote song lyrics. Sentence B stays in third person (*everybody, anybody*).

Seeing Double: Conjunction Pairs

Most joining words fly solo. Single words — *and, but, nor, or, because, although, since,* and so on — join sentences or parts of sentences. Some joining words, however, come in pairs. (In grammarspeak, joining words are called *conjunctions*. Double conjunctions are called *correlatives*.) Here are some of the most frequently used double conjunctions:

✔ not only/but also

✔ either/or

✔ neither/nor

✔ whether/or

✔ both/and

Some of these words show up in sentences without their partners. No problem! Sometimes they show up and don't act as conjunctions. Again, no problem. Just make sure that when they do act as conjunctions, they behave properly. Here's the rule: Whatever fills in the blanks after these pairs of conjunctions must match. The conjunctions have partners, and so do the things they join. You may join two nouns, two sentences, two prepositional phrases — two whatevers! Just make sure the things that you join match. Check out this example:

> Not only Ludwig but also his bride yearned for a day at the beach. (The conjunction pair joins two nouns, *Ludwig* and *his bride*.)

> Either you or I must break the news about the backhoe encounter to Ludwig. (The conjunction pair joins two pronouns, *you* and *I*.)

Nouns and pronouns are equals when it comes to parallelism. Because pronouns take the place of nouns, you may mix them without ill effect:

> Neither Murgatroyd nor he has brought a proper present to Ludwig's wedding. (The conjunction pair joins a noun, *Murgatroyd,* and a pronoun, *he.*)

Here's another example:

> Both *because he stole the garter* and *because he lost the ring,* Lochness is no longer welcome as best man. (This conjunction pair joins two subject-verb combinations.)

Because he stole the garter and *because he lost the ring* are subordinate adverbial clauses. For more information on clauses, see Chapter 24.

To help you spot parallelism errors in sentences with conjunction pairs, here are a few mismatches, along with their corrections:

> NOT PARALLEL: Either *Lulu will go with Ludwig to the bachelor party* or *to the shower,* but she will not attend both.

WHY IT'S NOT PARALLEL: The first italicized section is a subject-verb combination. The second italicized section is a prepositional phrase.

PARALLEL: Lulu will go with Ludwig either *to the bachelor party* or *to the shower,* but she will not attend both. (Now both are prepositional phrases.)

NOT PARALLEL: Both *her lateness* and *that she was dressed in white leather* insulted the royal couple.

WHY IT'S NOT PARALLEL: First italicized section is a noun, but the second is a subject-verb combination.

PARALLEL: Both *the fact that she was late* and *the fact that she was dressed in white leather* insulted the royal couple. (Now the italicized sections are both subject-verb combinations.)

PARALLEL: Both *her lateness* and *her white leather clothing* insulted the royal couple. (Now the italicized sections are both nouns.)

Which sentence is correct?

A. Lulu neither needled Ludwig nor his bride about the fact that Mrs. Ludwig has a slight but noticeable moustache.

B. Lulu needled neither Ludwig nor his bride about the fact that Mrs. Ludwig has a slight but noticeable moustache.

Answer: Sentence B is correct. In sentence A, *neither* precedes a verb *(needled)* but *nor* precedes a noun *(his bride)*. In sentence B, *neither* precedes a noun *(Ludwig)* and so does *nor (his bride)*.

Try another. Which sentence is correct?

A. Both the way she danced and the way she sang convinced Legghorn to award Lola a starring role in Legghorn's new musical, *The Homework Blues*.

B. Both the way she danced and her superb singing convinced Legghorn to award Lola a starring role in Legghorn's new musical, *The Homework Blues*.

Answer: Sentence A is correct. In sentence B, the first half of the conjunction pair *(both)* is followed by a noun *(way)* and then a subject–verb combination *(she danced)*. The second part of the conjunction pair *(and)* is followed only by a noun *(singing)*. In sentence A, a noun–subject–verb combination *(the way she danced, the way she sang)* follows both parts of the conjunction pair.

Either way I need a verb: Subjects with either/or, neither/nor statements and questions

Suppose you're talking about Ludwig and the poor people who have the misfortune to live in his country:

> Either Ludwig or his browbeaten subjects. . .

What comes next? *Is* or *are?* In a sentence with only one subject — *Ludwig,* for example — the choice is easy. *Ludwig is,* because *Ludwig* is a singular subject. Or, if the sentence has only one subject, and the subject is plural — say, *his browbeaten subjects* — the choice is also easy. *His browbeaten subjects are.* But what if a singular and a plural subject are in the same sentence? Then what do you do?

When you have a pair of subjects, one singular and one plural, grab a ruler. Okay, you don't actually need a ruler, but you do have to measure. Which subject is closer to the verb? The closer subject determines the type of verb that you need. If the closer subject is singular, use a singular verb. If the closer subject is plural, use a plural verb. Thus,

> Either *Ludwig* or his browbeaten *subjects* are going to regret this marriage.

The closest subject is *subjects,* a plural, so you need the plural verb *are.* (The subject is *subjects?* What are the odds of that?)

If you rearrange the sentence, you get the following:

> Either his browbeaten *subjects* or *Ludwig* is going to regret this marriage.

The closest subject now is *Ludwig,* a singular, so you need the singular verb *is.*

The same trick works for pairs of subjects connected by *neither* and *nor.*

Now for the questions. To change a statement into a question in English, you have to fool around with the word order of the sentence. Also, questions in English are usually constructed with two-word verbs — a main verb and a helping verb. The hard part comes when you're choosing a subject for a question with an *either/or* pair. Such sentences have two subjects. What if one subject is singular and one is plural? Which one should you match? The answer is easy. Take out your ruler. Find the subject that is closer to the part of the verb that changes (the helping verb) and make a match. For example:

> *Does* either *Ludwig* or his ex-wives live in a castle?

The singular subject *Ludwig* is closer to the helping verb *does. Does* is the part of the verb that matches a singular subject.

Here's another version of the same question, with the order changed:

> *Do* either his *ex-wives* or Ludwig live in a castle?

The plural subject *ex-wives* is closer to the helping verb *do. Do* is the part of the verb that matches the plural subject.

Theoretically, you may use the same trick when you're writing a question with *neither/nor* in it. As I write these examples, however, I must tell you that I've never actually heard anyone ask a *neither/nor* question. Still, if you're burning with curiosity or dying to make a *neither/nor* question, here are two:

> *Do* neither the *students* nor the teacher know anything at all about grammar?

> *Does* neither *the teacher* nor the students know anything at all about grammar?

Avoiding Improper Comparisons

The grammar police will arrive, warrant in hand, if your comparisons aren't parallel. Comparisons to watch out for include the following:

✔ more/than

✔ but not

✔ as well as

Comparisons with these words are tricky but not impossible. Just be sure that the elements you are comparing match grammatically. Check out these examples:

> Lulu was more *conservative* than *daring* in her choice of clothes for Ludwig's wedding.
>
> Even so, Ludwig liked *the way Lulu moved* but not *the way she looked*.
>
> Lulu enjoyed the ceremonial *dancing* as well as the ritual *bonfire*.

The italicized words in each sentence pair off nicely. In the first sample sentence, *conservative* and *daring* are both descriptions. In the second sample sentence, *the way Lulu moved* and *the way she looked* are similar constructions — nouns described by adjective clauses, if you absolutely must know. In the third sample sentence, *dancing* and *bonfire* are both nouns.

To illustrate parallel comparisons further, here are some incorrect and corrected pairs:

> WRONG: Lola sang more forcefully than with the correct notes.
>
> WHY IT'S WRONG: *forcefully* and *with the correct notes* don't match.
>
> RIGHT: *Lola sang* more *forcefully* than *correctly*.
>
> WHY IT'S RIGHT: The sentence compares two adverbs.

Here's another example:

> WRONG: Ludmilla assumed *that she would live in a separate castle* but not *spending every hour with Ludwig*.
>
> WHY IT'S WRONG: The words *but not* join a subject–verb combination and verb form.
>
> RIGHT: Ludmilla assumed *that she would live in a separate castle* but not *that she would spend every hour with Ludwig*.
>
> WHY IT'S RIGHT: The sentence compares two subject–verb combinations.

A question may have occurred to you: How do you know how many words of the sentence are being joined? In other words, in the preceding sample sentences, how do you know how much to italicize? The decision comes from the meaning of the sentence. Forget grammar for a moment and put yourself into reading comprehension mode. What are you comparing? Decide what you're comparing based on the ideas in the sentence. Now check the two ideas being compared and go back into grammar mode. Do the ideas match *grammatically?* If so, you're fine. If not, reword your sentence.

Which sentence is correct?

A. Legghorn told Ratrug that the ceremony was canceled but not that the couple planned to elope.

B. Legghorn told Ratrug that the ceremony was canceled but not about the elopement.

Answer: Sentence A is correct. *That the ceremony was canceled* matches *that the couple planned to elope.* In sentence B, *that the ceremony was canceled* has a subject–verb pair, but *about the elopement* is a prepositional phrase with no subject–verb pair.

Part V
Rules Even Your Great-Aunt's Grammar Teacher Didn't Know

In this part . . .

Learned philosophers in the Middle Ages used to argue about the number of angels that could fit on the head of a pin. That debate was only a little less complicated than the grammar rules in this part. Chapter 22 explains the moods of verbs (yes, they have moods). Chapter 23 shows you how to choose the proper pronoun for all sorts of weird sentences. The next chapter deals with the inner workings of the sentence — dependent and independent clauses and verbals. Chapter 25 gives you a master's degree in punctuation.

Bottom line: If you want to learn some of the pickiest grammar rules ever devised, this part's for you.

Chapter 22

The Last Word on Verbs

In This Chapter

▶ Getting in touch with your indicative mood

▶ Commanding the imperative

▶ Writing subjunctive verbs for conditions contrary to fact

▶ Avoiding common double-negative constructions

Murgatroyd stomps in, slams the door, and grabs the remote. As he raises the volume on the wrestling match to supersonic level, Lola asks politely, "Is anything wrong?" In reply, Murgatroyd lowers his eyebrows to the tip of his nose and glares silently. Lola shrugs and goes out to spread the word: Murgatroyd is in one of his Moods. Beware.

*V*erbs have moods too, but they're a lot more polite about showing them than Murgatroyd. A little change of form, and presto, the verb is in a different mood.

Modern English has three basic moods of verbs: indicative, imperative, and subjunctive. Indicative is the most common; the two other moods — imperative and subjunctive — enter speech and writing only occasionally. In this chapter, I give you the lowdown on these three verb types so you're sure to know the mood of any verb without consulting a mind reader.

Getting a Feel for Everyday Verbs: The Indicative Mood

Almost all verbs are in indicative mood. *Indicative* is the everyday, this-is-what-I'm-saying mood, good for questions and statements. All the lessons about verbs in this book — aside from those later in this chapter — discuss verbs in the indicative mood. (This fact, by the way, is totally useless. Forget it immediately.)

Think of indicative verbs as the permanent cast of a TV show. They are always around and are familiar to everyone.

The indicative verbs are italicized in the following sentences:

> Felonia *displayed* her musical range when she *played* a Bach concerto and a heavy-metal hit in the same concert.

> Ludwig *will be* the principal tenant of the honeymoon hotel as soon as Ludmilla *agrees* to marry him.

> Eggworthy often *dreams* about bacon.

Commanding Your Verbs: The Imperative Mood

Don't worry about imperatives; they're fairly simple. *Imperative verbs* give commands. Most imperative verbs don't have a written (or spoken) subject. Instead, the subject in an imperative (command) sentence is *you-understood*. The word *you* usually does not appear before the imperative verb. The reader or listener simply understands that *you* is implied.

Here are a few examples to get you thinking:

> *Eat* a balanced diet.

> *Climb* every mountain.

> *Calculate* the odds.

> No matter what happens, *hit* the road.

> *Fake* a sincere smile and you've got it made.

Rising to the occasion

Rise and *raise* are two very confusing verbs. *Rise* means "to stand," "to get out of bed," or "to move to a higher rank" under one's own power. *Raise* means "to lift something or someone else up" or "to bring up children or animals." In other words, Eggworthy *rises* whenever any sort of poultry enters the room. He *raises* roosters on his farm. When a nest is too low, Eggworthy *raises* it to a higher shelf.

Here's another way to think about these two words: *Rise* is a self-contained action. The subject acts upon him- or herself. *Raise* is an action that begins with one person (or thing) and moves to another person or thing. You *rise* by yourself; you *raise* someone or something else.

Think of imperative verbs as recurring guest stars on a sitcom, the characters who show up every three or four episodes just to add a little flavor to the mix.

There's almost nothing you can do wrong in creating an imperative sentence, so this topic is a free pass. *Go* fishing, or if you're in the mood to torture yourself, *move* on to the subjunctive.

Discovering the Possibilities: The Subjunctive Mood

Headache time! The subjunctive mood is rare, but it draws errors like a magnet. Master this topic and you'll qualify for the title "Grammarian of the Year." Subjunctive verbs show up when you state something that is contrary to fact. They may also express indirect commands and wishes. I tackle each of these situations in the following sections.

Subjunctive verbs make only a few cameo appearances. Like a pampered superstar, a subjunctive shows up only when the situation is exactly right.

Using subjunctives with "were"

Tevye, the main character in the musical *Fiddler on the Roof,* sings "If I Were a Rich Man" with the sadness of a man who knows that he'll never be anything but poor. Tevye's song is about a *condition contrary to fact* — something that is not true. Take note of the verb in the title: *were.* Normally (that is to say, in an indicative sentence) the subject–verb pair would be *I was.* But Tevye sings *If I were* because he isn't a rich man. The verb *were* is in subjunctive mood.

Unless someone is going to quiz you on it, don't worry about the terminology. Just know that if you're expressing a condition contrary to fact, you need the verb *were* for present and future ideas. (Past tense is different. See the next section, "Using subjunctives with 'had.'") Here are some examples of present and future tense:

> SUBJUNCTIVE: If Lochness *were* an honorable spy, he would not reveal the atomic secret hidden in the bean burrito.

> WHY IT'S SUBJUNCTIVE: Lochness is not an honorable spy, and he's going to blab the secret.

> WHAT THE NORMAL SUBJECT–VERB PAIR WOULD BE: Lochness was.

> SUBJUNCTIVE: If Analivia *were* less talented in mathematics, she would have taken fewer algebra courses.

WHY IT'S SUBJUNCTIVE: Analivia's a math genius, the kind of student who always says that the test was "so hard" and then wrecks the curve with a 96.

WHAT THE NORMAL SUBJECT–VERB PAIR WOULD BE: Analivia was.

To sum up, in subjunctive sentences, *were* is usually all you need (unlike in the Beatles' song, when love is all you need). Here are a few details about subjunctive for present or future statements of conditions contrary to fact:

- ✔ Use *were* for all subjects in the part of the sentence that expresses what is not true. (If she *were* entranced by Ratrug's explanation.)
- ✔ For the other part of the sentence, use the helping verb *would*. (Lola *would stare* at him in silence.)
- ✔ Never use the helping verb *would* in the untrue part of the sentence. For example:

WRONG: If I would have been president, I would ask the Martian colony to secede.

RIGHT: If I were president, I would ask the Martian colony to secede.

WRONG: Murgatroyd acted as though he would have been grammarian-in-chief.

RIGHT: Murgatroyd acted as though he were grammarian-in-chief.

Which sentence is correct?

- A. Ludmilla would have been happier if she would have been in the Marines.
- B. Ludmilla would have been happier if she were in the Marines.

Answer: Sentence B is correct. The *if* part of the sentence contains a subjunctive verb *(were)* because it expresses something that is not true. The *if* part of the sentence should never contain the helping verb *would*.

Using subjunctives with "had"

The other subjunctive that pops up from time to time is created with the helping verb *had*. For past tense sentences, the *had* belongs in the part of the sentence that is contrary to fact. The contrary-to-fact (that is, the lie) part of the sentence may begin with *if,* or the *if* may be understood.

Now I lie me down to sleep. . . .

Whoever invented the verbs *lie* and *lay* had an evil sense of humor. *Lie* means "not to tell the truth," but that meaning isn't a problem. *Lie* also means "to rest or to plop yourself down, ready for a snooze," or "to remain." *Lay* means "to put something down, to place something." Here are some examples:

> Scintilla likes to *lie* down for an hour after lunch. Before she hits the couch, she *lays* a soft sheet over the upholstery.

> Lochness *lies* in wait behind those bushes. When unsuspecting tourists *lay* down their picnic blankets, he swoops in and steals their lunches.

So far, this topic isn't too complicated. The problem — and the truly devilish part — comes in the past tense. The past tense of *lie* (to rest, to recline, to remain) is *lay*. The past tense of *lay* (to put or place) is *laid*. Check out these examples:

> Scintilla *lay* down yesterday, but a car alarm disturbed her rest. She immediately went to the street and *laid* a carpet of nails in front of the offending vehicle.

> Yesterday, while Lochness *lay* in wait, a police officer *laid* a hand on Lochness's shoulder. "You are under arrest," intoned the cop.

One more complication: When you add *has, had,* or *have* to the verb *lie* (to rest, to recline, to remain), you say *has lain, had lain, have lain.* When you add *has, had,* or *have* to the verb *lay* (to put or place), you say *has laid, had laid, have laid.* In other words:

> Scintilla *has lain* in the hammock for most of the morning, and her brothers *have laid* a basket of red ants on the ground beneath her. When Scintilla gets up, she is in for a big surprise!

> Lochness *has lain* in the lumpy jail bunk for an hour, but no one *has laid* a sheet over him to keep him warm.

Normally — that is, in non-subjunctive sentences — the past tense would be expressed by a single-word, past tense verb. The *had* form, in a non-subjunctive sentence, is used only to show one action happening before another. (See Chapter 18 for more information.) Here are a few examples of the past subjunctive:

> SUBJUNCTIVE WITH THE WORD *IF:* If Lola *had known* about the atomic secret, she would not have eaten that burrito.

> SUBJUNCTIVE WITHOUT THE WORD *IF: Had* Lola *known* about the atomic secret, she would not have eaten that burrito.

> WHY IT'S SUBJUNCTIVE: Lola knew nothing about the atomic secret; Lochness told her that the crunch in the burrito came from a new type of bean.

> WHAT THE NORMAL SUBJECT–VERB PAIR WOULD BE: Lola knew.

SUBJUNCTIVE WITH THE WORD *IF:* If Ludwig *had married* less often, he would have enjoyed the ceremony more.

SUBJUNCTIVE WITHOUT THE WORD *IF: Had* Ludwig *married* less often, he would have enjoyed the ceremony more.

WHY IT'S SUBJUNCTIVE: Ludwig has been married more times than he can count.

WHAT THE NORMAL SUBJECT–VERB PAIR WOULD BE: Ludwig has married.

Which sentence is correct?

A. If Felonia would have played the tuba, the gang would have listened to her CD more often.

B. If Felonia had played the tuba, the gang would have listened to her CD more often.

Answer: Sentence B is correct. Felonia played the piano, not the tuba, so subjunctive is appropriate. The word *would* is never part of an *if* statement.

Using subjunctives with "as though"

Sometimes conditions contrary to fact are expressed using the words *as though.* Check out the following:

SUBJUNCTIVE: Eggworthy hurtled through the air *as though* giant metal devices had intended to scramble him.

WHY IT'S SUBJUNCTIVE: Eggworthy was not being pursued by giant eggbeaters. He was actually hurtling through the air because Murgatroyd was in a bad mood, and Eggworthy was trying to escape on a skateboard with one bad wheel.

WHAT THE NORMAL SUBJECT–VERB PAIR WOULD BE: Giant metal devices intended.

Using subjunctives with commands, wishes, and requests

Ludwig loves to exercise his royal power:

His Majesty decrees that all his subjects *be* counted and then beheaded.

His Majesty asks that the governor of each province *climb* the nearest Alp and *jump* off the top.

His Majesty further insists that his favorite wedding planner *remain* in the palace.

When "if" isn't subjunctive

As you're reading about the subjunctive *if,* you may think that all sentences with the word *if* need a subjunctive verb. Nope. Some *if* sentences don't express a condition contrary to fact; they express a possibility, something that may happen. The *if* sentences that express a possibility take a plain old, normal, indicative verb. Here are some examples:

NON-SUBJUNCTIVE *IF* SENTENCE: If Lochness goes to prison, he will take a burrito cookbook with him.

WHY IT'S NOT SUBJUNCTIVE: Prison is a possibility.

NON-SUBJUNCTIVE *IF* SENTENCE: If Ludwig divorces, he will remarry within a year.

WHY IT'S NOT SUBJUNCTIVE: Divorce is a possibility. In fact, Ludwig is already looking around.

In an *if* sentence, if something is possible, use a normal, everyday verb to say it. If something is untrue, use a subjunctive verb.

The italicized verbs are all subjunctive. These sentences need subjunctives because they express wishes, requests, or indirect commands. (Commands that are given directly to the person who is supposed to follow them are in imperative mood. See " Commanding Your Verbs: The Imperative Mood," earlier in this chapter.)

In the previous sample sentences, the normal subject–verb pairs (the indicative pairs) would be *subjects are, governor climbs, wedding planner remains.* In these subjunctive sentences, all subjects take the same form of the verb — the infinitive minus the *to.* (For more information on infinitives, see Chapter 2.) Thus you have

> to sleep: subjunctive = sleep
>
> to slobber: subjunctive = slobber
>
> to sneak: subjunctive = sneak

and so forth.

In everyday communication, many speakers of perfectly good English avoid the subjunctive and use an infinitive or the helping verb *should* instead. Here are Ludwig's requests, with infinitives or *should* instead of subjunctive verbs:

> His Majesty wants his subjects *to be counted* and then *beheaded.*
>
> His Majesty says that the governor of each province *should climb* the nearest Alp and *jump* off the top.
>
> His Majesty wants his favorite wedding planner *to remain* in the palace.

Try and figure these out: Verbs and infinitives

Now that you've read the heading above, do you see what's wrong with it? *Try and* means that you are going to do two different things: *try* (first task) and *figure out* (second task). But you don't have two tasks in mind, do you? *Try and* is a common expression, but not a correct one. Here's what you really mean: *try* to *figure this one out*. *Try to* follows the normal English pattern of a verb and an infinitive:

> Lochness *plans to go* to the moon next week. (*plans* = verb, *to go* = infinitive)

> Ludmilla *likes to speak* in monosyllables. (*likes* = verb, *to speak* = infinitive)

Ratrug *hates to cry* in public. (*hates* = verb, *to cry* = infinitive)

By the way, infinitives look like verbs, but they never act as verbs in the sentence. In the sample sentences above, all the infinitives are direct objects. (For more information on direct objects, see Chapter 6; for more information on infinitives, see Chapter 24.)

Let me sum up: *Try to remember* the verb-infinitive rule and *try to forget* about *try and*.

Which sentence is correct?

A. Ludwig requests that his honeymoon attendants are paid by the hour.

B. Ludwig requests that his honeymoon attendants be paid by the hour.

Answer: Sentence B is correct. The subjunctive verb *(be)* expresses the request. (The infinitive *to be* minus the *to* equals subjunctive.)

Using subjunctives with "let us"

Have you been to church lately? If so, perhaps the religious leader said, "Let us pray" or "Let us sing all 5,987 verses of hymn #2." The *let us* sentence is actually in subjunctive mood. Follow *let us* with the subjunctive form of the verb: the infinitive minus the word *to*. In each of the following examples, the subjunctive verb is italicized:

> Let us *gather* together.

> Let us *eat* salad.

> Let us *ban* iceberg lettuce from Shakey's salad.

If you've read all the preceding sections on the subjunctive mood, by now you're probably in a mood yourself — a bad mood. Take heart! Although it may seem as if the subjunctive were all over the English language, in reality you need it only occasionally. If you speak another language — Spanish or French, for example — you've probably noticed by now that the subjunctive is a much bigger deal and far more common in those languages. One last thought: If the rules for subjunctive in this chapter seem overwhelming, forget about them. The grammar police won't execute you if you completely ignore the subjunctive. Many literate, educated people work around it, and errors of the subjunctive are not nearly so serious as, say, jaywalking.

I Can't Help But Think This Rule Is Crazy: Deleting Double Negatives

In some lucky languages, the more negatives the better. In English, however, two negatives are a no-no. (By the way, no-no is *not* a double negative! It's just slang for something that's prohibited.) I explain several basic forms of double negatives in Chapter 8. Here I tell you about some of the less obvious forms of double trouble.

One of the most common double negatives doesn't look like one: *cannot help but*. How many times have you heard someone say something like

> Eggworthy *cannot help but* act in that dramatic style because he was trained by a real ham.

Sometimes, *help* is left out:

> Eggworthy *cannot but* think that it is his job to bring home the bacon.

Unfortunately, both of these sentences are wrong because they both contain double negatives. The *not* and the *but* both express negative ideas. Use one or the other. Don't use both. Here are the correct versions:

> Eggworthy *cannot help acting* in that dramatic style because he was trained by a real ham.

> Eggworthy *can* but think that it is his job to bring home the bacon.

This last sentence sounds terrible, doesn't it? The next version is much better:

Eggworthy *can* think only that it is his job to bring home the bacon.

or

Eggworthy *cannot help* thinking that it is his job to bring home the bacon.

You can also write

Eggworthy *thinks* that it is his job to bring home the bacon.

Ironically, in English two negatives make a positive. So when you say *cannot help but,* you actually convey the opposite of what you imagine you're saying (or writing). For example:

Ratrug told his boss, "I cannot help but ask for a raise."

WHAT HE THINKS HE SAID: I have to ask for a raise.

WHAT HE REALLY SAID: I can't ask for a raise.

The boss told Ratrug, "I cannot help but say no."

WHAT THE BOSS THINKS SHE SAID: No.

WHAT THE BOSS ACTUALLY SAID: Yes.

Which sentence is correct?

A. I cannot help but think that this double negative rule is ridiculous.

B. I cannot help thinking that this double negative rule is ridiculous.

Answer: Sentence B is correct. Also, the idea of the sentence is correct! The double negative rule is dumb.

Can't Hardly Understand This Rule: Yet Another Double Negative

No matter what you do, avoid saying or writing *can't hardly* when you are using formal English. *Can't* is short for *cannot,* which contains the negative *not. Hardly* is another negative word. If you combine them, by the logic of grammar, you've said the opposite of what you intended — the positive instead of the negative. Here are a few examples:

Legghorn commented, "Lulu can't hardly count her tattoos."

WHAT LEGGHORN THINKS HE SAID: Lulu can't count her tattoos.

WHAT LEGGHORN ACTUALLY SAID: Lulu can count her tattoos.

According to Lola, Ludmilla can't hardly wait until her divorce becomes final.

WHAT THE WRITER THINKS THE SENTENCE MEANS: Ludmilla is eager for her divorce to become final.

WHAT THE SENTENCE ACTUALLY MEANS: Ludmilla can wait. (The palace is comfy and Ludwig isn't around very much.)

A variation of this double negative is *can't scarcely, aren't scarcely,* or *isn't scarcely.* Once again, *can't* is short for *cannot,* clearly a negative. *Aren't* and *isn't* are the negative forms of *are* and *is. Scarcely* is also negative. Use them together and you end up with a positive, not a super-negative.

Here's another double negative, in a couple of forms: *hadn't only, haven't only, hasn't only, hadn't but, haven't but,* and *hasn't but.* All express positive ideas because the *not (n't)* part of the verb and the *only* or *but* are both negatives:

WRONG: Agwamp *hadn't but* ten seconds to defuse the bomb before civilization as we know it ended.

WHY IT'S WRONG: As it reads now, the sentence says that Agwamp had more than ten seconds to defuse the bomb, but the little red numbers on the trigger were at seven and decreasing rapidly.

RIGHT: Agwamp *had but* ten seconds to defuse the bomb before civilization as we know it ended.

ALSO RIGHT: Agwamp *had* only ten seconds to defuse the bomb before civilization as we know it ended.

WRONG: Lochness *hasn't only* ten nuclear secrets.

WHY IT'S WRONG: The sentence now says that Lochness has more than ten secrets, but he just counted them and there are only ten.

RIGHT: Lochness *has only* ten nuclear secrets.

Which sentence is correct?

A. Ubetcha can't hardly understand those pesky grammar rules.

B. Ubetcha can't help but be confused by those pesky grammar rules.

DEMONS

It takes two to make a mistake

In English you find three "to's," all sounding exactly alike but spelled differently. (Words that sound alike but are spelled differently are known as *homonyms*). And no, they don't add up to six. *To* may be part of an infinitive *(to speak, to dream)* or it may show movement towards someone or something *(to the store, to me). Two* is the number *(two eyes, two ears). Too* means also *(Are you going too?)* or more than enough *(too expensive, too wide)*. In other words:

> If you *two* want *to* skip school and go *to* the ball game, today's a good day because the teacher will be *too* busy *to* check.

The *two* basketballs that hit Ludwig in the head yesterday were *too* soft *to* do much damage, but Ludwig is suing anyway.

Two things you should always remember before you decide *to* break a grammar rule: it is never *too* late *to* learn proper English and you are never *too* old *to* get in trouble with your teacher.

Answer: Both are wrong. (The official teacher manual orders teachers to play annoying tricks with quizzes.) In sentence A, *can't hardly* is a double negative. In sentence B, *cannot help but* is a double negative. Now look at these:

A. Ubetcha can scarcely understand those pesky grammar rules.

B. Ubetcha can't help being confused by those pesky grammar rules.

Answer: Sentences A and B are both correct. Ubetcha is serving five to ten in the penitentiary for breaking grammar rules. In sentence A, he has only a little understanding of grammar. In sentence B he is confused.

Chapter 23

The Last Word on Pronouns

You've come to it at last: the dreaded pronoun chapter where you find out the intricate details of who/whom and the like. Be warned: In three nanoseconds, you can easily find something to do that is more interesting than these concepts — training fleas for circus duty, for example, or picking lint out of your belly button.

You're still reading, aren't you? Okay, you asked for it. Here is the last word on pronouns, including who/whom sentences and a host of other really picky pronoun points. People have led perfectly pleasant (albeit grammatically incorrect) lives without knowing this stuff. But if you insist. . . .

Knowing the Difference Between Who and Whom

The rule for knowing when to use *who* and *whom* is simple; applying the rule is not. First, the rule:

> ✔ *Who* and *whoever* are for subjects.
>
> *Who* and *whoever* also follow and complete the meaning of linking verbs. In grammarspeak, *who* and *whoever* serve as linking verb complements.

> ✔ *Whom* and *whomever* are for objects — all kinds of objects (direct, indirect, of prepositions, of infinitives, and so on).

For more information on subjects, see Chapter 4. For more information on objects and linking verb complements, see Chapter 6.

Before applying the rule concerning who/whoever and whom/whomever, check out these sample sentences:

> *Whoever* needs help from Lochness is going to wait a long time. (*Whoever* is the subject of the verb *needs*.)

> *Who* is calling Lulu at this time of night? (*Who* is the subject of the verb *is calling*.)

> "I don't care *whom* you ask to the prom," exclaimed Legghorn unconvincingly. (*Whom* is the direct object of the verb *ask*.)

> The mustard-yellow belt is for *whomever* she designates as the hot dog eating champion. (*Whomever* is the direct object of the verb *designates*.)

> For *whom* are you bellowing? (*Whom* is the object of the preposition *for*.)

Now that you know the rule and have seen the words in action, here are two tricks for deciding between *who/whoever* and *whom/whomever*. If one trick seems to work, use it and ignore the other. Here goes. . . .

Trick #1: Horse and carriage

According to an old song, "love and marriage go together like a horse and carriage." Grammarians might sing that song with slightly different lyrics: "A subject and verb go together like a horse and carriage." (What do you think? Grammy material?) To use Trick #1, follow these steps:

1. Find all the verbs in the sentence.

2. Don't separate the helping verbs from the main verb. Count the main verb and its helpers as a single verb.

3. Now pair each of the verbs with a subject.

4. If you have a verb flapping around with no subject, chances are *who* or *whoever* is the subject you're missing.

5. If all the verbs have subjects, check them one more time. Do you have any linking verbs without complements? (For more information on complements, see Chapter 6.) If you have a lonely linking verb with no complement in sight, you need *who* or *whoever*.

6. If all subjects are accounted for and you don't need a linking verb complement, you've reached a final answer: *whom* or *whomever* is the only possibility.

Here's a sample sentence, analyzed via Trick #1:

SENTENCE: *Who/Whom* shall I say is calling?

The verbs = *shall say, is calling.*

The subject of *shall say* = *I.*

The subject of *is calling* = Okay, here you go. You need a subject for *is calling* but you're out of words. You have only one choice: *who.*

CORRECT SENTENCE: *Who* shall I say is calling?

Now you try: Which word is correct?

Agnes buys detergent in one-ton boxes for Lochness, *who/whom* she adores in spite of his odor problem.

Answer: *Whom,* because it's the direct object of *adores. Agnes buys, she adores* = subject–verb pairs. Both are action verbs, so no subject complement is needed.

Trick #2: Getting rhythm

This trick relies on your ear for grammar. Most English sentences follow one pattern: Subject–Verb–Object or Subject Complement. Trick #2 is to say the parts of the sentence in this order, even if you have to rearrange the words a little. Here are the steps to follow:

1. Identify the verb in the sentence that seems connected to the *who/whom* choice. Usually it's the verb nearest *who/whom.* It's also the verb logically connected by meaning — that is, in the same thought as *who/whom.*

2. Say (aloud, if you don't mind scaring your classmates or co-workers, or silently, if you plan to keep a reputation for sanity) the three parts of the sentence.

   Anything before the verb is *who* or *whoever.*

   If you're working with an action verb, anything after the verb is probably *whom* or *whomever.*

   If you're working with a linking verb, anything after the verb is probably *who* or *whoever.*

Here is a sample sentence analyzed with Trick #2:

Who/Whom will Lochness choose for the vacancy in his nuclear spy ring?

The verb is *will choose.*

Will choose is an action verb, so forget about linking verb complements.

Say aloud: Lochness will choose *who/whom*.

Choice = *whom* because the word is after the verb.

Whom = direct object of will choose.

CORRECT SENTENCE: *Whom* will Lochness choose for the vacancy in his nuclear spy ring?

Which word is correct?

Who/Whom do you like better, Lochness or Legghorn?

Answer: *Whom* is correct. Change the order of the words to *you do like whom*. Choose *whom* after an action verb. In this sentence, *whom* is the direct object. (By the way, the answer is Legghorn, no contest. He's much nicer than Lochness.)

Studying Improper Antecedents

The *antecedent* of a pronoun is the word that the pronoun replaces. The antecedent and the pronoun should be completely interchangeable. In other words, you should be able to replace the pronoun with its antecedent (or the antecedent with the pronoun) without changing the meaning of the sentence. To follow this rule, you must make sure that the pronoun has an antecedent to replace. If the pronoun has no antecedent, the pronoun flaps around loose. A loose pronoun is an unhappy pronoun. Furthermore, the pronoun is a picky little part of speech. It refuses to replace any old word. If an antecedent is almost but not quite right, every self-respecting pronoun turns up its nose at the antecedent and calls the grammar police. (For more information on pronouns and their antecedents, see Chapter 10.) Here are a couple of correct and incorrect examples:

WRONG: She's a lawyer, and I want to study it.

What does *it* replace? *Law,* I suppose. But the word *law* is not in the sentence; *lawyer* is. *Law* and *lawyer* are close, but not close enough.

RIGHT: She's a lawyer, and I want to be one also.

WHY IT'S RIGHT: *One* refers to *lawyer.*

ALSO RIGHT: I'd like to study law, as she did.

WHY IT'S ALSO RIGHT: There's no pronoun in the sentence.

ALSO RIGHT: I want to make a lot of money, so I'm going to law school.

Another (trickier) example is:

WRONG: In Murgatroyd's poetry, he frequently uses cow imagery.

Who's *he?* Murgatroyd, I imagine. But *Murgatroyd* isn't in the sentence. *Murgatroyd's* — the possessive noun — is in the sentence. You can replace *Murgatroyd's* by *his* (because *his* is a possessive pronoun), but not by *he.*

RIGHT: Murgatroyd frequently writes poetry with cow imagery.

WHY IT'S RIGHT: There's no pronoun in the sentence.

ALSO RIGHT: Stay away from Murgatroyd's poetry readings unless you are really, really, really fond of cows.

Which sentence is correct?

A. Lola has always been interested in archaeology because she thinks they spend a lot of time in the dirt.

B. Lola has always been interested in archaeology because she thinks archaeologists spend a lot of time in the dirt.

Sentence B is correct. In sentence A, no proper antecedent exists for *they.* Sentence B replaces *they* with the noun *archaeologists.*

Matching Verbs to Pronouns in Complicated Sentences

Singular pronouns must be paired with singular verbs, and plural pronouns must be paired with plural verbs. Easy rule, right? *He says. They say.* No problem. But not all pronouns are as simple as *he* and *they.* Some pronouns — *who, which,* and *that* — are chameleons. (See Chapter 25 for details on punctuating sentences with *which* and *that.*) They always look the same, but they may be either singular or plural depending upon their antecedents. You have to decode the sentence to decide whether the antecedent is singular or plural. Then you must match the verb to the antecedent. In some sentences with simple structure, the choice is fairly obvious. For example:

English Grammar For Dummies is the book that you're reading. (*that* = book = singular)

The tax guides that fell off the shelf cost me a million dollars. (*that* = *tax guides* = plural)

In complicated sentences, those that single out something or someone from a group, the choice is not so obvious. To pair the pronoun with the correct verb , use your reading comprehension skills to figure out the meaning of the pronoun. After you know the meaning of the pronoun, the choice between a singular and plural verb is clear. Check out the following examples:

SENTENCE A: Lulu is one of the few choir members who *has/have* more than 11 tattoos.

The *who* statement is about having more than 11 tattoos.

According to the sentence, how many choir members are in that category? One or more than one? More than one.

The *who* refers to *choir members*.

Choose the plural verb *(have)*.

CORRECT SENTENCE: Lulu is one of the few choir members who *have* more than 11 tattoos.

SENTENCE B: Lulu is the only one of the choir members who *has/have* a tattoo of a motorcycle on her arm.

The *who* statement is about having a tattoo of a motorcycle.

The sentence makes it clear that Lulu is the only one with that tattoo.

Who is singular, referring to Lulu.

Choose the singular verb *(has)*.

CORRECT SENTENCE: Lulu is the only one of the choir members who *has* a tattoo of a motorcycle on her arm.

Which word is correct?

Ratrug claims he is one of the many men who *has/have* been unfairly rejected by Lola.

Answer: *Have.* Lola has rejected more than one man, according to the sentence, so the verb must be plural.

This, That, and the Other: Clarifying Vague Pronoun References

One pronoun may refer to one noun. A plural pronoun may refer to more than one noun. But no pronoun may refer to a whole sentence or a whole paragraph. Consider the following scenario:

Lulu likes to arrive at school around 11 each day because she thinks that getting up at any hour earlier than 10 is barbaric. The principal, not surprisingly, thinks that arriving at school over two hours late each day is not a good idea. *This* is a problem.

This certainly is a problem, and not because of Lulu's sleeping habits or the principal's beliefs. This is a problem because the antecedent of the word *this* is unclear. What does *this* mean? The fact that Lulu arrives around 11? That Lulu thinks getting up before 10 is out of the question? Or that the principal and Lulu are not, to put it mildly, in sync? Or all of the above?

The writer probably intends *this* to refer to *all of the above,* a perfectly good answer on those horrible multiple choice tests you have to take far too often these days. Unfortunately, *all of the above* is not a good answer to the question, "What does the pronoun mean?"

Thus

WRONG: The orange dye looks horrible, and the cut looks as though it were done with pinking shears. *This* persuaded Lola to attend the dance wearing her purple wig.

WHY IT'S WRONG: *This* is referring to the 17 words of the preceding sentence, not to one noun.

RIGHT: Because the orange dye looks horrible and the cut looks as thought it were done with pinking shears, Lola decided to attend the dance wearing her purple wig.

ALSO RIGHT: The fact that the orange dye looks horrible and the cut looks as though it were done with pinking shears persuaded Lola to attend the dance wearing her purple wig.

WHY IT'S RIGHT: Eliminating *this* eliminates the problem.

In ordinary speech (conversational English) you may occasionally use *this, which,* or *that* to refer to more than one word, as long as your meaning is clear. For example:

Lochness refused to defuse the explosive postage stamp, which angered all the postal workers.

The pronoun *which* in the preceding example refers to the fact that Lochness refused to defuse the explosive stamp. Your audience grasps the meaning easily. However, grammatically, the sentence is incorrect because *which* should replace only one noun. Bottom line: In formal writing you should follow the rule. Reject the sentence. In informal situations, go ahead and use it.

In both conversational and formal English, avoid vagueness. Never use a pronoun that may refer to two or more ideas; don't leave your reader or listener wondering what you mean. For example:

Lulu's history term paper was ten days late and ten pages short. This earned her an F on the assignment.

What convinced the teacher to fail Lulu? The lateness or the fact that she wrote exactly 34 words on "The French Revolution: Its Causes and Effects in Relation to the Concept of Democracy"? One of these factors? If so, which one? Or both? Inquiring minds want to know, and the pronoun doesn't tell. Possible corrections include the following:

Because Lulu's history term paper was ten days late and ten pages short, the teacher failed her. (Now you know that both factors influenced the grade.)

Lulu's history term paper was ten days late, so the teacher failed her. Even if it had arrived on time, the fact that it was ten pages short would have earned her an F on the assignment anyway.

To sum up this simple rule: Be clear when using pronouns.

Which sentence is correct?

A. The roof leaked and the floor creaked, which kept Ratrug up all night.

B. The leaky roof and the creaky floor kept Ratrug up all night.

Answer: Sentence B is correct. In sentence A, *which* refers to two ideas, not to one noun.

Its or Their? Selecting Pronouns for Collective Nouns

Collective nouns present a problem when it comes to choosing the right pronouns. Collective nouns (*committee, team, squad, army, class,* and the like) refer to groups. When the group is acting as a unit — doing the same thing at the same time — the noun is singular and the pronouns that refer to it are also singular. When the sentence refers to individual members of the group, use a plural pronoun.

The audience rises and is ready to leave after a stirring performance of Legghorn's new play. (Actually, the audience was ready to leave after the first act, but Lulu had locked the doors.)

In this sentence, I paired the subject, *audience,* with singular verbs — *rises, is* and *was.* Those verbs are correct because the audience acts together, a collection of people molded into one unit. To put the concept into grammarspeak, *audience* is a collective noun.

In the paper it says.. . .

Are you writing about literature or even trashy tabloid journalism? If so, beware of *it* and *they*. Some common errors follow those pronouns. Check out these examples:

In *Hamlet,* it says that Claudius is a murderer.

Oh really? What does *it* mean? The play can't speak, and the author of the play (Shakespeare) is a *who.* Actually, in *Hamlet,* the ghost says that Claudius is a murderer, but even the ghost is a *he.* In other words, *it* has no antecedent. Reword the sentence:

In *Hamlet* Claudius is a murderer.

In *Hamlet* the ghost declares that Claudius is a murderer.

My teacher says that in *Hamlet* Claudius is a murderer, but I'm not sure, because I never understand Shakespeare's plays anyway. Why couldn't he write in plain English? What's up with that?

Here's another example:

In today's paper *they* say that more and more schools are dropping Shakespeare's plays because of incomprehensible language.

(I should probably say, before I get back to the grammar, that I actually *like* Shakespeare's plays, and not just because I'm an English teacher. Now, back to pronouns.) Who is *they?* Perhaps the authors of an article, but the sentence doesn't make that fact clear. More likely the author of the sentence thinks that *they* is a good, all-purpose pronoun for talking about anonymous or nameless authors. In other words, the antecedent of *they* is "I don't know and I really don't care." Wrong! The antecedent of *they* must be a real, identifiable group of people. Some possible corrections include:

Today's paper reports that more and more schools are dropping Shakespeare's plays because of incomprehensible language.

In today's paper, education critic I. M. Ignorentz explains that more and more schools are dropping Shakespeare's plays because of incomprehensible language.

So if the audience is a unit, should the audience clap *its* hands or *their* hands? At first glance *its* would seem appropriate, because *its* is singular, and *audience* is paired with singular verbs. However, the audience doesn't own a big, collective hand. Every person in the audience has two individual hands (every person except for Ludmilla, who has three, but I won't go into that because she's very sensitive about her body image). Body parts, no matter how unified the group, must belong to separate people. Dump the collective noun and substitute *members of the audience.* Now insert *their.* Therefore

The members of the audience rise to *their* feet and clap *their* hands.

Members is now the subject. *Members* is plural, so the verbs and pronouns are all plural also.

Are there any sentences in which *its* is correct? Yes. Here's one:

> The cast will hold *its* annual Thank-God-Legghorn's-Latest-Play-Is-Over Party tomorrow.

Its is appropriate in this sentence because the party belongs to the cast as a whole, not to the individual members of the cast.

Here's another sentence to figure out:

> As the orchestra raises *its/their* instruments, Lochness searches for the sheet music.

Orchestra is another collective noun. The verb is singular, because the orchestra acts in unison, but *its instruments* sounds strange. Okay, maybe the *orchestra* owns all the tubas, violins, and other instruments of destruction. (You should hear them play.) So if the sentence were talking about ownership, *its* would fit:

> The orchestra insures *its* instruments with Lloyds of Topeka.

However, the orchestra can't raise a collectively-owned instrument. Each musician raises his or her own. So *their* and *musicians* make more sense:

> The musicians in the orchestra raise *their* instruments and prepare to demolish Beethoven.

To sum up the general rules on pronouns that refer to groups:

- ✔ Collective nouns performing one action as a unit take a singular verb.
- ✔ Possessive pronouns referring to collective nouns are singular if the item possessed belongs to the entire group.
- ✔ If the members of the group are acting as individuals, drop the collective noun. Possessive pronouns referring to the members of the group are plural.
- ✔ Body parts always belong to individuals, not to groups.

Which sentence is correct?

A. The class will hold its annual picnic during the monsoon season because of poor planning by the administration.

B. The class will hold their annual picnic during the monsoon season because of poor planning by the administration.

Answer: Sentence A is correct. The picnic belongs to everyone as a group.

Pronouns, Inc.: Using Pronouns with Company Names

What about businesses? Is Bloomingdale's having *its* sale or *their* sale? (I'll answer you in a little while. First I have to check out the sale. I need new towels.) Think of the issue this way: Even if the business's name looks plural (*Bloomingdale's, Sears, AT&T,* and so on), the business is a singular noun because one company is, after all, just one company. Therefore, the verb is singular. Now for the pronouns: The business is an *it,* not a *they,* because a company is, as I just pointed out, a company. So possession for companies is always expressed by *its.* Thus

> Bloomingdale's is having *its* sale today.

> Sears is having *its* sale tomorrow.

Which sentence is correct?

A. The sales personnel at Gumley Brothers always say that *their* water filters are the absolute best.

B. The sales personnel at Gumley Brothers always say that *its* water filters are the absolute best.

Answer: Sentence B is correct, assuming that the sales personnel are referring to the water filters that are being sold in the store. If, however, the sales personnel are referring to filters that they themselves bought and installed (in their own separate homes) to keep the toxic waste away, go for sentence A.

A historic or historical occasion

If something is *historical,* it happened and is now history. If something is *historic,* it happened and was important. In one way or another, a *historic* event influenced the course of history as you now understand it. Consider the following:

The little-known American labor leader, Junius P. Legghorn, shaved at least three times a day because of accusations that he had sabotaged the disposable razor industry by promoting the five-o'clock-shadow look.

This information is *historical;* you can look it up in Legghorn's autobiography, *My Life in the Fast Lane with No Turn Signal.* Other *historical* events in Legghorn's tumultuous life include his trip by jet ski through the Erie Canal and his week-long visit to the White House, where he was not invited to sleep in the Lincoln bedroom.

Despite his long life in public service, Junius P. Legghorn was not involved in any *historic* events whatsoever. Nothing he did merits a moment's consideration by serious historians. (Even when he attended important ceremonies or congressional debates, he had a knack for disappearing into the men's room at the crucial moment, possibly because of his habit of drinking large quantities of iced tea.)

Thus, Junius P. Legghorn was a *historical,* not imaginary, figure who did not participate in any *historic* events.

Chapter 24

The Last Word on Sentence Structure

• •

In This Chapter

▶ Distinguishing between independent and subordinate clauses

▶ Untangling one clause from another

▶ Using subordinate clauses to make your writing more fluid

▶ Identifying verbals and using them to add variety to your writing

• •

Say I give you a new car. What do you do? Open the hood and check the engine, or hop in and drive it away? The engine-checkers and the drive-awayers are the two sub-groups of car owners. The engine-checkers have to know what's going on inside the machine. The other group doesn't care what's going on inside the machine. They just want the car to run.

You can also divide speakers of English into two groups. Some people want to understand what's going on inside the sentence, but most just want to communicate. In this chapter I provide some information for each — the lift-up-the-hood-of-the-sentence group and the drive-English-down-the-block group. The first part of this chapter digs into the structure of the sentence, defining clauses and verbals. The second part of the chapter shows you how to make your writing more interesting by varying sentence patterns. You use clauses and verbals to create those patterns, but you don't need to obsess over the terminology.

Understanding the Basics of Clause and Effect

No matter what food you put between two pieces of bread, you've got a sandwich. That's the definition of *sandwich:* bread plus filling. Clauses have a simple definition too: subject plus verb. Any subject–verb combination creates a clause. The reverse is also true: no subject or no verb, no clause.

You can throw in some extras (descriptions, joining words, lettuce, tomato . . . whatever), but the basic subject–verb combination is key. Some sentences have one clause, in which case the whole sentence is the clause, and some have more than one.

Be sure to check your sentences for completeness. Each sentence should contain at least one complete thought, expressed in a way that can stand alone. In grammarspeak, each sentence must contain at least one independent clause (check out "Getting the goods on subordinate and independent clauses," later in this chapter). For more information on complete sentences, see Chapter 5.

Here are a few examples of one-clause sentences:

> Has Eggworthy cracked the Case of the Missing Chicken? (subject = *Eggworthy*, verb = *has cracked*)

> Lulu crossed the Alps in the dead of winter without help from a single elephant. (subject = *Lulu*, verb = *crossed*)

> Cedric and his enemies have reached an agreement about the number of spitballs thrown each day. (subjects = *Cedric and his enemies*, verb = *have reached*)

> Agwamp swam for 15 minutes and rowed for an hour before nightfall. (subject = *Agwamp*, verbs = *swam, rowed*)

Notice that some of the clauses have two subjects and some have two verbs, but each expresses one main idea. Here are a few examples of sentences with more than one clause:

> SENTENCE: Legghorn struggled out from under the blankets, and then he dashed for the secret microfilm.

> CLAUSE 1: Legghorn struggled out from under the blankets (subject = *Legghorn*, verb = *struggled*)

> CLAUSE 2: then he dashed for the secret microfilm (subject = *he*, verb = *dashed*)

> SENTENCE: After Cedric had developed the secret microfilm, Eggworthy sent it to whatever federal agency catches spies.

> CLAUSE 1: After Cedric had developed the secret microfilm (subject = *Cedric*, verb = *had developed*)

> CLAUSE 2: Eggworthy sent it to whatever federal agency catches spies (subject = *Eggworthy*, verb = *sent*)

> CLAUSE 3: whatever federal agency catches spies (subject = *agency*, verb = *catches*)

There is something odd about the last example. Clause #3 is actually part of clause #2. It's not a misprint. Sometimes one clause is actually entangled in another. (This topic is deep in the pathless forests of grammar! Get out now, while you still can!)

Here's one more example that's really complicated:

> SENTENCE: Whoever ate the secret microfilm is in big trouble.
>
> CLAUSE #1: Whoever ate the secret microfilm (subject = *whoever*, verb = *ate*)
>
> CLAUSE #2: Whoever ate the secret microfilm is in big trouble. (subject = *whoever ate the secret microfilm*, verb = *is*)

Yes, one clause is the subject of another clause. Good grief! What a system. (For those who truly love grammar: The subject clause is a noun clause. See "Knowing the three legal jobs for subordinate clauses" later in this chapter for more information.)

Getting the goods on subordinate and independent clauses

Some clauses are mature grown-ups. They have their own apartment, pay their own rent, and wash the dishes frequently enough to ward off a visit from the health inspector. These clauses have made a success of life; they're *independent*.

Other clauses are like the brother-in-law character in a million jokes. They still live at home, or they crash on someone's couch. They're always mooching a free meal, and they never see Mom without handing her a bag full of dirty laundry. These clauses are not mature; they can't support themselves. They're *dependent*. These clauses may be called *dependent clauses* or *subordinate clauses*. (The terms are interchangeable.)

Following are two sets of clauses. Both have subject–verb pairs, but the first set makes sense alone and the second doesn't. The first set consists of independent clauses, and the second of subordinate clauses.

Independent clauses:

> Cedric blasted Blathersby with a radar gun.
>
> Blathersby was going 50 m.p.h.
>
> The cougar could not keep up.
>
> Did Blathersby award the trophy?

Subordinate clauses:

> After Cedric had complained to the race officials

> Because Blathersby had installed an illegal motor on his skateboard

> Which Eggworthy bought from an overcrowded zoo

> Whoever ran the fastest

Independent clauses are okay by themselves, but writing too many in a row makes your paragraph choppy and monotonous. Subordinate clauses, however, are not okay by themselves because they don't make complete sentences. To become complete, they have to tack themselves onto independent clauses. Subordinate clauses add life and interest to the sentence (just as the guy crashing on your couch adds a little zip to the household). But don't leave them alone, because disaster will strike. A subordinate clause all by itself is a grammatical felony — a sentence fragment.

The best sentences combine different elements in all sorts of patterns. In the following example, I join the independent clauses and subordinate clauses to create longer, more interesting sentences:

> After Cedric had complained to the race officials, he blasted Blathersby with a radar gun.

> Because Blathersby had installed an illegal motor on his skateboard, he was going 50 m.p.h.

> The cougar, which Eggworthy bought from an overcrowded zoo, could not keep up.

> Did Blathersby award the trophy to whoever ran the fastest?

Combine the ideas in each of these sets into one sentence.

Set A:

> Felonia screamed at the piano mover.

> The mover dropped the piano on the delicate foot of the vivacious violinist.

Set B:

> Analivia solved a quadratic equation.

> The equation had been troubling the math major.

Set C:

Legghorn gave special trophies.

Some people wanted those trophies.

Those people got the trophies.

Answer: Several combinations are possible. Here are three:

A. Felonia screamed at the piano mover who dropped the piano on the delicate foot of the vivacious violinist.

B. Analivia solved a quadratic equation that had been troubling the math major.

C. Legghorn gave special trophies to whoever wanted them.

Knowing the three legal jobs for subordinate clauses

Okay, subordinate clauses can't stand alone. What can they do? They really have three main purposes in life, as you see in the following sections.

Describing nouns and pronouns

Yep, subordinate clauses can describe nouns and pronouns. That is, the subordinate clause may give your listener or reader more information about a noun or pronoun in the sentence. Here are some examples, with the subordinate clause in italics:

The book *that Legghorn wrote* is on the best seller list. *(that Legghorn wrote* describes the noun *book)*

Anyone *who knows Legghorn well* will read the book. *(who knows Legghorn well* describes the pronoun *anyone)*

The book includes some information *that will prove embarrassing to Legghorn's friends. (that will prove embarrassing to Legghorn's friends* describes the noun *information)*

Subordinate clauses that describe nouns or pronouns are called *adjectival clauses* or *adjective clauses.*

Describing verbs, adjectives, or adverbs

Subordinate clauses can also describe verbs, adjectives, or adverbs. The subordinate clauses tell you *how, when, where,* or *why.* Some examples, with the subordinate clause in italics, are as follows:

Because Legghorn censored himself, the book contains nothing about the exploding doughnut. *(Because Legghorn censored himself describes the verb contains)*

We may find out more *when the movie version is released. (when the movie version is released* describes the verb *find)*

The government may prohibit sales of the book *wherever international tensions make it dangerous. (wherever international tensions make it dangerous* describes the verb *may prohibit)*

Legghorn is so stubborn *that he may sue the government. (that he may sue the government* describes the adverb *so)*

Subordinate clauses that describe verbs are called *adverbial clauses* or *adverb clauses.* Subordinate clauses that describe adjectives or adverbs (mostly in comparisons) are also *adverbial clauses.* Adverbial clauses do the same job as single-word adverbs. They describe verbs, adjectives, or other adverbs.

Acting as subjects or objects inside another clause

This one is a bit more complicated: Subordinate clauses may do any job that a noun does in a sentence. Subordinate clauses sometimes act as subjects or objects inside another clause. Here are some examples, with the subordinate clause in italics:

When the book was written is a real mystery. *(When the book was written* is the subject of the verb *is)*

No one knows *whom Legghorn hired to write his book. (whom Legghorn hired to write his book* is the object of the verb *knows)*

Legghorn signed copies for *whoever bought at least five books. (whoever bought at least five books* is the object of the preposition *for)*

Noun clauses are subordinate clauses that perform the same functions as nouns — subjects, objects, appositives, and so on.

Check out the italicized clause in each sentence. Subordinate or independent? You decide.

A. *Even though he had hit a home run,* Legghorn's team lost by more than 50 runs.

B. *Eggworthy danced for a while,* but then he said that his head was splitting and sat down.

Answer: In sentence A, the italicized clause is subordinate. In sentence B, the italicized clause is independent.

Untangling subordinate and independent clauses

You have to untangle one clause from another only occasionally — when deciding which pronoun or verb you need or whether commas are appropriate. (See the next section, "Deciding when to untangle clauses," for more information.) When you do have to untangle them, follow these simple steps:

1. Find the subject–verb pairs.

2. Use your reading comprehension skills to determine whether the subject–verb pairs belong to the same thought or to different thoughts.

3. If the pairs belong to different thoughts, they're probably in different clauses.

4. If the pairs belong to the same thought, they're probably in the same clause.

Another method also relies on reading comprehension skills. Think about the ideas in the sentence and untangle the thoughts. By doing so, you've probably also untangled the clauses.

Check out these examples:

SENTENCE: The acting award that Lola received comes with a hefty check.

SUBJECT–VERB PAIRS: *award comes, Lola received*

UNTANGLED IDEAS: 1.) The award comes with a hefty check 2.) Lola received the award.

CLAUSES: 1.) *The acting award comes with a hefty check.* (Independent clause) 2.) *that Lola received* (subordinate clause)

SENTENCE: When Lulu tattoos someone, they stay tattooed.

SUBJECT–VERB PAIRS: *Lulu tattoos, they stay*

UNTANGLED IDEAS: 1.) Lulu tattoos someone 2.) they stay tattooed

CLAUSES: 1.) *When Lulu tattoos someone* (subordinate clause) 2.) *they stay tattooed* (independent clause)

Untangle this sentence into separate clauses.

Lola's last motorcycle, which she bought second-hand, was once owned by Elvis.

Answer: Clause #1: Lola's last motorcycle was once owned by Elvis. Clause #2: which she bought second-hand.

Try another. Untangle the following sentence.

No one knows when Analivia sleeps.

Answer: Clause #1: *no one knows.* Clause #2: *When Analivia sleeps.*

Deciding when to untangle clauses

Why would you want to untangle clauses? Not just because you have nothing better to do. You should untangle clauses when you're choosing pronouns, verbs, and punctuation. Read on for the whole story.

When you're picking a pronoun

When you're deciding whether you need a subject or an object pronoun, check the clause that contains the word. Don't worry about what the entire clause is doing in the sentence. Untangle the clause and ignore everything else. Then decide which pronoun you need for that particular clause.

Many of the decisions about pronouns concern *who* and *whom.* (For tricks to help you make the *who/whom* choice, see Chapter 23. For a general discussion of choosing the correct pronoun, see Chapters 10 and 17.)

Here's one untangling example, with the pronoun problem in parenthesis:

SENTENCE: Ludmilla wasn't sure (who/whom) would want a used engagement ring.

UNTANGLED INTO CLAUSES: Clause #1: *Ludmilla wasn't sure.* Clause #2: *(who/whom) would want a used engagement ring.*

RELEVANT CLAUSE: *(who/whom) would want a used engagement ring.*

CORRECT PRONOUN: *who* (subject of *would want*)

When you're deciding on the correct verb

When you're deciding subject–verb agreement in one clause, the other clauses are distractions. In fact, if you're writing (not speaking), I recommend that you cross out or cover the other clauses for a moment. Check the clause that worries you. Decide the subject–verb agreement issue, and then erase the crossing-out line or remove your hand. (For more information on subject–verb agreement, see Chapter 11.)

Here's one untangling example, with the verb choices in parenthesis:

SENTENCE: Ludwig, whose brides are all thrilled to marry into the royal family, (needs/need) no introduction.

UNTANGLED INTO CLAUSES: Clause #1: *Ludwig (needs/need) no introduction.* Clause #2: *whose brides are all thrilled to marry into the royal family.*

RELEVANT CLAUSE: *Ludwig (needs/need) no introduction.*

CORRECT VERB: *needs* (Ludwig = singular, *needs* = singular)

When you're figuring out where to put commas

Sometimes you have to untangle clauses in order to decide whether or not you need commas. Go through the same untangling steps that I discuss earlier in the chapter (see "Untangling subordinate and independent clauses") and then flip to Chapter 25 to see how to use commas correctly.

Putting your subordinate clauses in the right place

Finding the correct place to put your subordinate clauses is simple. Clauses acting as subjects or objects nearly always fall in the proper place automatically. Don't worry about them!

Put the subordinate clause that describes a noun or pronoun near the word that it describes. (For lots more detail on placing descriptions in their proper places, see Chapters 8 and 18.)

If the subordinate clause describes the verb, it may land at the front of the sentence or at the rear. On rare occasions, the clause settles down in the middle of the sentence. Here are some examples, with the subordinate clause in italics:

> *Although Analivia understood the equation,* she chose to put a question mark on her answer sheet.

> She wrote the question mark *because she wanted to make a statement about the mysteries of life.*

> Analivia failed the test; but *until her mother found out about the question mark,* Analivia was not distressed.

An unbelievably obscure punctuation rule that no normal people follow calls for a semicolon in front of a conjunction when a comma appears elsewhere in the sentence. (For more information on conjunctions, see Chapter 7.) I followed that rule (an act which once and for all settles the question of my normalcy) in the preceding sample sentence. Because of the comma after *mark,* I placed a semicolon in front of the conjunction *but.* Warning: You should know that if you follow this rule, most of your readers will think that you've made an error. However, a few die-hard grammarians will break into tears of gratitude because someone else knows how to use a semicolon correctly. (Excuse me for a moment while I wipe my eyes.)

Choosing the content for your subordinate clauses

Although this topic is fairly easy, a few traps are sprinkled here and there. For example, what to put in each clause is generally a question of personal choice. Most writers believe that putting the important idea in the independent clause and the other ideas in subordinate clauses is best. Here are some examples:

IMPORTANT IDEA: Godzilla ate my mother.

LESS IMPORTANT IDEA: My mother was wearing a green dress.

GOOD SENTENCE: Godzilla ate my mother, who was wearing a green dress.

NOT-SO-GOOD SENTENCE: My mother was wearing a green dress when Godzilla ate her.

IMPORTANT IDEA: Agwamp just won a trillion dollars

LESS IMPORTANT IDEA: His name means "ancient bettor" in an obscure language.

GOOD SENTENCE: Agwamp, whose name means "ancient bettor" in an obscure language, just won a trillion dollars.

NOT-SO-GOOD SENTENCE: Agwamp, who just won a trillion dollars, says that his name means "ancient bettor" in an obscure language.

For more discussion on joining independent and subordinate clauses, see Chapter 7.

Getting Verbal

Ah, diversity. Wouldn't the world be boring if everyone and everything were the same? Ah, harmony. Isn't it wonderful when different backgrounds join forces to create a new, improved blend?

In grammar, the new, improved blend of two parts of speech is a *verbal*. Verbals are extremely useful hybrids. In this section, I tell you what's what, and then I show you how to use verbals.

Appreciating gerunds

The noun and the verb get married, move into a little house on the prairie, and pretty soon the patter of little syllables hits the airwaves. The children of this happy marriage are *gerunds*. Gerunds inherit some characteristics from their mother, the verb:

- ✔ They end in -ing and look like verbs — *swimming, dripping, being, bopping, bribing,* and so on.

- ✔ They may be described by words or phrases that usually describe verbs — swimming *swiftly,* dripping *noisily,* being *in the moment,* bopping *to the rhythm of a great new song,* bribing *yesterday,* and so on.

- ✔ The type of clause that usually describes verbs may also describe gerunds — swimming *after the race ends,* dripping *when the cap is not tightened,* being *wherever you should be,* bopping *although you are tired,* bribing *whenever you want something.*

- ✔ They may have objects or subject complements — swimming *laps,* dripping *drops of gooey glop,* being *president,* bopping *Lochness on the nose,* bribing *public officials and umpires,* and so on.

From their father, the noun, gerunds inherit only two characteristics, but one is a biggie:

- ✔ BIGGIE: They act as nouns in the sentence. Therefore, gerunds may be subjects, objects, and anything else that a noun can be.

- ✔ NON-BIGGIE: Words that usually describe nouns or pronouns — adjectives — may also describe gerunds — *my* swimming, *noisy* dripping, *illegal* bribing, and so on. (Is there any legal bribing?)

Here are a few examples, with the gerund and all the words associated with it (the *gerund phrase,* in grammarspeak) italicized:

> *Swimming the Atlantic Ocean* was not exactly what Ludmilla had in mind when she married Ludwig. *(swimming the Atlantic Ocean* = subject of the verb *was)*

> Analivia, a neat person in every possible way, hates *my dripping ice cream on the rug. (my dripping ice cream on the rug* = direct object of the verb *hates)*

> The importance of *being earnest in one's playwriting* cannot be over-emphasized. *(being earnest in one's playwriting* = object of the preposition *of)*

> After *bopping Lochness on the nose,* Legghorn took off at about 100 m.p.h. *(bopping Lochness on the nose* = object of the preposition *after)*

> Felonia gave *bribing the umpire* serious consideration when her team lost its 450th game in a row. *(bribing the umpire* = object of the verb *gave)*

Working with infinitives

The *infinitive* is another happy child of two different parts of speech. (See Chapter 2 for more information on infinitives.) The infinitives' mother is the verb, and from her, infinitives inherit several important characteristics:

✔ Infinitives look like verbs, with the word *to* tacked on in front — *to dance, to dream, to be, to dally, to prosecute,* and so on.

✔ Words or phrases that usually describe verbs may also describe infinitives (to dance *divinely,* to dream *daily,* to be *in the kitchen,* to dally *for hours,* to prosecute *ferociously,* and so on).

✔ Similarly, the type of clause that usually describes verbs may also describe infinitives to dance *until the cows come home,* to dream *when your heart is breaking,* to be *wherever you want to be,* to dally *even though homework awaits,* to prosecute *because justice demands it,* and so on.

✔ Infinitives may have objects or subject complements — to dance *a jig,* to dream *an impossible dream,* to be *silly,* to prosecute *Lochness* for high crimes and misdemeanors, and so on.

The infinitive inherits its job in the sentence from the father. Who, you may ask, is the father of the infinitive? Well, the infinitive's mom gets around, and the father may actually be any one of three parts of speech (shocking, isn't it?):

✔ Most infinitives act as subjects, objects, or subject complements. (Dad is a noun.)

✔ A few infinitives describe nouns. (Dad is an adjective.)

✔ A few infinitives describe verbs. (Dad is an adverb.)

Here are a few examples of infinitives in their natural habitat, the sentence. I have italicized the infinitive and the words associated with it (the *infinitive phrase,* in grammarspeak):

> *To dance on Broadway* is Lola's lifelong dream. *(to dance on Broadway* = subject of the verb *is)*
>
> During cabinet meetings, Ludwig likes *to dream with his eyes open. (to dream with his eyes open* = object of the verb *likes)*
>
> Lulu's lifelong goal is *to be silly* when everyone else is serious. *(to be silly* = subject complement of the verb *is)*
>
> Ludmilla went to that nightclub just *to dally. (to dally* describes the verb *went)*
>
> The case *to prosecute* is the one about the exploding doughnut. *(to prosecute* describes the noun *case)*

Participating with a participle

Last but not least of the verbals (a word that is a blend of two different parts of speech) is the participle. *Participles* are actually parts of verbs (hence the amazingly original name). In some sentences participles act as part of the verb, but in those situations, they're not called verbals. I ignore the acting-as-verb participles here, but if you want more information about them, see Chapter 3. When participles are verbals, they, like the other two verbals, inherit some important traits from their mom the verb:

✔ Participles look like verb parts, though they may have several different forms. Some end with *-ing*, some with *-ed*, and some with other letters. Also, they may have helping verbs. *Driven, coping, elevated, having crossed,* and *gone* are a few examples of participles.

✔ Words or phrases that usually describe verbs may also describe participles (driven *home*, coping *bravely,* elevated *to the position of Emperor,* having crossed *illegally,* gone *with the wind,* and so on).

✔ Similarly, the type of clause that usually describes verbs may also describe participles driven *although he has two perfectly good feet,* coping *bravely when tragedy strikes,* elevated *because he bribed three officials,* having crossed *where no man has crossed before,* gone *after the sun sets,* and so on.

✔ Participles may have objects or subject complements — driven *mad,* elevated *Ludmilla to the position of Empress,* having crossed *the road,* and so on.

From their father, the adjective, participles take one characteristic: They describe nouns and pronouns.

Participles may appear in several different spots in the sentence:

✔ They may precede the noun or pronoun that they describe: *tired* feet (the participle *tired* describes the noun *feet*), *sneezing* dwarves (the participle *sneezing* describes the noun *dwarves*), *burped* baby (the participle *burped* describes the noun *baby*).

✔ They may follow a linking verb, in which case they describe the subject. (A linking verb is a form of the verb *to be* or a sensory verb. See Chapter 2 for more information.):

> Ludmilla is *exhausted.* (The participle *exhausted* follows the linking verb *is* and describes *Ludmilla.*)

> Felonia's concerto sounds *enchanting.* (The participle *enchanting* follows the linking verb *sounds* and describes *concerto.*)

✔ They may follow the noun or pronoun that they describe. In this position, participles often include descriptive words or objects. The participles and the words associated with them — the *participial phrases* — are italicized here:

> Someone, *having angered the herd of cattle,* is running for the fence at the speed of light. *(Having angered the herd of cattle* describes *someone.)*

> I want to read the new anti-bubble gum law *passed by the senate. (Passed by the senate* describes *law.)*

✔ Participles may begin the sentence, in which case they must describe the subject of the sentence:

Poked in the tummy, the doll immediately said, "Watch it, Buster!" (*Poked in the tummy* describes *doll.*)

Smashed against the picture window, Lola's nose looked sore. (*Smashed against the picture window* describes *nose.*)

Spicing Up Boring Sentences with Clauses and Verbals

Which paragraph sounds better?

Legghorn purchased a new spy camera. The camera was smaller than a grain of rice. Legghorn gave the camera to Lola. Lola is rather forgetful. She is especially forgetful now. Lola is planning a trip to Antarctica. Lola accidentally mixed the camera into her rice casserole along with bean sprouts and orange marmalade. The camera baked for 45 minutes. The camera became quite tender. Legghorn unknowingly ate the camera.

Legghorn purchased a new spy camera that was smaller than a grain of rice. Legghorn gave the camera to Lola, who is rather forgetful, especially now that she is planning a trip to Antarctica. Accidentally mixed into Lola's rice casserole along with bean sprouts and orange marmalade, the camera baked for 45 minutes. Legghorn unknowingly ate the camera, which was quite tender.

I'm going to take a guess; you said that the second paragraph was better, didn't you? It's a bit shorter (62 words instead of 69), but length isn't the issue. The first paragraph is composed of short, choppy sentences. The second one flows. Grammatically, the difference between the two is simple. The second paragraph has more subordinate clauses and verbals than the first.

You don't necessarily need to know how to find or label clauses or verbals. However, you should read your writing aloud from time to time to check how it sounds. Are your sentences monotonous? Are they all more or less the same length? Do all your sentences follow the same pattern? Is everything subject–verb or subject–verb–complement? Have you strung a lot of short sentences together with *and* or a similar joining word? If so, your sentences need some first aid. In this section, with a minimum of grammatical labels, I give you some suggestions to pep up tired sentences.

The clause that refreshes

Have you ever seen those diet ads on late-night television? The before picture shows someone who has apparently eaten a rainforest, and the after picture shows a toothpick-thin body. In this section I show you some before-and-after sentences. No diets — just a change from boring to interesting. For label lovers, I have put in subordinate clauses, which are italicized.

> BORING BEFORE VERSION: Ratrug sat on a tuffet. Ratrug did not know that he was sitting on a tuffet. Ratrug had never seen a tuffet before. He was quite comfortable. Then Ms. Muffet came in and caused trouble.

> EXCITING AFTER VERSION: Ratrug, *who was sitting on a tuffet,* did not know *what a tuffet was because he had never seen one before. Until Ms. Muffet came in and caused trouble,* Ratrug was quite comfortable.

Doesn't the after paragraph sound better? It's two words shorter (33 instead of 35 words), but more important than length is the number of sentences. The before paragraph has five, and the after paragraph has two. Tucking more than one idea into a sentence saves words and makes your writing less choppy.

Verbally speaking

Verbals pull a lot of information into a little package. After all, they represent a blend of two parts of speech, so they provide two different perspectives in just one word. Look at this sentence, taken from the gerund section, earlier in this chapter:

> Felonia gave *bribing the umpire* serious consideration when her team lost its 450th game in a row.

Without the gerund, you use more words to say the same thing:

> Felonia's team just lost its 450th game in a row. Should she bribe the umpire? Felonia thought seriously about that possibility.

Okay, you saved four words. Big deal! Well, it is a big deal over the course of a paragraph or a whole paper. But more important than word count is sentence structure. Verbals are just one more color in your crayon box when you're creating a picture. Who wants the same old eight colors? Isn't it fun to try something different? Gerunds, infinitives, and participles help you vary the pattern of your sentences. Here's a before-and-after example:

> BORING BEFORE VERSION: Lulu smacked Ludwig. Ludwig had stolen the sacred toe hoop from Lulu's parrot. The sacred toe hoop was discovered 100 years ago. Lulu's parrot likes to sharpen his beak on it.

EXCITING AFTER VERSION: *Smacking Ludwig* is Lulu's way of telling Ludwig that he should not have stolen the sacred toe hoop from her parrot. *Discovered 100 years ago,* the toe ring serves *to sharpen the parrot's beak.*

LABELS FOR THOSE WHO CARE: *Smacking Lulu* = gerund, *discovered 100 years ago* = participle, *to sharpen the parrot's beak* = infinitive.

Combine these ideas into one or more sentences.

Ludwig bakes infrequently. He does bake with enthusiasm. His best recipe is for king cake. King-cake batter must be stirred for three hours. Ludwig orders his cook to stir the batter. The cook stirs and Ludwig adds the raisins. Sometimes he throws in a spoonful of tuna fish.

Answer: Many combinations are possible, including the following:

Ludwig's *baking* is infrequent but enthusiastic. His best recipe, king cake, requires three hours of *stirring,* which Ludwig orders his cook to do. *Adding* raisins and the occasional spoonful of tuna fish is Ludwig's job. (The italicized words are gerunds.)

Ludwig, who bakes infrequently but enthusiastically, excels at cooking king cake, which requires three hours of stirring. Ordering his cook to stir, Ludwig adds raisins and the occasional spoonful of tuna fish. (*who bakes infrequently but enthusiastically* = subordinate clause, *cooking king cake* = gerund, *which requires three hours of stirring* = subordinate clause, *ordering his cook* = participle, *to stir* = infinitive)

You're hanged, but a picture is hung

In Legghorn's new movie, Lulu stars as the righteous rebel leader *hanged* by the opposition. After the stirring execution scene, the rebels rally, inspired by a picture of Lulu that someone *hung* on the wall of their headquarters.

To hang is a verb meaning *to suspend.* In the present tense the same verb does double duty. You *hang* a picture and you also *hang* a murderer, at least in countries with that form of capital punishment. Past tense is different; in general, people are *hanged* and objects are *hung.*

Chapter 25

The Last Word on Punctuation

*P*unctuation is one topic that you don't have to worry about when you're speaking. But oh, those little specks of ink do make your life miserable when you're writing. Commas, ellipses (little dots . . .), hyphens, parentheses, and brackets can wreak havoc on your mind. (Who invented them, anyway?) I haven't even mentioned the slash, which isn't the name of a horror movie, but it could be.

Despite the terror most people feel when confronted with punctuation dilemmas, the rules actually follow a logical pattern. In this chapter I tackle some advanced punctuation rules. (For the basics of commas, see Chapter 14. For information about semicolons, colons, and dashes, see Chapter 15.) With just a little effort, you'll find that your punctuation improves and your writing takes a giant step towards grammar nirvana.

Making Your Point Clear with Commas

When you're writing, keep in mind that each comma in your sentence should have a reason for being there. The most important reason, of course, is to make your meaning clear. Commas act as a signal to your reader. Each comma calls for a slight pause — not so long as a period, but a pause nonetheless. Commas also separate some words from the rest of the sentence. The reader knows that words enclosed by commas are not part of the main idea of the sentence.

Essential or extra? Your commas tell the tale

To begin, here's the rule that tells you when to use commas with descriptions: If a description is essential to the meaning of the sentence, don't put commas around it. If the description is extra, non-essential information, set it off with commas. Consider this situation:

In her quest to reform Ludwig's government, Ludmilla made this statement:

> Taxes, which are a hardship for the people, are not acceptable.

Eggworthy, who is a member of Ludwig's Parliament, declared himself in complete agreement with Ludmilla's statement. However, his version had no commas:

> Taxes which are a hardship for the people are not acceptable.

What's the difference? Do the commas really matter? Yes. They matter a lot. Here's the deal: *which are a hardship for the people* is a description. If the description is set off from the rest of the sentence by commas, the description is extra — not essential to the meaning of the sentence. You can cross it out and the sentence still means the same thing. If commas do not set off the description, however, the description is essential to the meaning of the sentence. It may not be removed without altering what you are saying. Can you now see the difference between Ludmilla's statement and Eggworthy's? Here's the original and expanded version of each:

> LUDMILLA'S ORIGINAL STATEMENT: Taxes, which are a hardship for the people, are not acceptable.
>
> MEANING OF LUDMILLA'S STATEMENT: The government should not impose taxes. Taxes are a problem for the people. They have little money as it is. We can run the government perfectly well by selling postage stamps to foreign tourists. I suggest a tasteful portrait of the royal bride (me) on a new stamp. No taxes — that's the bottom line.

Because Ludmilla's original sentence includes commas, the description *which are a hardship for the people* is extra information. You can omit it from the sentence. Thus Ludmilla is against all taxes.

> EGGWORTHY'S ORIGINAL STATEMENT: Taxes which are a hardship for the people are not acceptable.
>
> MEANING OF EGGWORTHY'S STATEMENT: The government is against any taxes which are a hardship for the people. Of course we don't want to place a burden on the working families of our great nation. However, the new 90 percent income tax is not a hardship; it allows the people of this great nation to show their patriotism by contributing to the government and paying my salary. This particular income tax is acceptable.

Eggworthy's proposal is much less extreme than Ludmilla's. Without commas the description is a necessary part of the sentence. It gives the reader essential information about the meaning of *taxes.* Eggworthy opposes only some taxes — those taxes that he believes are a burden. He isn't against all taxes. This description doesn't simply add a reason, as Ludmilla's does. Instead it identifies the taxes that Eggworthy opposes.

The pronouns *which* and *that* may help you decide whether or not you need commas. *That* generally introduces information that the sentence can't do without — essential information that isn't set off by commas. The pronoun *which,* on the other hand, often introduces non-essential information that may be surrounded by commas. Keep in mind, however, that these distinctions are not true 100 percent of the time. Sometimes *which* introduces a description that is essential and therefore needs no commas. The pronoun *that* almost never introduces non-essential material.

Check out these additional examples, with the description in italics:

> SENTENCE: The students *who are planning a sit-in tomorrow* want to be paid for doing homework.

> PUNCTUATION ANALYSIS: The description is not set off by commas, so you may not omit it.

> WHAT THE SENTENCE MEANS: Some of the students — those who are planning a sit-in — want to be paid for doing homework. Not all the students want to be paid. The rest are perfectly content to do math problems for absolutely no money.

> SENTENCE: The senators, planning to revolt, have given the television network exclusive rights to cover their rebellion.

> PUNCTUATION ANALYSIS: The commas indicate that the description is extra, non-essential information.

> WHAT THE SENTENCE MEANS: All the senators are involved. They're quite upset, and all have prepared sound bites.

Which sentence means that you can't fly to Cincinnati for your cousin's wedding?

A. The pilots who are going on strike demand that mood music be piped into the cockpit.

B. The pilots, who are going on strike, demand that mood music be piped into the cockpit.

Answer: Sentence B means that all the pilots are going on strike. The description between the commas may be omitted without changing the meaning of the sentence. In sentence A, only the pilots who like heavy metal music are going on strike.

The elements of the sentence that I discuss in the previous examples are adjective clauses and participles. See Chapter 24 for more information on clauses and participles.

Do your commas have appositive influence?

If you're seeing double when you read a sentence, you've probably encountered an *appositive*. An appositive is a noun or a pronoun that is exactly the same as the noun or pronoun that precedes it in the sentence. Some appositives are set off by commas, and some aren't. The rule concerning commas and appositives: If the appositive is more specific, don't use commas; if the appositive is less specific, use commas.

Now put the rule into practice: What's the difference between these two sentences?

> Legghorn's play *Dinner at the Diner* is the least understandable of all that he has written.

> *Dinner at the Diner*, Legghorn's play, is the least understandable of all that he has written.

In the first sample sentence, *Dinner at the Diner* is the appositive of *Legghorn's play*. In the second sample sentence, *Legghorn's play* is the appositive of *Dinner at the Diner*.

To put the rule another way: If you're sure that your reader will know what you're talking about before he or she gets to the appositive, set off the appositive with commas. If you're not sure your reader will know exactly what you're talking about by the time he or she gets to the appositive, you should not use commas. (This rule is a variation of the rule that I explain in the preceding section.) If the appositive gives identifying, essential information, don't use commas. If the appositive gives extra information, do use commas.

In the first sample sentence the reader does not know which one of Legghorn's plays is being discussed. The appositive supplies the name. Hence, the appositive is essential and isn't set off by commas. In the second sample sentence the reader already knows the name of the play. The fact that Legghorn wrote the play is extra information and must therefore be surrounded by commas.

Here are a few more examples:

> SENTENCE: Lulu has five sisters, but her sister Mary is definitely her favorite.

> APPOSITIVE: *Mary* is the appositive of *sister*.

PUNCTUATION ANALYSIS: Because Lulu has five sisters, you don't know which sister is being discussed until you have the name. *Mary* identifies the sister and shouldn't be placed between commas.

SENTENCE: Lochness has only one sibling. His sister, *Mary,* does not approve of Lochness's espionage.

APPOSITIVE: *Mary* is the appositive of *sister.*

PUNCTUATION ANALYSIS: Because Lochness has only one sibling, the reader knows that he has only one sister. Thus the words *his sister* pinpoint the person being discussed in the sentence. The name is extra information, not identifying information. Therefore, you should place the name between commas.

Which sentence is correct?

A. Lola's mother, Lala, doesn't approve of her daughter's pierced toe.

B. Lola's mother Lala doesn't approve of her daughter's pierced toe.

Answer: Sentence A is correct. Lola has only one mother, so the name is extra, not identifying information.

Try another. Which sentence is correct?

A. Lochness's book *I Am Not a Monster* sold only three copies.

B. Lochness's book, *I Am Not a Monster,* sold only three copies.

Answer: This question is a bit tricky. How many books has Lochness written? If he has written only one, sentence B is acceptable. If he has written more than one, sentence A is the better choice because the title supplies identifying information.

Punctuating independently

When you join two complete sentences with the conjunctions *and, or, but, nor, yet, so,* or *for,* place a comma before the conjunction. Some examples include:

Ratrug robbed the bank, and then he went out for a hamburger.

Analivia recorded the measurements in her notebook, and then she wrote a computer program to calculate the amount of orange shag carpeting needed to cover the floors of Ludwig's new castle.

Lochness spies, but apart from that lapse he is not a bad fellow.

The pumpkin that Lulu carved will win first prize, or Lulu will demand to know the reason why.

Cedric bribed the judges of this year's state spitball contest, for he is determined to qualify for the national tournament.

For more information on conjunctions, see Chapter 7. For more information on complete sentences, see Chapter 5.

Some sentences have one subject (who or what you're talking about) and two verbs joined by *and, but, or,* and *nor.* Don't put commas between the two verbs. You aren't joining two complete sentences, just two words or groups of words. Here are some examples:

WRONG: Ludmilla wrote a statement for the media, and then screamed at Ludwig for an hour.

WHY IT IS WRONG: The sentence has one subject *(Ludmilla)* and two verbs *(wrote, screamed).* You aren't joining two complete sentences, so you shouldn't place a comma before *and.* Either way, Ludmilla should learn to control her temper.

RIGHT: Ludmilla wrote a statement for the media and then screamed at Ludwig for an hour.

WRONG: Ludwig has proposed a toast to his bride, but has given her nothing but a headache.

WHY IT IS WRONG: The sentence has one subject *(Ludwig)* and two verbs *(has proposed, has given).* The word *but* joins the two verbs, not two complete sentences. You don't need a comma. Also, Ludwig should give her a wedding gift.

RIGHT: Ludwig has proposed a toast to his bride but has given her nothing but a headache.

Which sentence is correct?

A. Agwamp slits the envelope with his teeth, but Eggworthy opens the mail with a fork.

B. Agwamp answers every letter on the day he receives it but doesn't pay any bills.

Answer: Both sentences are correct. In sentence A, the conjunction *but* joins two complete sentences. A comma must precede the conjunction *but.* In sentence B, *but* joins two verbs *(answers, does pay).* No comma precedes the conjunction.

Using Those Dot-Dot-Dots

Are you seeing spots before your eyes? The spots are called *ellipses*. (One set is an *ellipsis*.) An ellipsis is made up of three dots. Ellipses show the reader where you've omitted a word or words from the middle or end of a quotation. (Don't use them at the beginning of a quotation.) Ellipses may also show that the speaker you are quoting is hesitating.

Indicating missing words

When you're quoting someone else's words, place three dots wherever you've left out words from the original. If you've removed words from the end of a sentence, place four dots — three for the ellipsis and one for the period at the end of the sentence.

Here's a selection from Lochness's autobiography, edited by his publisher, who didn't want the tender minds of children to become corrupted by Lochness's words:

> As I slowly swam towards the. . . I saw. . . and decided then and there to take. . . if I could get it. The path of my life became clear. I would. . . and then retire to my estate in Antarctica, where I would write my memoirs and breed penguins. Soon after that decision I took action. . . .

What do you notice about the quotation from Lochness's book, apart from the appalling censorship? The missing words, of course! Notice how the ellipses take the place of one or more words.

Some additional examples:

> SENTENCE WITH ELLIPSIS: Lola cried, "I can't take that math exam! I studied the equations for hours. . . and had no time for the geometry chapter."

> PUNCTUATION ANALYSIS: An ellipsis (three dots) takes the place of the missing words.

> WHAT'S LEFT OUT: last year, but last night I went to the movies

Showing hesitation

You can also use ellipses to show hesitation, particularly in dialogue:

> What shall I do about that atomic bomb? It's. . . ticking and I. . . .

Using ellipses in this way can get really annoying really fast. Think of the dots as knock-knock jokes. Don't overuse them!

Here's Lola's explanation for the fact that she has no homework. The parts that she'll leave out are in italics. Punctuate the quotation properly.

> I sat down at the computer last night to write the essay. I truly love writing essays, and I certainly want to do well in this class. I began to write shortly before eight o'clock. *The phone rang almost immediately. I spoke with Lulu for no more than three hours. Then my mother asked me if I wanted a snack. I said yes. I ate four or five buckets of popcorn and settled down at the computer.* My stomach hurt, and I was very tired. I went to bed. I will do the essay tonight.

Answer: Use four dots. One dot is the period at the end of the sentence *(I began to write shortly before eight o'clock.)* and three dots are the ellipsis.

> I sat down at the computer last night to write the essay. I truly love writing essays, and I certainly want to do well in this class. I began to write shortly before eight o'clock. . . . My stomach hurt, and I was very tired. I went to bed. I will do the essay tonight.

I've been having some fun with the examples, leaving out key information. Don't follow my example! One of the most important issues in writing is credibility. If you change the meaning of what you're quoting by leaving out crucial details, your reader will discount everything you say. (Also, your teacher may fail you.) Check the passage you're quoting before and after you've cut it. Does each convey the same message? If not, don't cut.

H-y-p-h-e-n-a-t-i-n-g Made Easy

You need hyphens to help you maneuver through unexpected line breaks and for a couple of other reasons as well — to separate parts of compound words, to write certain numbers, and to create one description from two words. This section provides you with a guide to the care and feeding of the humble hyphen.

Understanding the great divide

Computer users have to worry about hyphens less often than other writers. Most of the time, the word processing program moves a word to a new line if there isn't enough room at the end of a line for the entire word. But sometimes, when you're writing by hand or typing on an old-fashioned typewriter, for example, you need to divide a word. And sometimes, even computer users need to divide a word.

The British system

The practice of dividing a word between syllables is American. In Britain, words are often divided according to the derivation (family tree) of the word, not according to sound. For example, in the American system, *democracy* is divided into four parts — *de-moc-ra-cy* — because that's how it sounds. In the British system, the same word is divided into two parts — *demo-cracy* — because the word is derived from two ancient Greek forms, *demos* and *kratia*. Let the dictionary of the country you're in be the final authority on dividing words.

Why should you divide a word? Mostly to make your writing look better. The computer allows a ragged right margin, but if you have a very long word — antidisestablishmentarianism, for example — the computer will move it to a new line when you've typed only half of the preceding line. (By the way, antidisestablishmentarianism is a real word. Look it up, but not in a pocket dictionary. It's too long and too unimportant for an abridged dictionary.)

If you have to divide a word, follow these simple rules:

- ✔ Place the hyphen between the *syllables,* or sounds, of a word. (If you're not sure where the syllable breaks are in a word, check the dictionary.)

- ✔ Don't leave only one letter on a line. If you have a choice, divide the word more or less in the middle.

- ✔ Don't divide words that have only one syllable.

- ✔ To divide a word, be sure to use a hyphen, which is a short line. Don't use a dash, which is a longer line and a completely different punctuation mark. (See Chapter 15 for more information on dashes.)

Using hyphens for compound words

Hyphens also separate parts of compound words, such as ex-wife, pro-choice, one-way, and so forth. When you type or write these words, don't put a space before or after the hyphen. If you don't know whether a particular expression is a compound word, a single word, or two separate words, check the dictionary.

Are you wondering how to capitalize compound words? Most of the time, you should capitalize both words. All the parts of a person's title are capitalized, except for prepositions and articles: Secretary-General, Commander-in-Chief. Don't capitalize the prefix *ex-:* ex-President Carter, ex-Attorney-General. Words that are capitalized for some other reason (perhaps because they're part of a book title or a headline) follow a different rule. Always capitalize the first half. Capitalize the second half of the compound if it's a noun, or if the second half of the compound is equal in importance to the first half: Secretary-General Lola, President-elect Lulu. (For more information on capitalization, see Chapter 15.)

Placing hyphens in numbers

Decisions about whether to write a numeral or a word are questions of style, not of grammar. The authority figure in your life — teacher, boss, parole officer, whatever — will tell you what he or she prefers. In general, larger numbers are usually represented by numerals:

> Lochness has been arrested 683 times, counting last night.

However, on various occasions you may need to write the word, not the numeral. If the number falls at the beginning of a sentence, for example, you must use words because no sentence may begin with a numeral. You may also need to write about a fractional amount. Here's how to hyphenate:

- ✔ Hyphenate all the numbers from twenty-one to ninety-nine.

- ✔ Hyphenate all fractions used as descriptions (three-quarters full, for example).

- ✔ Don't hyphenate fractions used as nouns (three quarters of the money; one third of all registered voters).

Utilizing the well-placed hyphen

Here's another simple rule concerning hyphens, but one that may be on the way out. (A little personal story here: A young man I know was thrilled to be accepted to the staff of the law review of his school. At the first meeting, the editor addressed the new recruits on the hyphen issue, explaining that the magazine had decided to drop the hyphen from two-word descriptions. "I knew then that it was going to be a very long year," he sighed.) Anyway, if you want to follow the rule, here it is: If two words are being used as a single description, put a hyphen between them if the description comes before the word that it's describing. For example:

> a well-placed hyphen — BUT — the hyphen is well placed.

Don't hyphenate two-word descriptions if the first word ends in *-ly:*

nicely drawn rectangle

fully understood idea

completely ridiculous grammar rule

Place hyphens where they're needed.

Lulu was recently elected secretary treasurer of her club, the All Star Athletes of Antarctica. Lulu ran on an anti ice platform that was accepted by two thirds of the members.

Answer: Here's the paragraph with the hyphens inserted, along explanations in parentheses:

Lulu was recently elected secretary-treasurer (hyphen needed for compound title) of her club, the All-Star (hyphen needed for two-word description) Athletes of Antarctica. Lulu ran on an anti-ice (hyphen needed for two-word description) platform that was accepted by two thirds (no hyphen for fractions not used as descriptions) of the members.

Sprinkling Parentheses and Brackets throughout Your Writing

What's the difference between brackets and parentheses? *Brackets* are straight and *parentheses* are curved, of course. They both serve the same function: separating information from the rest of the sentence. If you've studied math, you know that brackets generally enclose expressions with parentheses inside. In one of the more annoying customs of English grammar, the opposite is true in writing. If you have material in parentheses and you need to separate some of it from the main idea, use brackets:

Ludwig declared that the new tax rate would be 95 percent (not 90 percent as had been reported earlier [see "Tax Rate Rises" in last week's issue]).

You also need brackets when you quote to show a comment that you, the writer, have inserted into someone else's words. Writers often use brackets in this way to enclose a useful little word — *sic.* When you quote something that is spelled wrong, said wrong, or is just dead wrong, the word *sic* means that the mistake was made by the person you're quoting, not by you. Here's an example:

Eggworthy declared, "I shall not surrender the presidentiary [sic] until all the ballots are counted."

A few more rules (sigh) for parentheses:

- ✔ Don't overuse them. (Seeing parentheses sprinkled all over a paragraph is boring and annoying.) Work the material in the parentheses into the main, logical thread of the paragraph (if at all possible). (See what I mean about annoying?)

- ✔ If the parenthetical expression needs any punctuation, put the punctuation *inside* the parenthesis.

- ✔ If the rest of the sentence (not the parenthetical material) requires any punctuation, put the punctuation *outside* the parenthesis.

Slashing Your Sentences

If any grammarian is worried about the slash, he/she should simply relax. The slash seldom appears in your writing, and/or you're unlikely to need it. The computer has probably done more to increase the number of slashes than any other machine/event/application. Are you tired/irritated/angry with this paragraph yet? Answer yes/no.

Okay, here's the deal. Use the slash when you need to present two or more alternatives, but pretend that it's the hottest chili pepper imaginable and you have just had dental surgery. How many chili peppers do you want in your food? That's how many slashes you should place in your writing — very, very few.

Slashes have one other important job. If you're writing about poetry and quoting some lines, the slash shows the reader where the poet ended one line and began another. Here's an excerpt from Legghorn's essay on a poem written by Lulu:

> The exertion of mountain climbing has contributed to the imagery Lulu employs in her poem "Everest or Nothing": "and then the harsh/breath of the mountain/meets the harsh/breath of the climber/I am/the climber."

The slashes tell us that the lines of Lulu's poem were arranged as follows:

> and then the harsh
>
> breath of the mountain
>
> meets the harsh
>
> breath of the climber
>
> I am
>
> the climber.

Part VI
The Part of Tens

The 5th Wave   By Rich Tennant

©RICHTENNANT

"Oh, he's brilliant all right. But have you ever noticed the grammar in his memos? 'Org need helicon antenna... Org need ion cyclotron... Org need neutron analyzer....'"

In this part . . .

This section opens the door to a grammatical life beyond *English Grammar For Dummies*. After you've absorbed the rules of grammar, you've still got to apply them. Chapter 26 provides ten strategies to improve your proofreading. (After reading this chapter, you'll never sign a letter "Yurs turly" again.) Chapter 27 lists ten ways to train your ear for good English, a process that inevitably improves your speech and writing. You may not follow all the suggestions that I give you (especially the one that tells you to hang out with nerds), but you'll find at least some appealing.

Chapter 26

Ten Ways ~~Two~~ to Improve Your Proofreading

In This Chapter

▶ Checking your work with the help of a computer

▶ Proofreading more effectively

*Y*ou read it 50 times and finally put it in the mail. It was so important that you cried when the clerk at the post office threw it into a bin and a corner of the envelope creased. You dried your eyes, went home, and, unable to calm your fears, sat down to read the text for the 51st time. And that's when you finally saw it — an error. Not a little error, but a big one. An embarrassing one. The ink equivalent of a pimple on the tip of your nose.

Sound familiar? If so, you need some proofreading help. In this chapter, I give you ten tricks to improve that all-important final check.

Read Backward

Okay, I know that reading backward sounds crazy, but successful proofreading is about breaking habits. If you read something over and over, after a while you're on automatic pilot. Your eye jumps at exactly the same spot simply because that's where it jumped before. So if you missed the error the first time, you'll miss it again. You've got to do something different to break the monotony of reviewing your work. If you read backward (word by word, not the letters that make up a word), you're in a good frame of mind to catch spelling errors because reading in the wrong direction means that you must check each word separately. If you read backward, you can't swing through a sentence by hopping to every fifth or sixth word.

Wait a While

Your work is done, you've read it, and you've made the corrections. Now what do you do? Put it away and do something else. Go water-skiing, run for president, or clean the closet, and then come back to the writing — refreshed and with a new point of view. You'll see your work with new eyes — and find mistakes.

Of course, this method works only if you've left some time before the deadline. If you finish your report three nano-seconds before the boss wants to see it, you'll have to forgo this method of proofreading.

Read It Aloud

I know, I know. You don't want to sound like a dork. But reading aloud helps you *hear* your writing in a different way. So put the radio on or lock yourself in the bathroom. Take the paper and read the words in a normal speaking voice. Did you stumble anywhere? If so, you may have come across an error. Stop, circle the spot, and continue. Later, check all the circles. Chances are you'll find something that should be different.

Delete Half of the Commas

During the last two weeks of the grading period, students visit me with their rough drafts in hand for a quick check before the final, graded copy is due. Privately I think of that time as *Comma Season.* I spend most of the day deleting hundreds of punctuation marks. (I also add a handful or two.) If you're like most people, your writing has commas where none are needed. Go back and check each one. Is there a reason for that comma? If you can't identify a reason, take the comma out.

Swap with a Friend

The best proofreading comes from a fresh pair of eyes. After you've written your essay, report, parole petition, or whatever, swap with a friend. You'll see possible errors in your friend's writing, and he or she will see some in yours. Each of you should underline the potential errors before returning the paper. Make sure you check those sections with special care.

Let the Computer Help

Not foolproof, by any means, the computer is nevertheless helpful. After you've finished writing, go back and check the red and green lines (or whatever signal your grammar and spelling checkers supply). Don't trust the computer to make the corrections for you; the machine makes too many mistakes. The computer identifies only *possible* mistakes and misses many errors (homonyms, for example). Let your own knowledge of grammar and a good dictionary help you decide whether you need to change something.

Check the Verbs

Traps sprinkled in every sentence — that's the way you should look at verbs. Give your work an extra verb check before you declare it finished. Consider *number:* Should the verb be singular or plural? Consider *tense:* Have you chosen the correct one? Do you have any sentences without verbs? If so, take care of the problem.

Check the Pronouns

Pronouns present potential pitfalls and are also worthy of their own special moment. Give your work an extra once over, this time checking all the pronouns. Singular or plural — did you select the appropriate number? Does each pronoun refer to a specific noun? Did you avoid sexist pronoun usage? Did you give a subject pronoun a job suited to an object pronoun, or vice versa?

Know Your Typing Style

I have a tendency to hold the shift key down a little too long, so many of my words have two capital letters: THe, KNow, and so on. Do you have a mistake that results from your typing style? Notice when you have to backspace as you type and then check for similar errors when you finish typing.

The Usual Suspects

Look at your earlier writing, preferably something that was corrected by a teacher or someone else in a position to point out your mistakes. Where is the red ink concentrated? Those red-ink areas are the usual suspects that you should identify in future writing. For instance, if you have a number of run-on sentences in an old paper, chances are you'll put a few in a new paper. Put "run-on" on your personal list of common errors. Don't let any piece of writing leave your desk until you've searched specifically for those errors.

Chapter 27

Ten Ways to Learn Better Grammar

In This Chapter

▶ Going beyond *English Grammar For Dummies* to improve your grammar

▶ Using real-world resources to train your ear for good grammar

Yes, I admit it. This book helps you learn grammar, but (sigh) it's not the only way to improve your communication skills. A few other resources may also help you in your quest for perfect language. In this chapter, I suggest ten ways to learn better grammar.

Read Good Books

You probably won't get far with *Biker Babes and Their Turn-ons* or *You're a Butthead: The Sequel to Snot-Nose.* But good books usually contain good writing, and if you read some, pretty soon your own speech and writing will improve. How do you know whether a particular volume contains good writing? Check the reviews, ask the bookstore clerk, or read the blurb (the comments on the book's jacket). Classics are always a choice, but you may also find modern texts, both fiction and non-fiction, written according to the best grammar rules.

The point is to expose your mind to proper English. When you read, you hear the author's voice. You become accustomed to proper language. After a while correct grammar sounds natural to you, and you detect non-standard English more easily.

Watch Good TV Shows

When I say to watch good TV shows, I'm not talking about programs with audio tracks that are mostly grunts, such as wrestling. I'm referring to shows in which people actually converse. Programs on the nerd networks are a good bet. You know the shows I mean; the producers assume that the audience wants to learn something. The screen has a lot of talking heads (images of commentators, not the rock band) with subtitles explaining why each is an expert. Watch them in secret if you're afraid of ruining your reputation, and pay attention to the words. Don't expect to pick up the finer points of grammar on TV, but you can get some pointers on the basics.

Peruse the News

News broadcasts on radio, television, and the Internet are fine sources of literate (okay, semi-literate on some networks) role models. You can train your ear for grammar at the same time that you learn a lot about current events. Just think of the advantage when you need a pick-up line. Instead of "Come here often?" or "What's your sign?" you can mention the Russian policy on Afghanistan. (On second thought, maybe you should stick to astrology.)

Read the Newspaper

Well, read some newspapers. Years ago I started to "pay" my students one point for each grammar error that they found in print. I eventually had to rule out a couple of publications because it was just too easy to gather material. Avoid publications that report Elvis sightings and have headlines like "Man with Four Arms Tests Deodorant for a Living." Read with a grammarian's eye (if the thought isn't too frightening for you), absorbing *how* the writer expresses an idea.

Flip through Magazines

If all the words in a magazine are in little bubbles above brightly colored drawings, you may not find complete sentences and proper pronoun usage. However, most published writers have at least the fundamentals of good grammar, and you can learn a lot from reading publications aimed at an educated audience. How do you know whether a publication is aimed at an educated audience? Check the articles. If they seem to address issues that you associate with thoughtful readers, you're okay. Even if they address issues that aren't associated with thoughtful readers, you may still be okay. Reading well-written magazine articles will give you some models of reasonably correct grammar. And as a side effect, you'll learn something.

Visit Nerd Hangouts

Before I say anything else, let me mention that *nerd* is a word based on value judgments. What most people deem nerdy (or whatever the current slang equivalent is), others may call *educated.* I'm not saying that the locker room or the corner bar is filled with uneducated people. I'm saying that you ought to investigate some spots where people gather when they're in the mood to talk on a level above "the defense creamed us last night." Try a bookstore, a science lab, or a concert. Listen to what the people around you are saying and how they're saying it. Your ear for good grammar will sharpen over time.

Check Out Strunk and White

The best book ever written on writing, in my humble opinion, is *The Elements of Style* (Allyn and Bacon). This book is so tiny that it fits into your shirt pocket. Authors William Strunk, Jr. and E.B. White (yes, the fellow who wrote *Charlotte's Web* and *Stuart Little*) tackle a few grammar issues and make important points about style. You'll spend an hour reading it and a lifetime absorbing its lessons.

Listening to Authorities

Listen! Your teacher or boss probably says that word often, and you should (pause to arrange a dutiful expression) always do what your personal authority figure says. Apart from all the other reasons, you should listen in order to learn better grammar. By speaking properly, he or she is probably giving you English lessons along with descriptions of the Smoot-Whatever Tariff Act, the projected sales figures, and so forth.

Reviewing Manuals of Style

No, manuals of style won't tell you whether *eggplant* is one of this year's approved colors or what kind of nose ring Hollywood favors. They will tell you, however, in exhaustive (and exhausting) detail, where to put every punctuation mark ever invented, what to capitalize, how to address an ambassador, and lots of other things that you never really wanted to know. Some universities and a few groups of recognized rule-creators publish manuals of style. If you're writing a term paper or a business report, ask your teacher or boss which manual of style he or she favors. Use the recommended book as a reference for the picky little things and as a guide to the important issues of writing.

Surfing the Internet

I can't leave this one out, though the Internet contains as many traps as it does guiding lights. Type *grammar* in a search engine and press enter. Sit back and prepare yourself for a flood of sites explaining the rules of grammar. Some sites are very good; some are horrible. Look for university- or school-sponsored URLs (Web addresses).

Index

• W •

• Y •

BUSINESS, CAREERS & PERSONAL FINANCE

0-7645-5307-0

0-7645-5331-3 *†

Also available:
- Accounting For Dummies †
  0-7645-5314-3
- Business Plans Kit For Dummies †
  0-7645-5365-8
- Cover Letters For Dummies
  0-7645-5224-4
- Frugal Living For Dummies
  0-7645-5403-4
- Leadership For Dummies
  0-7645-5176-0
- Managing For Dummies
  0-7645-1771-6

- Marketing For Dummies
  0-7645-5600-2
- Personal Finance For Dummies *
  0-7645-2590-5
- Project Management For Dummies
  0-7645-5283-X
- Resumes For Dummies †
  0-7645-5471-9
- Selling For Dummies
  0-7645-5363-1
- Small Business Kit For Dummies *†
  0-7645-5093-4

HOME & BUSINESS COMPUTER BASICS

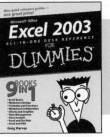

0-7645-4074-2

0-7645-3758-X

Also available:
- ACT! 6 For Dummies
  0-7645-2645-6
- iLife '04 All-in-One Desk Reference
  For Dummies
  0-7645-7347-0
- iPAQ For Dummies
  0-7645-6769-1
- Mac OS X Panther Timesaving
  Techniques For Dummies
  0-7645-5812-9
- Macs For Dummies
  0-7645-5656-8

- Microsoft Money 2004 For Dummies
  0-7645-4195-1
- Office 2003 All-in-One Desk Reference
  For Dummies
  0-7645-3883-7
- Outlook 2003 For Dummies
  0-7645-3759-8
- PCs For Dummies
  0-7645-4074-2
- TiVo For Dummies
  0-7645-6923-6
- Upgrading and Fixing PCs For Dummies
  0-7645-1665-5
- Windows XP Timesaving Techniques
  For Dummies
  0-7645-3748-2

FOOD, HOME, GARDEN, HOBBIES, MUSIC & PETS

0-7645-5295-3

0-7645-5232-5

Also available:
- Bass Guitar For Dummies
  0-7645-2487-9
- Diabetes Cookbook For Dummies
  0-7645-5230-9
- Gardening For Dummies *
  0-7645-5130-2
- Guitar For Dummies
  0-7645-5106-X
- Holiday Decorating For Dummies
  0-7645-2570-0
- Home Improvement All-in-One
  For Dummies
  0-7645-5680-0

- Knitting For Dummies
  0-7645-5395-X
- Piano For Dummies
  0-7645-5105-1
- Puppies For Dummies
  0-7645-5255-4
- Scrapbooking For Dummies
  0-7645-7208-3
- Senior Dogs For Dummies
  0-7645-5818-8
- Singing For Dummies
  0-7645-2475-5
- 30-Minute Meals For Dummies
  0-7645-2589-1

INTERNET & DIGITAL MEDIA

0-7645-1664-7

0-7645-6924-4

Also available:
- 2005 Online Shopping Directory
  For Dummies
  0-7645-7495-7
- CD & DVD Recording For Dummies
  0-7645-5956-7
- eBay For Dummies
  0-7645-5654-1
- Fighting Spam For Dummies
  0-7645-5965-6
- Genealogy Online For Dummies
  0-7645-5964-8
- Google For Dummies
  0-7645-4420-9

- Home Recording For Musicians
  For Dummies
  0-7645-1634-5
- The Internet For Dummies
  0-7645-4173-0
- iPod & iTunes For Dummies
  0-7645-7772-7
- Preventing Identity Theft For Dummies
  0-7645-7336-5
- Pro Tools All-in-One Desk Reference
  For Dummies
  0-7645-5714-9
- Roxio Easy Media Creator For Dummies
  0-7645-7131-1

* Separate Canadian edition also available
† Separate U.K. edition also available

Available wherever books are sold. For more information or to order direct: U.S. customers visit www.dummies.com or call 1-877-762-2974.
U.K. customers visit www.wileyeurope.com or call 0800 243407. Canadian customers visit www.wiley.ca or call 1-800-567-4797.

 WILEY

SPORTS, FITNESS, PARENTING, RELIGION & SPIRITUALITY

0-7645-5146-9

0-7645-5418-2

Also available:
- Adoption For Dummies
  0-7645-5488-3
- Basketball For Dummies
  0-7645-5248-1
- The Bible For Dummies
  0-7645-5296-1
- Buddhism For Dummies
  0-7645-5359-3
- Catholicism For Dummies
  0-7645-5391-7
- Hockey For Dummies
  0-7645-5228-7

- Judaism For Dummies
  0-7645-5299-6
- Martial Arts For Dummies
  0-7645-5358-5
- Pilates For Dummies
  0-7645-5397-6
- Religion For Dummies
  0-7645-5264-3
- Teaching Kids to Read For Dummies
  0-7645-4043-2
- Weight Training For Dummies
  0-7645-5168-X
- Yoga For Dummies
  0-7645-5117-5

TRAVEL

0-7645-5438-7

0-7645-5453-0

Also available:
- Alaska For Dummies
  0-7645-1761-9
- Arizona For Dummies
  0-7645-6938-4
- Cancún and the Yucatán For Dummies
  0-7645-2437-2
- Cruise Vacations For Dummies
  0-7645-6941-4
- Europe For Dummies
  0-7645-5456-5
- Ireland For Dummies
  0-7645-5455-7

- Las Vegas For Dummies
  0-7645-5448-4
- London For Dummies
  0-7645-4277-X
- New York City For Dummies
  0-7645-6945-7
- Paris For Dummies
  0-7645-5494-8
- RV Vacations For Dummies
  0-7645-5443-3
- Walt Disney World & Orlando For Dummies
  0-7645-6943-0

GRAPHICS, DESIGN & WEB DEVELOPMENT

0-7645-4345-8

0-7645-5589-8

Also available:
- Adobe Acrobat 6 PDF For Dummies
  0-7645-3760-1
- Building a Web Site For Dummies
  0-7645-7144-3
- Dreamweaver MX 2004 For Dummies
  0-7645-4342-3
- FrontPage 2003 For Dummies
  0-7645-3882-9
- HTML 4 For Dummies
  0-7645-1995-6
- Illustrator CS For Dummies
  0-7645-4084-X

- Macromedia Flash MX 2004 For Dummies
  0-7645-4358-X
- Photoshop 7 All-in-One Desk Reference For Dummies
  0-7645-1667-1
- Photoshop CS Timesaving Techniques For Dummies
  0-7645-6782-9
- PHP 5 For Dummies
  0-7645-4166-8
- PowerPoint 2003 For Dummies
  0-7645-3908-6
- QuarkXPress 6 For Dummies
  0-7645-2593-X

NETWORKING, SECURITY, PROGRAMMING & DATABASES

0-7645-6852-3

0-7645-5784-X

Also available:
- A+ Certification For Dummies
  0-7645-4187-0
- Access 2003 All-in-One Desk Reference For Dummies
  0-7645-3988-4
- Beginning Programming For Dummies
  0-7645-4997-9
- C For Dummies
  0-7645-7068-4
- Firewalls For Dummies
  0-7645-4048-3
- Home Networking For Dummies
  0-7645-42796

- Network Security For Dummies
  0-7645-1679-5
- Networking For Dummies
  0-7645-1677-9
- TCP/IP For Dummies
  0-7645-1760-0
- VBA For Dummies
  0-7645-3989-2
- Wireless All In-One Desk Reference For Dummies
  0-7645-7496-5
- Wireless Home Networking For Dummies
  0-7645-3910-8